"This book is a prophetic call for a more discip[...] and inspirational form of leadership in our time. And it further proves why Neil Cole is one of the most important voices in the Western church today."

—**Alan Hirsch**, author, *The Forgotten Ways* and *ReJesus*; co-founder, shapevine.com

"Though I frequently read leadership books, it has been a very long time since I've read a book on leadership that moved me, challenged me, gave me fresh insights, and went beyond the typical 'here's how you get it done' approach. Neil takes the person, the context, and God's Word, and mixes them in a powerful way for a life of leadership. Absent from this mix is the Western-driven spirit of 'how to use people to get your stuff done'! This is a book on how leaders do life, develop others, and flow in the kingdom of God."

—**Bob Roberts Jr.**, senior pastor, Northwood Church; author, *Transformation* and *Glocalization*

"Neil Cole does it again! With prophetic clarity he shares with us an honest look at the sacred cows of church and leadership development in his book *Organic Leadership*. I enjoy how Neil isn't afraid to examine presuppositions that can paralyze the church, especially since we naturally gravitate toward centralization, institutions, models, and calcified attitudes."

—**Dave Gibbons**, author, *The Monkey and the Fish*

"Neil Cole wants to make the complex simple—and he does it again in *Organic Leadership*. My head moved a lot as I read the book—mostly up and down, sometimes back and forth. Sometimes I just hung my head, thought, and prayed. *Organic Leadership* will trouble you—but more importantly, it will challenge you. And you should read it because the church could use some troubling and a new challenge."

—**Ed Stetzer**, author and researcher (www.edstetzer.com)

"At the core of my being, I am passionate and committed to getting big kingdom results. So is Neil Cole. In his latest book, *Organic Leadership*, you will find many additional insights and tools to help you and your church expand your kingdom reach."

—**Bob Buford**, founder, Leadership Network; author, *Halftime* and *Finishing Well*

ORGANIC LEADERSHIP

Leading **Naturally** Right Where You Are

NEIL COLE

BakerBooks

a division of Baker Publishing Group
Grand Rapids, Michigan

© 2009 by Neil Cole

Published by Baker Books
a division of Baker Publishing Group
P.O. Box 6287, Grand Rapids, MI 49516-6287
www.bakerbooks.com

Paperback edition published 2009
ISBN 978-0-8010-7238-3

Printed in the United States of America

The Library of Congress has cataloged the hardcover edition as follows:
Cole, Neil, 1960–
    Organic leadership : leading naturally right where you are / Neil Cole.
      p.   cm.
    Includes bibliographical references and index.
    ISBN 978-0-8010-1310-2 (cloth)
    1. Christian leadership. 2. Leadership—Religious aspects—Christianity. I. Title.
BV652.1.C635 2009
253—dc22
                                          2008040240

Published in association with the literary and marketing agency of C. Grant and Company.

This book is dedicated to the memory of
Hank Montoya
and all who exhibit a similarly powerful
weakness in the service of our King.
May your tribe multiply in the days that are coming.

CONTENTS

FOREWORD

Copernicus challenged and eventually overturned a millennium of church dogma with his heliocentric view of the solar system. His proofreader was a mathematician and pastor who wrote that the radical model Copernicus was presenting "need not be true" except as a mathematical model to predict planetary positions in the sky. I guess that's called hedging your bets.

The missional movement currently under way is a similar shift from a church-centric perspective to a kingdom-centric reality—a radically different way of seeing the world. It has enormous leadership implications. In the church culture, leadership is unequally distributed, institutionally based, and positional—in other words, clergy dominated and clergy driven. After all, clergy are charged with the responsibility of guiding the church institution, guarding it from doctrinal heresy, and leading it to corporate success. The increasing demands on clergy present a growing issue of sustainability as professional ministry becomes increasingly complex. The good news is, God is not tied to a clergy model in terms of leadership of the movement.

Church-culture leadership focuses on gifts and offices. Through the centuries this has generated a lot of theological discussion and many disagreements between various tribes and traditions. A fair amount of wrangling has occurred over what apostleship entails, whether or not prophets still function, the qualifications of pastors and teachers, and the proper role of evangelists. The wide range of application has created quite a menagerie of church-leader taxonomies, from apostle of apostles to novitiate in monastic brotherhoods and sisterhoods.

In the missional movement, the concept of church shifts from church based to kingdom based. Leadership has to make this shift. Kingdom leadership is widely distributed (across all domains of culture—business, education, health care, and so on), organic in its expression (responding to and shaping its environment), and personal in its authority (the leader is the message). It is leadership for a movement, not for an institution.

Kingdom-oriented leadership discussions conjure up results, not offices. These outcomes flow from the characteristics of kingdom leadership that show up in the lives of kingdom leaders. Kingdom leaders are spiritual leaders. To be around them is to be struck with their God dependence and Jesus centeredness. They operate from vision—not one they create but one that translates what God is doing so others can see it and participate in it. These leaders are missional, engaged in the world as partners with God in his redemptive mission that targets all of human experience, not just church life. They develop others, investing in people. Kingdom leadership flourishes in community, frequently deployed and expressed in teams of leaders. And these leaders are not afraid of risk and failure. They are spiritual entrepreneurs, figuring out how the church is expressing itself in today's cultural milieu. They are leading the church that shows up at Walmart, performs in the city symphony, works together in the university research center, collaborates in the movie industry, competes in the sports industry, and yes, gives leadership even in traditional church gatherings.

Neil Cole is giving his life to foster the development of kingdom leaders. While some think he is in the church-planting business, he is really in the leadership-development business. After giving us a view of what the missional church looks like in *Organic Church*, he now gives us insight into the kind of leadership that is necessary for this movement. He not only pulls back the curtain so we can see the leader in action; he goes behind the scene to tell us what it takes to shape the leader.

This book highlights the important truth that God is raising up spiritual leaders in every part of culture. That's because God's redemptive mission extends to the world, not just to the church. Church-centric thinking about leadership development focus on producing leaders who can build and operate great churches. Kingdom-focused thinking maintains that God is deploying his mission leaders to bless the world.

The latter is the perspective that shapes Neil's message and the story line he is following with his life's work. This volume is an important element in the developing plot. If you want to script yourself into the epic, read on.

Reggie McNeal, Missional Leadership Specialist, Leadership Network; author, *The Present Future* and *Missional Reniassance*

PREFACE

Live the Adventure

The key to change . . . is to let go of fear.

Rosanne Cash

Change is the essence of life.
Be willing to surrender what you are for what you could become.

Anonymous

The kingdom of Rohan is under attack. An army of dark creatures bred for destruction has invaded and is killing everyone in its path. They are headed toward Edoras, the capital of Rohan and the location of the Golden Hall; there King Théoden sits on his throne. The king has issued a command; all are to retreat to the defense of Helm's Deep, an ancient stone fortress deep in a high ravine.

With darkness encroaching and haste in everyone's steps, there is a revealing and intimate scene in the second movie of the Lord of the Rings trilogy, *The Two Towers*. It is a quiet moment, a transitional time when the people are preparing for the inevitable conflict with the dark forces that are mounting.

In the scene, Éowyn, a royal princess, believing she is alone, except for a few servants who are occupied with packing for a long journey, practices using her sword.

First, she holds it with a sense of reverence—a warrior has respect for her weapon. She almost caresses it. A subtle smile comes on her face as if she is about to dance with a very old and dear friend. She is.

As if in time with string instruments that have begun to play, she steps back, then forward. She begins wielding her sword with deliberation and precision. Each strike is a blow against imaginary foes that have her surrounded. First, she advances: *swoosh, swoosh*. Then she spins, and with force swings the sword around behind her. To her surprise her blade meets another. *Clank*.

Instantly everything stops. A sudden tension fills the air.

It is Aragorn's small knife that has interrupted Éowyn's waltz. Shocked to find that he has been watching her, feeling her personal space and private imagination have both been brutally violated, the princess's embarrassment is mixed with rage.

"You have some skill with a blade," remarks Aragorn, calmly trying to diffuse her embarrassment. But instead, feeling mocked, and worse, patronized, her anger increases.

Éowyn is never one to back down. With fire in her eyes, she wields the sword with a speed and force not expected from her small frame. Her thrust at once moves Aragorn's blade away and leaves the tip of her sword directly in his face as if to say "checkmate." She will go the distance without hesitation. Aragorn, yielding to the more powerful weapon, lowers his small dagger. This is not a fight.

"Women of this country learned long ago that those without swords can still die upon them," she explains.

But the hero in her is not willing to excuse *anything*. As she places the sword back in its place, she adds almost matter-of-factly, "I fear neither death nor pain."

Intrigued by this strong, beautiful woman, Aragorn feels compelled to ask, "What *do* you fear, my lady?"

As courageous as she is, she does have a fear. She cannot deny it or escape it. She knows exactly what it is. Still, it is difficult for her to answer, because the very telling of it makes her vulnerable. But the question was asked, and she does not back down from anything or anyone. While she has a fear, she also has courage, so she answers.

"A cage," she says. "To stay behind bars until use and old age accept them. And all chance of valor has gone beyond recall or desire."

All her life the real Éowyn has been overlooked, brushed aside as weak and needing protection. But inside she is a warrior, even if she is the only one in the kingdom who knows it. Everyone expects her to wear silk dresses, look pretty, and sit in court, but this princess is truly a noble warrior who will go on to defeat one of the most feared and powerful enemies in all the world. Her courage will reveal that she is not just a pretty woman, not a fragile little bird perched on a throne. Beneath her beauty is a raging warrior, so zealous for the cause of her kingdom that she would risk death to protect it. As the events in this epic tale play out, all will see she is not to be ignored.

Aragorn hears her words and responds in a manner she does not expect. As he listens, his brow furrows slightly with compassion for this warrior trapped in a woman's body. He knows what it is to be prejudged and labeled. They have a strange unseen connection. He is royalty, hidden behind a warrior. She is a warrior, hidden behind royalty.

"You are a daughter of kings," he reminds her, "a shield-maiden of Rohan."

Her face brightens as she senses that he sees the nobility in her that others have neglected.

With a wise confidence he goes on, "I do not think that will be your fate."

For perhaps the first time in her life, she feels acceptance. Hope shines in her eyes, as if to say, *Can it be that someone else sees me as I truly am?*

Aragorn bows slightly, turns, and walks away, leaving her flushed with hope and vigor.

Éowyn has experienced what anyone does whose true self has been exposed, then accepted and even admired. There is a great sense of relief and freedom. When someone else sees real nobility in us, it gives us a sense of empowerment.

Oh, to have a heart like Éowyn's, a bold heart that will not be satisfied with less than the nobility we have been given in Christ! Our fear, like hers, should be that we would go through life and not make a difference, that we would be stuck, a captive for life in a safe but meaningless existence.

There are many in the kingdom of God who feel like warriors trapped behind normalcy and the expectations of what has always been. Their nobility and courage lie deep inside, waiting for the right moment to be unleashed. Even many of those who know and love them do not see their strength. It is hidden behind the cloak of everyday life.

You may be such a person. You need the reminder that Éowyn received. You are a son or daughter of the King! Your fate, your destiny, is to be so much more than ordinary. You may live life in a business suit or in a blue-collar shirt with your name over the pocket or in an apron with two toddlers hanging on to your legs, but inside you are royalty—a fellow heir with Christ. Do not forget who you truly are, who you were destined to be. No matter what you do each day for your livelihood, do not forget the identity that Christ, at great expense, has put inside of you.

Fear and Courage

Éowyn was courageous but she was not fearless. We may think courage and fear are opposites that can never be found together, but this is wrong. These two qualities can be together; in fact, while it is possible to have fear without courage, courage is always found with fear. Courage without fear is ignorance or foolishness or both. The very essence of courage is to acknowledge the risk and move forward boldly, not succumbing to fear. Courage is not the absence of fear; it is the mastering of it.

Faith requires that we take risks, so faith requires courage in the face of fear. The greater the risk we take, the greater our fear will be, but when we master our fear, great faith is gained.

Do not feel ashamed of your fears; otherwise you may be tempted to deny their existence. Delusion is not courage. The true path to faith is to swallow your fear, like a lump in your throat, and boldly move forward, clinging to the God who goes with you.

This is a time for God's people to be courageous. This is a day of challenge, when we are called on to face our greatest fears and then to step forward in faith.

About This Book

This book is a follow-up to *Organic Church*. After its release, some people thought it provoked many questions but didn't supply enough answers, so here I begin to answer some of those questions. This book will not be enough. It is not that I haven't thought through the issues in depth, but I can fit only so much in each book. I hope this one both answers questions and also whets appetites for more to come in future works. Two books will follow this one, continuing my effort to flesh out the concepts of leadership and its role in organic church movements. So this is the beginning of the conversation, not the totality of it.

Organic Church cast the vision for a new expression of God's people in this world—healthy, holistic, and spiritual families that reproduce naturally. An organic church is a vibrant spiritual family that is on mission together. Such churches usually begin with changed lives, meet in the places where the seed was originally planted, and reproduce naturally and more easily than traditional churches because they are simple in structure.

The fully devoted followers in the organic church, who are able to reproduce themselves, are indeed the foundation for both organic churches and organic leadership. That is why I wrote *Search & Rescue* before writing this book on organic leadership. In *Search & Rescue* I set out to capture the imaginations of ordinary Christ-followers and challenge them to live lives that are heroic and sacrificial for the sake of Christ's kingdom.[1]

In this book I wish to build on the foundation laid in the previous books and address how healthy, growing disciples can emerge naturally as leaders right where they are. That is basically what organic leadership is all about. What is consistent in both *Organic Church* and *Organic Leadership* is my belief that the kingdom of God is relational, spiritual, and natural—without all the artificial stuff we tend to use to prop up our ministries today. It is not necessary for people to work as professionals in the church to make it happen. When church and her leadership are natural and organic, they reproduce spontaneously and movements will result.

I challenge many ideas about leadership and church life that we all take for granted. Many of them are faulty ideas about leadership, which we continue to support but which have never really been evaluated in the light of Scripture. Ideas that corrupt our understanding of the kingdom are addressed, such as our tendency to view the church as simply a religious institution with a top-down authoritative structure; and some of the temptations that tend to hijack leadership away from healthy fruitfulness and can actually cause leaders to become detrimental to the work of God's kingdom; as well as some of the ways we try to force people to live up to a religious code of conduct with manipulative tactics. In all of these examples, spirituality is seen as something that can be put on us from the outside, rather than growing and emerging from the heart. In each case, leadership is core to maintaining these false paradigms of spiritual life and development. Thus the first section of this book addresses honestly and directly many of the factors that keep true and natural leadership from emerging organically and growing.

The second section focuses on how healthy leadership emerges naturally from the inside out. We will discover how a true leader is formed and how to measure his or her success.

The third section of the book will share some sound scriptural principles about leaders who emerge organically and serve humbly yet are spiritually powerful in their leadership role. We will come to see that the kingdom of God is countercultural. It is, in fact, counterintuitive, the opposite of what we would expect. From this vantage point we will see how leaders emerge from the soil of brokenness and blossom with great fruitfulness, affecting generations to come. In this sense leaders are no different from other Christians. Living a life of Christ incarnate within us is the key to making a difference.

The fourth section presents practical leadership-development practices built on the foundations laid in the previous sections. These recipes for homegrown leaders are both practical and simple.

The fifth section is about resources for the life, growth, and health of leaders and churches.

I will conclude with some examples of the kind of leaders that exemplify the concepts in this book. These are true stories of real people who are carving out communities of light in the midst of the heavy darkness in our land.

As you read this book, you may find you are challenged to a level of discomfort. This book is about leadership, and leadership moves forward—often into uncharted territory, which may be an uncomfortable place. Anytime we are asked to move beyond the familiar, we will feel some level of discomfort and fear. The question is not whether you feel fear, but whether you allow fear to be your master.

I encourage you to break free from the cage of fear, refusing to accept the bars that confine you to what has been. Begin living a life of valor. It is not too late to be the warrior you were meant to be.

Live like the royalty you are.

ACKNOWLEDGMENTS

Perhaps the pinnacle description of what it means for a man to be a leader in God's kingdom is simply to be a father. While anyone can claim that title with very little effort these days, not many become the type of father the Bible describes as a godly father—the type of father we all feel we need deep down inside. It is a title God chooses for himself and should be held in high esteem.

So first I thank my heavenly Father for not leaving me alone in the world.

Second, I have been given great mentors in life to teach me how to be a man of God and a father to others—both literally and spiritually. I learned leadership from these men. Though the years have passed and time has separated us, I want each of you to know that you are not forgotten and your investment in me has not been wasted. My heartfelt thanks:

- To Lance Stowe, who saw potential in me when no one else did and was the first to take the time to listen to me and challenge me to fulfill my dreams.
- To Randy Creswell, who was a great example to me of a man who pursues God with reckless abandon to the ends of the earth.
- To Jay Bell, who passed on to me a heart for the nations of the world.
- To Dr. David Allen Black, who gave me a love for and faith in God's Word.
- To Dr. Robert Logan, who opened doors for me and helped me to crystallize and publish many of the concepts I have learned.
- To Tom Julien, who showed me how to be a patient and gracious change agent.

- To Ralph Moore, who always let me feel like one of his men even at a distance and showed me how to lead by giving away.
- To George Patterson, who instilled the wisdom of church multiplication learned on other soil and then helped me contextualize it for the West.
- To Dr. Thom Wolf, who unlocked the truths of God's Word that have shaped my ministry, which has now been replicated all over the world.
- To Ray Walker, who showed me how to be a real man and both a husband and a father. I miss you, Ray.

Third, I have walked through the years with brothers and together we have learned and lived the principles found on these pages. I am indebted:

- To Phil Helfer, Chris Suitt, Ed Waken, Paul Kaak, and Dezi Baker. You are my band of brothers and each of you has watched my back in difficult times.
- To Alan Hirsch, Wolf Simson, and Tony and Felicity Dale, who have seemingly come from across the world to walk and learn together in these amazing times.

Fourth, I have striven to be a good father because God has given me great children: Heather, Erin, and Zachary.

Finally, to Dana, my partner, my lover, and my companion.

INTRODUCTION

A Fate Worse than Failure

No man will make a great leader who wants to do it all himself
. . . or to get all the credit for doing it.

Andrew Carnegie

When you're finished changing, you're finished.

Benjamin Franklin

Most Americans have never heard of General William Winder. His song is not sung, nor will you find a statue of him in any park. No public school or boulevard is named for him. He has been forgotten.

But we ought to remember him. Winder was an American brigadier general during the War of 1812. In one attack he had a four-to-one advantage but still managed to lose the battle and was captured.

In a stroke of genius, the British decided this incompetent leader was actually more of an advantage to them free than if he was in prison, so they let him go.

Thirteen months later in the sultry August heat, the British surrounded the Americans in Washington, D.C., and captured our nation's capital. Yes, our own capitol building was under enemy occupation, with the British Union Jack flying in place of Old Glory. A small footnote in our history books reveals General William Winder was in charge of our capital's defense.

After the war, some attempted to court-martial Winder, but his only real crime was his inept leadership, which would have been difficult to prove in court. So through his foolish incompetence, he escaped imprisonment again.

Winder had all the right motives. He wanted only to serve his nation at a time of need. He was an educated man with a law degree from the University of Pennsylvania. His uncle, who had served well in the Revolutionary War, was governor of Maryland. Everyone assumed Winder would succeed as a military leader, but he did not. I am tempted to say he failed, but that is not the whole of it. He did far *worse* than fail. He became more of an asset to the enemy's cause than to his own.

I guess there really are fates worse than failure.

Unfortunately we can see this phenomenon in the lives of Christian leaders today. Many Christian leaders mean well, but I fear they are doing the cause of Christ more damage than good. Of course they don't think so; they believe they are defending the cause. In reality, however, they are aiding and abetting the Enemy, who will never take them out; they are too helpful to his purpose.

When leaders are nice guys with good motives, should we just ignore the negative impact they are having? This would not be a loving response. Bad leaders with good intentions are still bad leaders. If these leaders truly want to be useful, we need to speak the truth in love. If the emperor has no clothes, let's not allow the charade to go on.

I'm not saying we must be mean or spiteful. Do not misunderstand me. This is about love. These leaders who are causing damage today could be set free to become helpful leaders for the future, but only the truth spoken in love can set them free. I believe firmly that the heroes of tomorrow are in bondage to lies today, and I want to do everything I can to set these captives free.

The Bottleneck in God's Work

A few years ago my associates and I attended a consultation and workshop on leadership presented by Bob Logan. Bob is a good friend and my coauthor on two projects: *Raising Leaders for the Harvest* and *Beyond Church Planting*.[1] At this workshop Bob was going over our newest material about raising leaders for the harvest from the harvest. Because it was in Indiana, not too far from my denominational headquarters, we invited a few key leaders to drive the three or four hours to hear from Bob.

One of those who came was Roger, whom I had not met. Roger is tall, thin, and very intelligent. (He came in a little late due to a long drive on some rural back roads of Indiana.) He sat next to me and opened his Bible—a Greek New Testament.

Bob began by saying that in many cases, the bottleneck in the ministry of our churches is the pastors. He recounted ways that pastors actually prevent ordinary Christians from being used in God's kingdom. He went on to talk about some possible ways to reverse this problem, but Roger never heard that part. Roger heard only the phrase: pastors are the bottleneck in the ministry of the church.

Halfway through this talk, Roger, assuming all of us would be equally indignant, leaned over to me with disgust in his voice and said under his breath, "Do you have any idea what this guy is saying?" I had co-written most of the material Bob was using, so I simply replied, "Yes, I do," and left it at that. This short reply infuriated Roger.

It wasn't until a few years later that I heard the whole story. After the afternoon session, Roger had had enough. He left and went to the home he was staying at, but his thoughts could not be silenced. *The nerve of that guy! How could he say such a thing? How could I, an educated pastor, be a problem rather than the solution in the church?* But as he wrestled with these ideas, he began to ask himself, *Have I been a bottleneck that has held God's people back?* Though this Christian leader had been outraged by the implication of Bob's remarks, more than anything else Roger wanted to reflect God's heart.

He slept very little that night wrestling with God about this. His passion for truth would not let him be satisfied with pat answers or cliché ideas. In the end, he surrendered. This was a night of reckoning for Roger, but it was also a night of repentance and reconciliation. In the end he had to confess he had been at times more helpful to the Enemy's cause than the Lord's, and he repented. He would not be a bottleneck in God's work any longer.

The next day he came back to the workshop and explained what his night had been like. He drove home a changed man. In essence he had come all that way to hear just one sentence: pastors are the bottleneck in the ministry of the church. For Roger, the workshop had been worth far more than the registration cost.

I have known Roger now for well over a decade, but the man I met at the workshop I have never seen again. The new Roger is the man I know, love, and respect. Roger is now a humble man who empowers others to such an extent that he even gave his pastorate over to a younger man much sooner than necessary because he never wants to cause a bottleneck in the ministry of others.

Spiritually Plateaued Leadership

Some leaders, more than we care to admit, are spiritually plateaued and no longer growing. They have been educated and trained to be responsible for the growth of others, and they spend their lives meeting others' needs rather than growing themselves.

J. Robert Clinton has studied the lives of more than a thousand Christian leaders to discover what God does to form leaders who finish well. In a later chapter I will include some of his important observations. According to Clinton, either leaders grow forward in their development or they are stalled. A stalled leader is a plateaued leader, one who acts as though he or she has nothing more to learn. This leader is committed to maintaining the work he or she has begun but is no longer growing as a leader.

Terry Walling, a close associate of Robert Clinton, has developed a list of characteristics of a spiritually plateaued leader. The ten characteristics that follow are from Walling's list, with my adaptations and elaborations.

1. *A spiritually plateaued leader avoids relationships of personal accountability.* These leaders are removed from people. They have a degree of separateness that keeps them unaccountable to anyone. Often Christendom has reinforced such a separation and tried to justify it as biblical, to the detriment of the church, the world, and especially the leader.

   It is quite common, when I speak about the need to be honest and transparent and to confess our sins to one another, that people object to the idea of leaders doing these things. But the Bible is clear about leaders living as examples of honest transparency for others to follow (see 1 Peter 5:2–4; 2 Tim. 2:20–26; James 5:16; 1 John 1:5–10). Not only should spiritual leaders live transparent, honest lives, but they must be accessible and accountable so they can lead others into a healthy spiritual walk.

   Feeling the pressure to appear perfect, many leaders hide their spiritual failures behind closed doors and smiling masks. The result is that the world doesn't believe our message is truthful because they smell the hidden secrets and even delight in exposing the hypocrisy. Removing the masks and becoming accessible diffuses the world's desire to attack the leadership of the church and also removes a great barrier that keeps nonbelievers from respecting our message.

2. *A spiritually plateaued leader rarely applies the truths of God's Word to him- or herself personally.* Many Christian leaders have pursued education and have become experts on the Bible, thus believing they have no more to learn.

These leaders no longer read the Word for insight into their own lives, but rather apply it to the problems others have. They read the Bible only to find solutions to other people's issues rather than with their own needs in mind.

3. *A spiritually plateaued leader has replaced his or her joy, peace, and love with envy and resentment.* People cannot simply manufacture godliness by modifying their behavior to conform to Christ's ideals. The fruit of God's Spirit, seen in every aspect of our lives, is evidence of our redeemed character, not the works we force ourselves to perform to demonstrate our religious behavior.

Where the Spirit is not in control, the fruit is not evident, and no amount of hard work can make it so. Leaders who are no longer growing in their pursuit of the Lord cannot display the fruit of the Spirit and often exhibit instead sour religious attitudes. It's amazing how these ugly ways of thinking, when enough leaders display them, are accepted as the norm.

Instead of being bearers of Christ's love and forgiveness in the world, many leaders have begun to think it's their right, even their obligation, to judge and criticize others.

4. *A spiritually plateaued leader frequently looks for greener pastures in other places.* Often Christian leaders blame their church or organization for the lack of fruitfulness in their ministry. They attribute the success others have to the luck of landing in the right place at the right time. Leaders who think like this are always looking to move to a better place where their ministry will be truly appreciated and the success they deserve will finally come. This means that many pastors move frequently from one church to the next looking for success.

5. *A spiritually plateaued leader finds faults in others more often than in self.* These leaders find introspection difficult and rarely evaluate themselves, though they are often busy evaluating everyone else. This is certainly not a new phenomenon by any means. Jesus described such leaders humorously as ones who find the speck in their brother's eye but do not notice the plank protruding from their own (Matt. 7:3).

6. *A spiritually plateaued leader is burned-out from lots of busyness that has been substituted for simple intimacy with Christ.* Spiritually plateaued leaders are exhausted because they are usually deceived into thinking that more effort and more activity are ways to gain closer access and blessing from God. This is a devastating lie from hell itself.

There is no substitute for intimacy with Christ. More activity will never satisfy our deep need to connect with God and usually prevents us from having the intimacy we so desperately require. This is one of the reasons this particular deception is so sinister.

While carrying out religious business may grant us a sense of importance, it does not renew our hearts with joy and purpose. Instead it robs us of the strength we need. Only intimacy with Christ can renew our hearts and supply us with power and strength so we can accomplish the great things God wants to do through us.

7. *A spiritually plateaued leader compromises on ethical principles once held dear.* It is not uncommon to find such leaders have fallen deep into patterns of hidden sin. Using grace and liberty as excuses, they continue to function publicly without regret or remorse, while behind closed doors they carry out sinful practices.

It is difficult to keep sin hidden for long. It tends to leak out in embarrassing ways. Often spiritually plateaued leaders wake up one day to their greatest nightmare—their hidden sin has been revealed. For some, however, their sin will follow them into God's judgment, where it will finally be revealed (1 Tim. 5:24).

8. *A spiritually plateaued leader stays within safe areas of expertise rather than branching out into new learning endeavors.* This sort of leader wants to be seen as an expert rather than a learner and therefore has no intention of exploring new fields or gaining new understanding. This leader tells the same stories and uses the same sermons when he or she moves to a new pastorate. The idea of learning something new is scary because it implies that the leader does not have the expertise that has been part of his or her identity.

9. *A spiritually plateaued leader is unable to acknowledge the wisdom of others.* This leader talks more often than listens, is uninterested in what others have to say, and is easily offended if someone contradicts his or her idea. It is almost impossible to tell

this person anything new. When trying to share a new idea, you will often hear the words, "I know," from the plateaued leader.

10. *A spiritually plateaued leader has reduced the Christian life to a routine.* The plateaued leader is in a kind of holding pattern and is not moving forward in his or her walk with Christ. For this person life is a routine, trying to live the Christian life in the right Christian way. It is a static existence of maintaining what is, rather than developing anything new. It is a life of a few dos and many don'ts.

As you read through the list, did any of the descriptions of the plateaued leader sound like you? Perhaps you need to put this book down and have some time alone with the Lord. Confess to him the things in this list that have become part of your own identity and ask him to help you change. This is a vital step that you will not be sorry you take.

The Impact of Spiritually Plateaued Leadership

Being a plateaued leader is not only costly to the leader but also to all who follow this leader. Here are six ways poor leadership often becomes a bottleneck to releasing God's powerful kingdom on a world ready for change. These will all be discussed in much greater length as this book progresses.

1. *Poor leadership needs to control all ministry.* When leaders feel that all programs of the church need their approval, they have a very unhealthy understanding of leadership, the church, and Christ himself. Such Christian leaders behave as though Christ is on vacation and has put them in charge because they have special leadership abilities. But Christian leaders do not always know what is best for the church nor should they. As leaders they are to help the people of God connect with their Head and follow his lead, because our Father knows best.

2. *Poor leadership needs to filter God's voice.* Too often Christian leaders believe that other Christians are unable to understand God's Word adequately. As a result, they become God's interpreters, revealing what God meant to say, as though God doesn't know our language, context, or challenges. And even if these leaders believe God can explain himself quite well, they still think most

Christians are incapable of truly understanding his Word without the help of the leaders' expertise.

3. *Poor leadership promotes upper-class Christianity.* For almost two thousand years Christendom has been plagued with a sinister doctrine that has corrupted all that the church should be and do in this world. It is the separation of clergy and laity. Despite the Reformation and the priesthood of all believers, ushered in by Protestantism, we still accept two classes of Christians in the kingdom, and this is just wrong.

Professional Christian leaders have a vested interest in continuing this perception rather than changing it. When someone is committed to following Christ and making a difference, he or she is usually challenged to do so professionally rather than as a "layperson." This pattern continues the class distinction and seems to give all other Christians permission to be less than wholly devoted. Unfortunately, lay leaders are often viewed as less potent change agents in the world.

4. *Poor leadership emphasizes knowledge at the expense of obedience.* When leaders believe their role is teacher and protector of God's Word, the church becomes more of an academic institution than a spiritual family on a mission. The emphasis on knowledge creates a false set of values that corrupts the church and thus the image of Christ in this world. When we confuse knowledge with maturity, we allow for a congregation to take in lots of teaching without any accountability for obedience, and the result is less maturity, not more. We can teach that obedience is important all day every day, but teaching about obedience is not the same as obedience. In fact one can question if you really know something until you put it into practice, so even our retention of knowledge is suspect if we're not practicing what we have learned.

5. *Poor leadership sees church as a worship service more than a service of worship.* For many people church has become nothing more than a Sunday morning religious event, and church growth means having more and more people attending the service. This is far removed from what the Bible teaches. The words *church* and *pastor* in the New Testament had completely different meanings than they do for us today, but we are unaware of this because we read the Bible with the understanding we have gained from our own experience. This has led us to some strange practices that we do not question because our baseline of truth about the church

is so far removed from biblical truth. For example, we see church as a standard order of service. We stick to it so religiously that we assume it must be prescribed somewhere in the Bible, since we all adhere to it so firmly—an upbeat song, followed by short announcements, followed by three more songs, an offering, and a skit. Then we have a sermon and a final song and closing benediction or prayer.

You may be thinking, *What's wrong with that?* Well, nothing really, except that we have done it every single week for centuries, so that in the conscience of people this defines church. It is so common today that we do not even see the "strangeness" of our practices. We assume they are right, without question, even though no such practice is found in the New Testament. Frankly, church services share more in common with *The Tonight Show* than they do with the New Testament.

6. *Poor leadership is lured by fame and fortune.* Leadership in the church today has become a career path, and certain well-known leaders are the standard against whom others are measured. Leaders who are seen as successful enjoy special perks, which makes this kind of success in leadership even more enticing. They have greater influence and bigger buildings; they write bestselling books, speak at bigger conferences, and enjoy larger salaries. However, lives of privilege are often corrupted, and these leaders are easily lured by fame and fortune. Usually such leaders expect to be served rather than serve others.

Despite the preceding lists of problems with the leadership in the church, this book is not intended to be merely a critical analysis of church leaders. As you read on, you will find a strong positive portrayal of ways to bring health, vitality, and fruitfulness to the church today. Understanding where we are and where we need to go is essential, so first we must look at some of the problem issues.

SECTION ONE

THE COUNTERFEIT KINGDOM OF OUTSIDE IN

Weeds That Infiltrate the Garden of Christian Leadership

There has been an alien invasion. In our kingdom garden where we hope to grow fruit-bearing followers of Christ, weeds have infiltrated. These weeds have turned a healthy garden into a hostile environment that chokes and suffocates life. Offering what appears to be a natural and life-giving environment, these weeds are in reality part of hell's conspiracy to counterfeit the real kingdom.

Before we can grow healthy leaders from the soil of changed lives, we must first dig up and remove the weeds that suck the life from good leaders who would ordinarily bear fruit. Because these weeds are so abundant and rooted deeply in our soil, we cannot just ignore them and hope to bear fruit in spite of them.

In this first section, we will pull out these weeds by the roots. The weeds we will address all have one thing in common: they promise life and empowerment if people conform to the pressures and structures established by the counterfeits, which work their way in from the outside. When the weeds take over, the ways of the world are valued, and we put more trust in the organization than in our King. The laborers work hard for approval from the outside or up the chain of command, which is not the way of Christ's kingdom but is a counterfeit expression.

The chapters that follow address the problems of institutionalization, corruption of leadership character, legalistic leadership, the monopolization of truth, the hierarchical chain of command, false views of reality, and parasitic "ministries." In each of these cases, lies from the counterfeit kingdom have taken root in the soil of the true kingdom and sucked out life to such an extent that fruit is either nonexistent or limited.

Because these weeds have been at home in the church for centuries (if not millennia in some cases), we are coaxed to believe they are natural and right. We have come to accept them as normal and have even endowed them with religious authority. As I address each one, you may even think I am trampling on holy stuff, but be patient with me. I am not antichurch. If you read my words correctly, you will find that I am adamantly *for* the church. Be brave as you read and fix your focus on the Scriptures rather than on your traditions and experience.

I risk coming across as negative here, but it's necessary to address the problems in an honest, biblical, and forthright manner. This section is important, but it is only the beginning of the book. Once the weeds are pulled, we can go on to some profound principles for growing leaders from the good soil, leaders who will change the world.

1

ON BEING INSTITUTIONALIZED

Depending on the Walls That Imprison You

All progress is initiated by challenging current conceptions, and executed by supplanting existing institutions.

George Bernard Shaw

The moment the slave resolves that he will no longer be a slave, his fetters fall. Freedom and slavery are mental states.

Mahatma Gandhi

Brooks was a well-liked and respected person in the inmate community. He ran the library and loved books and people. He was no one's enemy. A senior citizen of the prison populace, he had been in the Shawshank institution longer than anyone could remember. And he was about to be released.

Suddenly and without any warning, Brooks goes crazy and threatens to kill another inmate with a shank to his throat. The other cons try to figure out what went wrong with the normally calm and likeable old guy.

Listening to a later conversation in the prison yard, we get the sense that this is about more than just a literal prison.

Andy, played by Tim Robbins, remarks, "I just don't understand what happened in there. That's all."

Another inmate chalks it up to the old man going crazy, but Red, played by Morgan Freeman, takes issue with the remark. "Would you knock it off? Brooks ain't no bug. He's just . . . institutionalized. The man's been in here fifty years, Hayward, fifty years! This is all he knows. In here he's an important man. He's an educated man. Outside he's nothing. He's just a used-up con with arthritis in both hands. He probably couldn't even get a library card if he tried. Do you know what I'm trying to say?"

What It Means to Be Institutionalized

I have met many people like Brooks—prisoners, people who are institutionalized. I have been like that.

The organized church has become an institution and its leaders are much like Brooks. Inside the institution they are important people, educated people. Outside they are nothing, with no clout, no power, nothing impressive. It is dangerous when the institution becomes the leader's source of identity and purpose. Soon the leader feels compelled to give his or her life to maintaining the institution. In essence the leader is a prisoner and cannot imagine life on the outside.

Such leaders invest years in the furtherance of the institution and, in many cases, tens of thousands of dollars in education to be leaders in it. I remember the shock of one day realizing that my master of divinity degree, which cost me five years and fifty thousand dollars, was of no value at all in the world. It had value only behind the walls of the institution.

At the time of this realization, Paul Kaak and I were working together to create our Organic Church Greenhouse Training. He and I come from very similar backgrounds. By gift and calling Paul is a teacher. He was the teaching pastor of a large up-and-coming church when God called him to a more organic expression of church life.

As we grew in our convictions concerning organic church, Paul sought opportunities to teach in the secular world. He went to some local community colleges to see if he could teach there, but his MDiv degree did not prepare him to teach in any of their departments. In frustration he went to his seminary and asked them if he could trade his ninety-eight-unit MDiv for a thirty-three-unit master of communication degree, just so he could qualify for a job outside the walls of the church institution. His request was denied. He decided to get a PhD instead and is now a professor, teaching leadership in a university.

Most pastors do not make a great deal of money, despite the years of education required to qualify for the job. After three to five years and thousands of dollars spent on acquiring the degree, a pastor seldom makes enough money to support a family, let alone pay off the school loans.

My point is not that an education is a waste. I do not think that at all. I value my education. I enjoyed it, excelled in it, and in the future plan on continuing it. The burgeoning organic church movement of which I'm a part is not anti-education at all; many of us have doctorates and are teachers in colleges and universities.

The fact remains that those in professional ministry are deeply invested in the institution, seemingly from the very start. The institution reinforces the value of their education and their sense of importance, making life outside of the institution hard to imagine or attempt. Outside they are qualified to do little more than flip burgers or brew lattes. The institution sucks them in and leaves them no hope for a life outside.

I can't tell you how many times I have seen pastors get excited about the challenge of God's organic kingdom principles, only to face the inevitable surprise of a lack of credentials for working outside the institution. Unfortunately one of the first questions I usually get is: "How can I do this and still support my family?"

A few years ago I was asked to consult on an ordination process. I began to ask a lot of questions of the process, as was my role. The examining board was made up entirely of pastors who would test the doctrine of candidates and then recommend them (or not) to the churches for licensure and/or ordination. The process, not unlike that of most denominations, was an examination of the candidate that was similar to a bar exam.

In my opinion, this whole process was confusing people and reinforcing the unbiblical division between clergy and laity. By encouraging the professional Christian phenomenon, we were in a sense excusing ordinary Christians from having to take responsibility for the kingdom of God—after all, that's what we pay the pastor to do. So I asked very straightforward questions of the process, demanding that we substantiate it biblically and theologically.

Quickly I had to back off and excuse myself from the role because I found that my queries were touching very sensitive areas of the identities of some men whom I love and respect. My questions made many feel as if their entire life needed justification. This response was an eye-opener for me. Some had faithfully served the Lord for three to four decades, and their whole sense of identity was entwined with the idea of being professional Christian leaders who are responsible for the faith and understanding of God's people. These godly men could not comfortably question, without becoming unglued, the very institution they had helped reinforce for decades.

Though my questions were good and my intentions were sound, I became aware that some of God's dearest children are firmly entrenched in the institution. I realized the wisdom of Christ's words concerning new wine and old wineskins (see Matt. 9:17). Christ was not saying that new wineskins are good and old ones are bad. The point is that all the wine is important to Christ, and he has no intention of spilling even a drop. So new wineskins are necessary for new wine, which would cause old wineskins to burst and the wine to be lost. I am not saying we must get rid of the old wineskins, but I am challenging the church to see beyond the old and allow the new to emerge.

Two Lethal Problems

Christ did not come to establish an institution. His kingdom and his church are meant to be relational and spontaneous movements, not organizations. It is his followers who created the "church institution" with layers of authority and solidified programs and practices that take on a sacred nature in and of themselves. Wikipedia says:

> Institutions are structures and mechanisms of social order and cooperation governing the behavior of a set of individuals. Institutions are identified with a social purpose and permanence, transcending individual human lives and intentions, and with the making and enforcing of rules governing cooperative human behavior. The term, *institution*, is commonly applied to customs and behavior patterns important to a society, as well as to particular formal organizations of government and public service.

When we become part of the perpetuation of the institution so that our own identity and security are found there, we have become institutionalized like Brooks.

The Counterfeit Kingdom of Outside In

There are two lethal problems with being institutionalized. First, the leader who has been institutionalized in the church, often unwittingly, places his or her faith in the institution rather than in the Lord. The church's institutional form becomes the provider: the source of security, identity, and hope. As the institution goes, so goes this person's sense of worth and well-being. If the institution is threatened, the leader's own security is threatened. In this state, the leader's faith is reduced to maintaining and promoting the institution and its agenda.

The second problem is we elevate the institution to the level of being God's main, if not his only, instrument on earth. We limit God to working within the institution. This is by far the worst consequence of institutionalization. If we see the organization called "church" as God's special means of working on earth, it takes on divine importance. If this is our perception of the organization, then to resist it or exist outside of it is to resist or be outside of God himself. When we further the cause of the institution, we further God's cause. When we question it, we question God. Those who are not friends of the institution are not friends of God but enemies. Anyone who competes with the institution must be against God. The worth of people is determined by their value to the institution and its objectives. Even the buildings that are owned by the institution are said to be God's house.

Of course, God may well be working in and through the organized expression of the church, but I guarantee he is also at work outside of it. His kingdom is bigger than any church, denomination, or institution.

The first problem is personal and affects the leader and perhaps those closest to him or her. The second—believing the institution is God's main instrument for working in the world—can create an entire culture that affects many others. Both problems are forms of idolatry, because in both cases the institution replaces God. This is bondage. It is unhealthy and can destroy lives, and it certainly is not the reason Jesus died on the cross.

Freedom Behind or Beyond the Walls

I believe that some people are supposed to work within the walls of the organized church. They are called to serve there, and this is where God uses them. It is not my idea that all need to leave the Christian institution. It is essential, however, that those who stay in it function with freedom and faith and not in bondage. This is the only path to renewal. The institution itself is not evil, but when the church is institutionalized, this is wrong.

Getting back to the story of Red and Brooks, Red explains how someone becomes institutionalized. "I'm telling you these walls are funny. First you hate 'em, then you get used to 'em. Enough time passes and you get so you depend on 'em. That's institutionalized."

The film *The Shawshank Redemption*, based on a Stephen King novel, is a story of a man wrongly convicted of a double homicide and sentenced to life in the Shawshank prison. It is a story of redemption and freedom from bondage—physical, emotional, and mental.

Red concludes the scene with these words: "They send you here for life, and that's exactly what they take—the part that counts—anyway."

Many leaders hear about the thrill of seeing lost people redeemed, churches started, and God's kingdom transforming the world in organic church movements. They feel something deep inside them, something long forgotten, rise up once again. Then they count the cost of joining such a movement, and it suddenly becomes an immense challenge because they are dependent on the institution for their livelihood. When they first started a life in ministry, they were excited about making a difference. When they bumped up against the walls of the institution back then, it frustrated them. But after a while, they got used to the walls and one day they woke up and realized their entire existence was dependent on those very walls they once despised. They have become institutionalized.

Choosing to Be a Captive

My great-great-grandfather and original namesake—Cornelius Cole (yes, that's my real name)—was a leader in the abolitionist movement and a personal friend of Abraham Lincoln. Our nation was founded on the idea that freedom is important, and everything in me is about setting captives free. But one day I realized that there are many people who actually prefer captivity. If I'm honest, there are even some days that I wish it for myself.

It took much dramatic work for God to set the Israelites free from slavery in Egypt, but it didn't take much at all for them to want to go right back to slavery.

Freedom can be scary for those who have never known it and are ill-equipped to live on their own. The same is true of those who have been institutionalized for a long time. Being freed from the institution is a scary thing.

The Counterfeit Kingdom of Outside In

This is what was behind Brooks's rampage in Shawshank Penitentiary. After fifty years of life behind the walls of the institution, he was suddenly and unexpectedly paroled. Brooks was afraid of freedom because he had grown so comfortable and dependent on the institution. So he reasoned that he should do something bad, then maybe he could stay. His heart, though, wouldn't let him really hurt anyone.

In junior high I felt like a prisoner, and in some ways I was. I wasn't free to do what I wanted and I couldn't wait for that freedom. Of course I never considered that the freedom of adulthood included mortgage payments, deadlines at a dead-end job, or weekends spent mowing the lawn and painting the shutters.

I felt imprisoned at the time, but bore little responsibility. A bell would ring and I would go to the next task. I didn't have to worry about budgets, bills, or bank accounts. Decisions were made for me. If things went wrong, others were responsible, not me. If something was needed, someone else paid for it. Life was simple then.

Many people are unwilling to take responsibility. Some demand freedom without responsibility, but you cannot have one without the other. When we take responsibility, we can become free, and freedom is worth the cost.

There are many who not only prefer to remain locked away in the institution of the organized church but actually believe that God has called them to fight against anyone who would venture to have a spiritual life outside its walls.

A Subtle Distinction

There is a very subtle difference between being needed and being needy. When it comes to leadership, this subtlety is often trampled over. What we think of as being needed can in reality be our own neediness. While the rest of the church may need leaders for the ministry to carry on, the leaders may be just as needy, and some serve to satisfy this longing. A drive to feel significant compels them and being needed affirms their sense of importance. Their identity is found in the neediness of others.

We all have met people who are part of a dysfunctional family. Often there is one person who, despite constant vows to change, is never able to mend his or her ways to benefit the family. The husband who is a drug addict is one example. His addiction seizes control of his life and devastates everyone close to him.

There is more to the story, though. From the outside, the drug addict's wife seems to be in a much better condition. She doesn't do drugs, she is faithful in attending church, and she is responsible in paying the bills and keeping the family business going, even when her husband is out wreaking havoc. But she also contributes to the dysfunction. She is codependent.

Her husband is dependent on drugs; she is dependent on him. She needs to feel needed, and her husband's irresponsible behavior engenders that feeling. Thus she thrives on enabling her husband's irresponsible behavior. No matter how awful he behaves and what devastating actions he inflicts, she always takes him back, fixes the problems, and in essence gives him a kind of permission to do it all over again. She has become his safety net, and he feels free to fly irresponsibly through life.

The wife also enjoys the sympathy and admiration of others who believe she is the most patient and long-suffering person on earth. People comment, "I could never be as strong as you are." But strength has nothing to do with this ugly cycle her life has become. It is all about weak wills, not strong ones.

The church in the West functions in a pattern similar to that of a dysfunctional relationship. It is locked up in an unhealthy cycle in which the Christian leaders and the regular Christians are codependents. The Christians who are not the church leaders prefer not to take responsibility for the kingdom of God. They want to be free to invest in their own plans rather than God's. They are the irresponsible party in this dysfunctional relationship.

The Christian leaders, on the other hand, want to be responsible—to a fault. They continue to do all the work of the church, which enables other Christians to be irresponsible. Leaders need to be needed and admired, and often this is the result when they take all the responsibility for kingdom work. People place them on a pedestal because of the important things they do. Thus a cycle develops.

The cycle of codependency must stop, and it begins with the leader refusing to enable the irresponsible behavior of others. Christian leaders must step off the pedestal and no longer allow the average Christian to do nothing. As long as the leaders continue to fulfill all roles of responsibility, the others will not be able to do what God has called them to do.

The Counterfeit Kingdom of Outside In

From Stardom to Stoning

Acts 14 tells a story about Paul and Barnabas who are preaching in Lystra. A miracle occurs, and the people begin to think that Paul and Barnabas are gods; they start to worship them. Immediately Paul and Barnabas rush out into the crowd, tearing their robes and saying, "Men, why are you doing these things? We also are men of the same nature as you" (v. 15).

Christian leaders today need to do the same thing. They need to make clear that they are no different from their followers and that both they and their followers are accountable to God for how they use what he has given them for the kingdom of God. We must end the cycle of dysfunction.

It is important, however, that I be honest. When codependents decide they will no longer enable addicts, the response is usually harsh and immediate. Those who are dependent on some compulsive behavior do not like to have their irresponsible lifestyle cut off and their sin called out. They will strike swiftly and hard.

A short time after the people of Lystra wanted to worship Paul as a god, they turned against him and ended up stoning him and dragging his lifeless body out of the city.

It will cost us to break the cycle of dysfunction in the church, but it is the only way for God's people to gain the freedom necessary to carry the kingdom of God into the world.

Living or Dying

It's not a question of whether you are inside the walls, but are the walls inside of you? The actual walls of the institution, whether they are brick and mortar or bureaucratic channels and political process, are not the real problem. It is the mind-set of the leader that is most important. A leader must be free if he or she is to lead others into freedom. Some, who remain behind the walls of the institution, can still be free in their minds. Others, outside of the institution, may still be held captive. Often we get confused and blame the institution, when it is our own mind-set that is really the issue.

It is a sad thing when a leader nears the end of life and realizes that the institutional expression of the church in which he or she invested everything is in fact less than viable, spiritual, or able to do much good in this world. To have given your best years and fought tough battles for an institution and find that your faith was misplaced is perhaps the saddest story of all.

Today many leaders are awakening to the fact that the call they once received was long ago hijacked by an institutional mind-set that sucked all the life and gifts out of them. Actually it takes a very intentional and heartfelt breaking of self—our identity, sense of vested importance, and dependence—to experience the freedom we need from the institution, whether we remain behind the walls or venture beyond them. I will elaborate much more on this in chapter 19.

In a later scene of *The Shawshank Redemption*, Red and Andy are sitting alone in the yard, leaning against what seems like an ancient wall. In the shadow of an ominous prison wall a conversation ensues that is a pivotal moment in the film.

Red is known as the guy who can get you things in prison. Andy and Red have become friends. Red is concerned with Andy's well-being, since he just finished an extensive time in solitary. But in an ironic twist, Andy is more concerned with Red's well-being.

Andy has gone through an incredible ordeal of punishment, which he did not deserve. Another prisoner, who had testimony that vindicated Andy, was killed by the prison guards at the warden's order. At every turn Andy finds life slapping him in the face and knocking him down, but he always gets back up and continues with a seemingly unbelievable optimism. Andy is able to have this incredible outlook because he is free. Despite being behind the walls of the institution, his heart, his mind, and his emotions are still free and nothing will take that from him. This movie is a battle for Andy's freedom, for his soul, and in the end he will win. He will have his Shawshank redemption.

"You think you'll ever get out of here?" asks Andy of Red.

"Me? Yeah, one day when I got a long white beard and two or three marbles rolling around upstairs, they'll let me out."

With a faraway look in his eyes, Andy remarks, "Tell you where I'd go—Zihuatenejo."

Red is not sure he understood, so Andy explains further. "It's in Mexico. A little place on the Pacific Ocean." Then he asks, "Do you know what the Mexicans say about the Pacific?"

Red shakes his head.

Still with a dreamlike look, Andy says, "They say it has no memory. That's where I want to live the rest of my life. A warm place that has no memory."

He goes on, as if he is there, under the sun with his feet in the warm sand, "Open up a little hotel right on the beach. Buy some worthless old boat, 'n' fix 'er up new. Take my guests out charter fishing."

Red responds, "Zihuatenejo, eh?"

Then the conversation changes. Andy is mentally back with Red in the prison yard. He turns, looks him in the eyes, and says, "A place like that . . . I could use a guy who knows how to get things."

Red looks down, almost in defeat. Unable to see the possibility because the reality of the prison walls is truer for him, Red replies, "I don't think I could make it on the outside, Andy."

Red trusts Andy. In a prison culture where you have to always show your strength, Red reveals his vulnerability.

As he gazes up at the high, cold stone walls that have imprisoned him, he goes on, "I've been in here most of my life. I'm an institutional man now, just like Brooks was."

"Well, you underestimate yourself."

"I don't think so," Red replies. "I mean, in here I'm the guy who can get things for you, sure. But out there all you need is the yellow pages. Hell, I wouldn't even know where to begin. The Pacific Ocean? About scare me to death, something that big."

Andy, clearly disappointed, but still resolute, says, "Not me. I didn't shoot my wife and I didn't shoot her lover, but whatever mistakes I made I paid for them and then some. That hotel and boat, I don't think that's too much to ask."

Out of concern for his friend, and perhaps a little shame at his lack of faith in himself, Red responds forcefully, "I don't think you ought to be doing this to yourself, Andy. I mean, Mexico is way the hell down there and you're in here."

Once again, the reality of the prison comes crashing in on Andy. Everything is telling him to give up and surrender to the walls of the institution. But he won't. He knows that he is not guilty; he will hold out for his freedom.

"Yeah, right," Andy says, jaw clenched. "That's the way it is. It's down there and I'm in here. I guess it comes down to a simple choice really."

Red nods, assuming Andy is about to choose to surrender to life behind the walls and give up on Mexican fantasies, but Red is wrong. Andy is unsinkable. He summarizes in one sentence the choice all of us have to make if we are to break free from being institutionalized. Our simple choice is the same as Andy's: "Get busy living or get busy dying."

Leaving Red alone in the shadows, he stands up and walks away, into the sunshine of a day that is ending.

Andy would not surrender to the walls. He would be free. He was free before he was in prison, he was free while in prison, and he would be free outside of prison.

And you can be too.

Andy saw great potential in Red, more than Red himself could see. And eventually, they would both realize the freedom that Andy always had on the inside.

Will you be free of the institution? The choice is yours. Get busy living or get busy dying.

2

SLAVES ARE MADE
IN SUCH WAYS

The Corruption of Christian Leadership

Don't compromise yourself. You are all you've got.

Janis Joplin

A man who stands for nothing will fall for anything.

Malcolm X

In a time known to us as the Dark Ages, William Wallace rose to defend his nation, Scotland, from the tyrannical rule of England's King Edward I. The 1995 Oscar-winning film *Braveheart* tells the story. (This film is a great study of leadership. For this reason I will refer to it often in this book.)

Shortly after Wallace (played by Mel Gibson) had invaded and defeated the king's troops at York, King Edward, called "Longshanks," sent his daughter-in-law, Isabella of France, the Princess of Wales, to negotiate a peace settlement. For this fictional depiction of their meeting, Wallace is called to Isabella's tent to discuss the king's proposals.

She begins the conversation with small talk. "I understand you have recently been given the rank of knight."

Unwilling to concede on any point whatsoever, Wallace responds honestly, "I have been given nothing. God makes men what they are."

Isabella is no pushover. "Did God make you a sacker of peaceful cities?" she retorts.

Wallace responds by describing some of the ugly atrocities thrust on the Scots by Longshanks and the ruler of York.

Then Hamilton, the captain in charge of the princess's protection, whispers to her in Latin, assuming that Wallace will not understand, "He is a bloody, murdering savage, and he is telling lies."

Wallace responds in perfect Latin, "I never lie!"

The captain is obviously shocked by the fluent Latin coming from a man who has the appearance of having little education.

With eyes of steel, Wallace goes on to finish his thought, still in Latin: "But I am a savage." Wallace wants them to know that he is a wild man, an educated but untamed man.

To make his point plainly and settle all discussion, he challenges the princess to ask the king about the atrocities while looking into his eyes to see if she sees truth.

Isabella dismisses her guard to speak frankly with the rebel. She is a strong woman and once alone with Wallace, she goes right to the issue. "You invade England, but you are too far from shelter and supply to finish the conquest. The king desires peace; he swears it to me. He proposes that you withdraw your attack and in return he grants you title, estates, and this chest of gold, which I am to pay to you personally."

"A lordship and titles—gold—*that I should become Judas?*"

She replies with the wisdom of the world: "Peace is made in such ways."

Wallace, in his commanding voice, interrupts her and pronounces with zeal, "*Slaves* are made in such ways!"

After some personal interchange, Wallace ends the negotiation with these words, "One day you will be a queen and you must open your eyes. You tell your king that William Wallace will not be ruled, nor will any Scot while I live."

Three Paths to Corruption

It is not very hard to find stories of Christian leaders who have fallen victim to sin. Just about every year a major news story tells of another one who falls into immorality. Whether it's Jim and Tammy's air-conditioned doghouse and "creative" financing, Jimmy Swaggart's public weeping for having rendezvoused with prostitutes, or Ted Haggard's alleged involvement with drugs and homosexual prostitutes, the stories are splashed across the media and seared in our memories.

We hear about these leaders' sin when their fall is at its end. The fall doesn't begin with public humiliation, however; it begins very privately with small decisions that individually do not have nearly the same grave implications they will have when compounded by later choices. It is always at least one of three paths that leads to a broken leader who is no longer capable of exemplifying any moral authority. These paths of corruption are the pursuit of power, the pursuit of possessions, and the pursuit of pleasure.

The Pursuit of Power

I travel a lot and my travel exacts a cost from my body, my family, and the ministry. Over the years I have worked hard to keep things healthy. Often I take family members on trips overseas so that I am investing in family while also doing ministry. As a result we share memories that will last a lifetime. I try to maintain seasons at home and seasons of travel. Usually I do well with this but sometimes I find I have said yes to one too many engagements.

Because of my frequent flier status, airlines often grant me perks. Now I have entered into a more elite club where I can be upgraded to a better class of service. For years I flew economy class, never thinking business or first class were options. Suddenly I am flying in business class more often than economy, but never paying more than an economy price. This perk comes from logging a lot of flight miles and it is much appreciated, especially for long flights overseas when I have to get off the plane, ignore jet lag, jump right into my work, and then return home in a couple days.

I have noticed, however, a negative side effect to my new status that surprises me. I have come to expect that my airline will give me an upgrade. When they don't, I find that I'm offended. *Don't they know who I am?*

My wife, Dana, saw this firsthand on a recent trip to Europe when I was denied an upgrade but I persisted in pursuing one. Eventually I was able to finagle an upgrade for both of us. My wife looked at me with both relief and shocked disbelief. She did want to fly comfortably but she wasn't sure she wanted to sit next to this spoiled baby who felt entitled to the best service.

It wasn't the upgrade that was wrong, it was the sense of entitlement that was oozing from my ego that bothered her. And she was right. We get used to being treated like royalty, and we feel as though it is right for us to be treated this way, not like those common people in economy class. I needed to have Dana wake me up to the fact that I had become accustomed to and expected upper-class service. I'm amazed how easily this happened and now guard against an expectation of special treatment. To be honest, I still don't mind being upgraded on my flights; I just want to remain humble about it.

Inside all of us is a God-given desire to be loved, admired, and respected. Constantly Satan is enticing us to meet our God-given needs in less than honorable ways. One of those ways is the pursuit of power, and Satan has long used this lure to draw Christian leaders into biting on his bait and being hooked by him.

Christian leaders find that as we advance up the ladder of what is considered success, we gain greater influence and authority. Longing to be useful and successful in ministry, we continue to pursue success. As we gain more and more influence, we are placed in positions of power. Then too often we become hooked by the power we are able to wield. From this place, we feel the need to protect the institution that grants us the power, and we are now part of the problem.

In most evangelical circles, *power* is not the best word to describe this phenomenon; it is *fame*. We want the masses to accept us and acknowledge our value. We enjoy the privileges of fame: being invited into the rooms where key decisions are made, being included in the list of speakers at big events, seeing our photo included in advertisements for important conferences. Soon our smiling face dominates the covers of our books. Now *we*, more than the content of the book, are the draw.

But fame has a cost. Often it pulls us away from the place where we were effective, and we begin a traveling circuit of ministry in which there is little or no accountability. While wanting to be used in significant ministry, we end up achieving fame but having little impact on changing the lives of others.

Of course public speaking has some influence, but it does not produce the fruit that reproduces for generations. Because often the people attending conferences say kind things about the speakers, we are deceived into thinking that our lives are making an impact and our significance is huge. But the reality is that the impact of a conference speaker is

The Counterfeit Kingdom of Outside In

shallow compared to that of the one who pours his or her life into a few people in a mentoring relationship.

Jesus never settled into a public speaking ministry for this reason. He would never give his heart to the crowds and always withdrew to the few who would listen and be changed. Jesus had the capacity to draw huge crowds, but instead he invested his life in a handful of people who would turn the world upside down.

If anyone ever deserved royal treatment, it was Jesus when he came to earth. He should have been born in a mansion but he was born in the midst of manure. He lived life as a humble servant, always looking to empower others rather than get his own upgrade. He was not enamored by the shallow love of the crowds and never let the public seduce him.

There is a grave danger to fame. Everyone knows who you are but no one really knows *you*. Life on the road, surrounded only by people who praise you, entices leaders into a dangerous path of a never-satisfied ego. We begin to believe our press clippings and are trapped into thinking we are indeed more significant and important than the common people. Soon we prefer being around the people who think the world of us rather than with the people who ground us in reality. Our goals in life change, reflecting more selfish positions, though we mask them with language that sounds spiritual.

Sitting in our business class seats, we begin to notice the few who get to sit in first class and we wonder what life is like up there.

The ego is never satisfied with a little power; we want more. It is easy to become slaves to its pursuit, and this cruel master, whose hunger is never satiated, will take us to places we never wanted to be. While we are biting down on the delicious bait of fame, the hook of privilege digs into us and will never release us. It is hard to open our mouths and let go of the position, the power, and the prestige.

The Pursuit of Possessions

Oh, man, this chapter is hard for me to write. You see, not only do I like upgrades, but I also love Macintosh computers and other electronic gadgets. In fact I am writing these very words on my new Macintosh laptop with my iPhone on my chest, waiting for a call. Oops, there's the call . . .

This desire for new stuff is another longing that is never satisfied. The next model, even sexier than the last, is more powerful, has more features, and is sleeker looking. My new laptop is already out of date, and the newer iPhone is already demanding long lines. The seduction is insidious.

This is intentional. The steady seduction lures our affection to the wrong place. Before we know it, we wake up someplace we never expected to be. Like Edmund in *The Lion, the Witch and the Wardrobe*, we want our Turkish delight and are willing to sell off all that is precious to gain it.

What does the man who has everything want? The answer: more. We become slaves of the things we own. Soon, all we do is work to pay the interest we have on loans to own the things that actually own us.

It may start with upgrades on computers and cell phones, but the path descends from there. Soon we want better cars and a second home. Before long, the biggest TV is not enough; we need an in-home theater system. Surrounded by beautiful things we are still not satisfied, because there is always something we do not have. This is how people end up with an air-conditioned doghouse in the yard of their mansion or a Learjet to take them from one ministry assignment to the next, paid for by the ministry support of others. In such a spiral descent, it isn't long before we lose sight of the true treasure. We start to live for the possessions rather than our Lord.

I have to remind myself, more often than ever, that I will gladly give away everything I have just to hold on to Christ. We must remember what he said: "Where your treasure is, there your heart will be also" (Matt. 6:21). He is the hidden treasure. He is the pearl of great price. And I would gladly sell everything to be with him.

The Pursuit of Pleasure

Deep in all of us is a God-given need for pleasure. He has given us this need so that we will find pleasure in him and in the good things he gives us.

Satan is a deceptive and sinister enemy who hijacks God's creation any way he can. He always lies to us. He tempts us to think that God cannot or will not meet our needs, which he gave us in the first place. Then we think we have to take matters into our own hands. This is when we take the first step toward bondage to an evil and maniacal master.

Our Enemy knows where our weaknesses lie. He waits for moments when we are susceptible, and he strikes with just the right amount of temptation mixed with a healthy dose of deception. Our vulner-

The Counterfeit Kingdom of Outside In

ability is often most acute when we are feeling grave disappointment about our current endeavors. Our unfulfilled expectations soon turn to feeling sorry for ourselves. Usually, we are not thinking God is to blame for our lack of fulfillment. Typically we are mad at someone else, but we bite on the bait and it doesn't matter why, we are hooked. In our feelings of grief we want something to make us feel good, and Satan is glad to present us with just that, at least for a moment. A moment of sin is all it takes to be trapped into a lifelong prison sentence. The pursuit of pleasure has led many to plunge into the depths of depravity.

Because of the way we have envisioned leadership in our society—as a lone eagle soaring above the rest—leaders are susceptible to feeling alone and isolated. Often the Christian church expects the pastor to be better than the rest so that he or she can set the example for all others. This causes the leader to believe foolishly that there are spiritual reasons for not being open about one's weaknesses. This isolation often leads to a lack of accountability and relational transparency, which makes the leader even more vulnerable.

A leader needs regular rest, relational boundaries, open accountability in a trusted relationship, and the recognition that the weight of the church's success is not on his or her shoulders. When a leader blindly denies these needs, he or she will not know what to do when they arise. Feeling unappreciated by loved ones, having unmet physical needs, experiencing discouragement, insecurity, loneliness, mixed with a dose of ego and a need to be needed creates a volatile cocktail that could easily implode a life and ministry. So often sexual temptation presents an avenue of escape, and many good leaders have fallen victim to it.

From the very beginning, God said, "It is not good for the man to be alone" (Gen. 2:18). He designed us to need pleasure in relationships. Denying this need for long seasons does not help; it only accentuates the problem. Only a leader who finds the time necessary to enjoy life, love, and lasting relationships in a healthy manner will last.

The Oldest Trick in the Book . . . *Literally!*

If these three paths of corruption for leaders sound familiar, it is because they are not new at all. They are the oldest trick in the book. The apostle John writes about our Enemy's tactics. He summarizes them as "the lust of the flesh and the lust of the eyes and the boastful pride of life" (see 1 John 2:15–17).

You do not have to go far in the Bible to find these strategies at work; three chapters in and there they are. Even in a perfect paradise, while tempting unblemished people who do not have a sinful nature, Satan starts with these same three temptations and hits a home run with his first at bat. Why would he change his strategy if it works so well?

The Bible says that the fruit Adam and Eve were forbidden to eat was delicious (lust of the flesh), a delight to the eyes (lust of the eyes), and would make one wise (boastful pride of life). Eve took, ate, and gave it to her husband, who also ate (see Gen. 3:6). We've been biting onto the same bait ever since.

This is the same tactic Satan used to tempt another perfect representation of man. Before Jesus started his public ministry, he was led out into the wilderness alone to face the Enemy (Matt. 4:1–11). Jesus is called the second Adam (Rom. 5:15–17; 1 Cor. 15:45–49) because he represents us all. There are some striking similarities, and equally striking differences, between the two men. Both were perfect men without sin. Both were representatives of all of humanity. Both spent time in the company of animals and angels (Gen. 2:19–20; 3:24; Matt. 4:11; Mark 1:12–13). Both faced Satan head-to-head.

Jesus was tempted in the same ways Adam had been—"the lust of the flesh" ("command that these stones become bread," v. 3), "the lust of the eyes" ("all the kingdoms of the world and their glory . . . I will give you," v. 8), and "the boastful pride of life" ("throw yourself down [from the pinnacle of the temple]," vv. 5–6). Both were tempted at their point of weakness—Adam and Eve were innocent, pure, and physically perfect but lacked maturity and wisdom; Jesus was perfect but had been fasting for forty days. He was hungry and alone.

This is where the similarities end and the differences begin. Adam was in a garden paradise; Jesus was in a desert wilderness. Adam had companionship, and Jesus was alone. Adam had all the food he could eat with only one restriction. Jesus lived under many restrictions and spent forty days fasting. With Adam, the animals were friendly and the angels hostile (see Gen. 2:19–20; 3:24). With Jesus the animals were hostile, and the angels were friendly (Mark 1:13). Of course the most striking difference is that Adam fell into sin when tempted, and Jesus did not. It is not wrong to desire wisdom or to need food. It is wrong to disobey God to get them.

Satan's Strategy

All that is in the world (1 John 2:16)	Used against Eve (Genesis 3:6)	Used against Jesus (Matthew 4:3, 6, 9)
"the lust of the flesh"	"the tree was good for food"	"command that these stones become bread"
"the lust of the eyes"	"it was a delight to the eyes"	"showed Him all the kingdoms of the world"
"the boastful pride of life"	"the tree was desirable to make one wise"	"throw Yourself down [off the temple] . . . His angels . . . will bear You up"

Seven Comparisons of the First and Last Adam

	Adam	Jesus
1. Both were approached in weakness.	Gen. 3:1	Matt. 4:2–3
2. Both were tempted to doubt God's Word.	Gen. 3:1–4	Matt. 4:3
3. Both were sinless.	Gen. 2:25	Matt. 3:17
4. Both were tempted with . . .		
the lust of the flesh	Gen. 3:6	Matt. 4:3
the lust of the eyes	Gen. 3:6	Matt. 4:8–9
the boastful pride of life	Gen. 3:6	Matt. 4:5–6
5. Both were enticed to eat something.	Gen. 3:5–6	Matt. 4:3
6. Both were surrounded by animals.	Gen. 2:19	Mark 1:13
7. Both represented all of mankind.	Rom. 5:12	Rom. 5:19

For as through one man's disobedience the many were made sinners, even so through the obedience of the One the many will be made righteous.

Romans 5:19

Eight Contrasts of the First and Last Adam

Adam	Jesus
1. In a garden paradise.	In a desert wilderness.
2. Fully fed and satisfied.	Hungry.
3. With a companion.	Alone.
4. With no precedent for sin.	With *only* the precedent of sin.
5. Surrounded by *tame* animals.	Surrounded by *wild* animals.
6. Didn't expect Satan.	Did expect Satan.
7. Angels were hostile.	Angels were helpful.
8. Failed the test.	Passed the test.

Jesus resisted by using the truth of God's Word at the point of temptation. He never doubted God's love or care for him. He never believed that God was unable to care for him. The successful response to Satan's strategy is always the same: know and trust God and his Word. Once we doubt that God cares for us, we are vulnerable to Satan's schemes.

Christian leaders face the same temptations every day that Adam and Jesus did. We must rise above and recognize that there is truth that can save us. We must love God more than our bodies and our desire for pleasure (the lust of the flesh); we must love him more than all the things we want (the lust of the eyes); we must love him more than power or fame (the boastful pride of life).

In this chapter I have often used rather harmless and seemingly insignificant examples to illustrate these lures—wanting to sit in first class, enjoying a new laptop. The truth is that temptation usually begins in small things, but it never ends there. Whether it is a sense of entitlement or a desire for accolades, it is a dangerous path. Whether it is an upgrade to a better computer or gadget or wanting a second, third, or fourth vacation home and a private jet to get there, the path is the same, just farther along. Satan always lures us with seemingly harmless temptations at first, but soon we find ourselves sliding down into deeper and deeper traps. We must recognize the temptations at their most benign level if we are to stay clear of the more lethal hooks that are waiting to ensnare us farther along.

In his parables Jesus spoke of seed being planted in soil that is infested with weeds. The seed is the Word of God and it germinates and grows, but the life of the emerging plant does not bear fruit because the weeds suffocate it. Jesus identifies the weeds in the parable as "the worries of the world, and the deceitfulness of riches, and the desire for other things [that] enter in and choke the word, [so that] it becomes unfruitful" (Mark 4:19).

Weeds—the lust for pleasure, for possessions, and for power—are not simply harmless realities we all live with; they are sinister and insidious traps that will kill us if we grow complacent and allow them to take root in our life. These weeds threaten organic leadership by sucking the life out of the emerging leader and choking all his or her fruit.

As Christian leaders, we serve a higher purpose than our own satisfaction. But our own satisfaction can become our master if we begin to compromise in even small ways and yield to the temptation to satisfy our needs apart from God. I have often wondered, *What would the sin be if Jesus had turned stones into bread and eaten them? What*

The Counterfeit Kingdom of Outside In

command would he have broken? Is it a sin to be hungry or to eat? Is turning water into wine okay but stones into bread is a sin? The issue is not the act of eating or the miracle of transforming elements; it is in obeying the Enemy in defiance of God's leading. This is what ushers us into bondage: believing that God doesn't care for us and we need to take matters into our own hands. Slaves are made in such ways. If we are in bondage, how can we lead others to freedom, the freedom for which Christ died?

3
PHARISAISM TODAY
Protecting the Powerful

Great spirits have always encountered violent opposition from mediocre minds.

Albert Einstein

Insanity: doing the same thing over and over again and expecting different results.

Albert Einstein

A few years ago, the Lutheran Church put out a film based on Martin Luther's life, called *Luther*. Often films made by Christians are less than stellar, but this time, they spared no expense and put together a good cast including Joseph Fiennes, Alfred Molina, and Peter Ustinov. Granted, it is a positive look at Luther's life, absent of some of his foibles and costly errors in judgment, but it does accurately follow the life of this key historical figure whom God used to ignite the Protestant Reformation.

There is one clip from this movie I have watched and shown to people dozens of times, and every time I get a little teary eyed. It is a powerful scene. I will try to describe it, but my words will not do justice to the performance of the two actors. This was the late Oscar winner Peter

Ustinov's final screen role in which he portrays Luther's protector and benefactor Frederick III.

The Diet of Worms is not a middle-school boy's lunch dare but a historical and religious court that was held by the Roman Catholic Church in a town called Worms (on the Rhine River in what is now Germany). It was there that Martin Luther was put on trial as a heretic. He was asked to renounce or affirm his writings. He was unable to go against his conscience or the Scriptures, so he is reported as saying: "Here I stand. I can do no other. God help me. Amen."

From there he escaped before he was condemned as a heretic and charged as an outlaw. The church hired assassins to kill him and granted that anyone who succeeded would not face charges. Before Luther could be caught, Frederick III (sometimes called Frederick the Wise), a prince in Germany, had him seized and granted him secret asylum in his castle for eleven months. It was there, which Luther referred to as "his Patmos," that he translated the New Testament into German.

In this important scene from the movie, Luther comes into Frederick's study to present him with the German Bible he had dedicated to his benefactor. As Luther takes the leather-bound work from under his cape, he announces, "I dedicated this work to you, my lord, the translation of the New Testament." There is a short but very pregnant pause before he adds, "into our own language."

"Into German?" asks Frederick. He pauses and is obviously contemplating the implications of this momentous act. Frederick, though an admirer of Luther, was quite devoted to Catholicism and had invested much in a collection of Roman Catholic relics. Almost as if thinking out loud he says, "But this will separate us from Rome forever."

Luther, knowing well the consequences of his actions and the devotion of his benefactor to the institution, replies firmly but with kindness, "I have always sought Christian unity but not at the price of servitude." And with a spark of boldness that rises within him on occasion, he states more confidently, "I answer to God's law, not Roman."

With the wisdom of a seasoned politician, Frederick responds matter-of-factly, "Roman law is the reality."

Luther, a capable debater, retorts, "I believe in the reality of Christ."

"With no compromises?" queries Frederick.

In stoic resolve Luther replies, "None."

"You realize of course they will take this to be an act of sheer provocation?"

"Yes."

"And they will not hesitate to strike back."

"Yes, I know."

Luther's protector drops his hands in a gesture of futility. He looks up and remarks, "Well . . ." and after another pause he says, "so long as you knoooooow," stressing the word.

Luther directs his gaze at the floor as he considers the cost his work may exact.

After this exchange, there is a sudden shift in the whole mood of the scene. Frederick cannot conceal his excitement at the prospect of releasing the Scriptures to the common man. How powerful that will be!

Leaning forward and pointing to the Bible in Luther's hands, he asks, "Do you think I can have my present now?"

Luther smiles and with joy replies, "Yes, of course."

Like a child eager to open presents on Christmas morning, Frederick is practically shaking in anticipation of opening the Bible. His eyes are fixed on it as Luther brings it to him. Receiving the precious gift, he quickly opens it and is immediately so engrossed in reading that he doesn't even look up to say thank you.

There are two important observations we can make from this scene. First, when someone opens the Bible as if for the first time and hears God's voice clearly and directly, there is great joy and freedom. Nothing can compare to it on earth, anywhere. I live for those moments when a Christian, young or old, hears God speak to him or her in a clear and recognizable voice. To see such joy and enthusiasm for God's Word is the greatest reward in ministry I can receive. It is especially meaningful to me, because it reminds me of my own thirst for God's Word.

Second, some in power hold the Scriptures at a distance from ordinary Christians. I will address this further below. Just as in the days of Luther, some leaders gain power by trying to keep God's Word from the common person. This has always been the case in the church.

In this chapter and the next I will expose two ways in which Christian leadership has held the church hostage to their own power play. The first way is by promoting spiritual practices with presumed biblical authority when in actuality they do not have any biblical support. The second is by protecting Scripture from the "abuses" that common, untrained Christians inflict on it.

Indulgences Today?

When someone is perceived to have access to God, he or she has great power. In Luther's day, the church made a fortune selling indulgences, which provided forgiveness of sin and access to heaven for those who paid enough money. This is one of the things Luther was fighting against.

Today we divide the world into two categories. We emphasize that Christians are going to heaven and non-Christians are not. Sometimes we use the distinctions of "saved" and "unsaved," "saints" and "sinners," "Christians" and "non-Christians," "believers" and "unbelievers." Often we use "churched" and "unchurched" right along with the other distinctions. The logical assumption is that the unchurched need to change their Sunday morning routine if they want to avoid an eternity of suffering in hell. We may not truly believe this, but this is what our actions communicate, and people do pick up on our nonverbal sermons as much (or more) than our recorded ones.

So from the perspective of the non-Christian, does the church sell indulgences today? We tell non-Christians they need to decide to become Christians (like us) to escape hell. And part of becoming a Christian is going to church, and part of going to church is giving money in the offering. I've not heard any evangelical church threaten the fires of hell for those who refuse to give money, as they did in the time of Luther, but we are closer to that than we might think.

When we evangelize people, it usually ends with us taking them to church to hear the gospel and close the deal. We urge them to walk down the aisle to receive salvation. From the altar we escort them to a prayer room where we counsel them and sign them up for a newcomers class to become church members. In the new members class they are taught the importance of tithing to the church if they want to be good Christians.

Though the belief in most churches in America is not that church membership is a requisite for salvation, I am describing how it may appear to someone who is not yet a Christian.

Literal indulgences are no longer sold today, but we still wrestle with the same underlying issues: offering spiritual goods and services for a price (the subject of this chapter) and the power that some people wield over the church (which I will deal with in the next chapter).

The Competitive Church Market

Simply peruse the Christian television channels for a single evening, and you will observe how Christian goods and services are marketed. There are those who sell prayers, healings, blessings from God, and perhaps even salvation. If you send in your money, you may receive a signed copy of the speaker's latest book—a $24.99 value for a onetime gift of $100 or more. In one case a prayer cloth that was personally prayed over and anointed by the pastor was sent to anyone who would send in a "faith gift" of $25 or more. Donors were instructed to place the cloth over any ailing part of their body, and they would be healed. One leader, wanting to demonstrate his servant leadership, offered to "faith givers" a packet of moistened towelettes that he had prayed over so that donors could use them to wash their feet, thereby enabling the leader to do so by proxy.

Even in our enlightened age, Christian leaders can be abusive. We may not call them indulgences today, but the intent of these sales is strikingly similar to that of the church in Luther's day.

These are extreme abuses and such practices have been well documented by others. Actually, I am more concerned with less extreme practices we can find in most churches, because they can be even more dangerous. They have become so acceptable that we tend to see them as normative or, worse, spiritually right.

The practice of offering "indulgences" starts subtly, but it can end up going to extremes and, like the frog in the kettle of slowly boiling water, we don't realize what's happening until it's too late.

I have written before of a church planter who took out an ad in the newspaper offering to pay people $100 to attend his church. Today he has changed his philosophy and is quite embarrassed by his attempts at church growth no matter the cost. It's sad but true that even good folks can get caught up in some unsound thinking regarding these things.

Many gimmicks have been tried to get people to attend a church's services. One congregation raffled off a five-hundred-dollar gift card for gasoline. A fast-growing church in my own area advertised free raffle tickets to the first one hundred newcomers who showed up at their Easter service. The winner of the drawing would receive a new car. Another church in my area had added a new service time and offered free popcorn to anyone who would attend the new service, thus making room for other worshipers in the other services.

As churches in an area feel they must compete with each other, they begin to offer special perks to attract attenders. One church starts serving Starbucks coffee on Sunday mornings, and before you know it other churches in town are doing the same. Not only is this seen as a good thing, some would say it constitutes being relevant and hospitable.

I'm not objecting to serving good coffee but I do see danger in the spirit of competition that these tactics reveal. And I don't mind when my local movie theater offers special deals with free popcorn to get me to become a loyal customer. After all it is a business competing for my dollar. But when the church, feeling the need to compete for attendees and their offerings, adopts the way of the world, we are in trouble. Some churches have exiting pastors sign a "noncompetition contract," so they will not start a church within a certain distance of the one they leave. This is how far we have ventured into a capitalistic Christianity that treats church like a business, service like a product, and people like customers.

The Rampantly Consumeristic Mind-set

Many pastors complain about the consumeristic mind-set in their churches. It is a "what-have-you-done-for-me-lately" attitude that causes the pastor to feel pressure to keep up with the megachurch around the corner. But our people have a consumeristic attitude because we have trained them to think this way. When we try to "sell" our worship and programs to the largest crowd possible, we will attract and reinforce a consumer mind-set.

I know someone who chose to leave his home church of many years and started attending a megachurch because the opportunity for business contacts was far greater there. Granted, this sounds bad, but it just reflects the sort of church we have developed. In a sense, this person is simply living out the theology we have taught him to have.

Church growth used to be about adding souls to the church through the preaching of the gospel. Because we have foolishly come to equate church with the Sunday worship service, church growth has been reduced to increasing the attendance on Sunday mornings. Now we find ourselves competing with other churches for parishioners who are looking for the best service they can find.

Let me just ask straight up: why is the Sunday morning service so important anyway? We Protestants have the same religious zeal for it that the Roman Catholic Church has for the sacraments or the Pharisees had for the holy days and temple offerings. But we have much less Scripture to back up our making the Sunday morning service a priority than either the Catholics or the first-century Jewish leaders had for their practices.

Pick up your New Testament, open it, and read it as if for the first time. Search the Scriptures. Show me in the New Testament the verses that command us to gather together for a worship service, complete with sermons, announcements (commercials), tithes, and offerings. You will not find any verses that prescribe or even describe such a thing. What you will find are verses, chapters, and entire books dedicated to the church functioning as a spiritual family on a mission to redeem the lost.

Many point to the first few chapters of Acts to defend the practice of meeting publicly for worship and teaching. Never mind that these are not prescriptive texts but merely describing what was done for a very short time period, the practice was not preaching to the saints as much as to the lost. The rest of Acts does not describe such a gathering. Even in Ephesus where Paul says he was teaching them both publicly as well as from house to house (Acts 20:20), the public training was a discussion rather than a sermon, held in the school of Tyrannus (Acts 19:9). This was more likely a daily ministry training time than a worship service. In the New Testament the pattern of church life was not a once-a-week worship service but it was a spiritual family, gathering regularly to live life together under the common headship of Jesus Christ with everyone fully participating. All attempts to squeeze something else out of the text are nothing more than trying to defend a practice that is not biblically authoritative.

I am not saying that the Bible doesn't teach that we should get together as a family; I am arguing for the exact opposite. We *are* to be together, but not passively listening to a worship concert and a sermon.

We have hidden our Christian practices, which in the New Testament were carried out in the marketplace for all to see. We have "sanctified" them—our preaching, our baptism, our communion meal—and moved them behind stained-glass windows. We've even developed doctrines to keep them reserved for the saints and dispensed by special holy men.

Our true Enemy has been hard at work trying to pull the teeth out of the potent practices that Jesus established. The Enemy's scheme is to remove them from the context where they are indeed dangerous to his cause. Baptism was meant to be public. Communion was meant to be a shared everyday meal, which can "proclaim the Lord's death until

The Counterfeit Kingdom of Outside In

He comes" (1 Cor. 11:26). In the New Testament, preaching is always for the purpose of presenting the gospel of God's kingdom to those who are trapped in the darkness. It was not done from behind a pulpit to an audience of Christians to help inspire them in their own personal sanctification.

The Most Important Thing

We simply must move from seeing church as a religious event to seeing it as a spiritual family. Without this context, this soil, leadership will emerge deformed—mutated by corrupt views of church and mission. Contrary to the Scriptures, those considered the top leadership will be the ones who are best at entertaining the crowd or organizing a large weekly event.

I am not asking if a Sunday worship service is right or wrong. I am asking, Why is it so important to us? Obviously, worshiping together is a good thing—but is it the main thing? Is that what church is according to the New Testament? I believe that our practice and priorities are way off.

I read of a church in which two people were shot dead and many others were wounded by mad gang violence on their church property early Sunday morning before sunrise. Later that morning, police cars were all over and yellow police tape was cutting across the crime scene as an open investigation was taking place. The coroner was taking away body bags, while a sign, hastily hung below the police tape, read, "Church Service Will Go On As Usual."

Our first response might be admiration for such a thing. Nothing can keep God's people from obedience; they will worship no matter what happens. But obedience to what? There is no command in the New Testament to attend church services as we know them on Sunday morning.

Is it wrong that this church met despite the ongoing investigation of murder on their campus? No, it isn't wrong, just a bit extreme and portrays that we may have our priorities out of balance.

A pastor friend of mine does not understand the reason I think this is so extreme. He asked, "If a murder happened on the same block as the house where your organic church meets, would you cancel a get-together?"

I said, "No, but if the murder took place at the same house where we meet, and the police were still dusting for fingerprints and removing body bags, *yes!*"

I have heard pastors say that what we do on Sunday mornings is the most important thing we do all week. Such platitudes sound religious and inspiring, but I do not believe they are true. I think God is far more concerned with how you treat your family, your neighbors, and the strangers on the street than how well dressed, timely, and inspired you are on Sunday morning at church services. Just the fact that we can get away with convincing people that Sunday services are the most important thing we do all week is testimony to how far removed we are from the Scriptures. The devil has succeeded in deluding us and removing us from truth. We leaders are taking people down a path that is not the truth with all of the conviction of our belief in the Bible and none of the truth in it.

Two people died that morning on the church grounds. Police were still actively investigating the crime scene, taking testimony, and searching for evidence when parishioners started arriving for the service. The coroner was trying to remove the bodies before the choir started singing! In any other context the police would have prevented anyone from entering the scene of the crime, but I am sure a church on Sunday morning is an intimidating force.

A Spiritual Family

For Christians the worship service has top priority in the church, but it is not a high priority in the Bible we preach from. An interesting phenomenon has developed. In most churches in America, the people are encouraged to join small groups. These groups are like small spiritual families where all the "one anothers" of the New Testament are practiced. This is indeed the church. But participating in such groups is usually considered optional, whereas most Christians feel they must attend the Sunday morning worship service. They think it is the biblical mandate.

The truth is that the New Testament clearly makes mandatory participating in the spiritual family, the small group. The larger gathering is optional. This is the very opposite of contemporary practice. There are many mandates in the New Testament directing people to come together as a church, but it is for service to one another, not a worship service that includes preaching. We are so immersed in the current forms of ministry that when we read these verses, we read into them an understanding of church that is not contextually accurate.

Our persistence in attributing spiritual authority to religious practices not taught in Scripture is not far removed from that of the Roman Church and its observance of mass and the sacraments or the legalism of the religious leaders that Jesus confronted.

One Another

Let me just state it clearly: attending a church service is not the same as being a church family. The church, according to the New Testament, means being involved with one another in an open, vulnerable, and interactive relationship. There is not a single biblical command to attend Sunday morning worship services the way we insist on today. It just isn't there, and the verses that are used to support the idea are used out of context.

If God had intended the Sunday service to have top priority, he would have commanded the practice in the Bible, but he did not. Instead there are many passages that address what the church should be and what people need in the church. According to the New Testament, people in a church need to:

- Love one another (John 13:34).
- Be devoted to one another and give preference to one another (Rom. 12:10).
- Be of the same mind with one another (Rom. 15:5).
- Accept one another (Rom. 15:7).
- Wait for one another before eating (1 Cor. 11:33).
- Care for one another (1 Cor. 12:25).
- Greet one another with a holy kiss (2 Cor. 13:12).
- Bear one another's burdens (Gal. 6:2).
- Tolerate one another (Eph. 4:2).
- Be kind to one another and forgive each other (Eph. 4:32).
- Speak to one another in psalms, hymns, and spiritual songs (Eph. 5:19).
- Submit to one another (Eph. 5:21).
- Regard one another as more important than oneself (Phil. 2:3).
- Share God's message and admonish one another (Col. 3:16).

- Comfort one another (1 Thess. 4:18).
- Encourage and build up one another (1 Thess. 5:11).
- Live in peace with one another (1 Thess. 5:13).
- Confess sins to one another and pray for one another (James 5:16).
- Be hospitable to one another (1 Peter 4:9).
- Serve one another (1 Peter 4:10).
- Fellowship with one another (1 John 1:7).
- And yes, gather together (Heb. 10:25), but not in the form of a worship service but rather in such a way that we can challenge one another to love and good deeds (v. 24). In other words, to live out together all the other mandates given above.

By the way, "one another" does not mean a pastor interacting with a congregation; it means everybody interacting with everybody else. The artificial setting of the worship service makes this nearly impossible. For us to minister to one another as described in these verses, we must be in a family-like setting where we can interact.

I hope that I have been clear in this. I am not against weekly worship or the church. I am not saying in any way that it is wrong to gather together weekly for worship. I do question, however, the high value we place on the Sunday morning service, often at the expense of practicing the New Testament one-anothers, which are indeed the true expression of the church.

Four Tough Questions

For too long we have maintained the traditional understanding of the worship service without questioning whether it is a biblical understanding of how God wants us to be his body. It is time to ask some tough questions. Here are four.

Does God Need It?

Do we believe that we must have a service every week because God needs it? Do we think that if we do not gather together weekly and worship him, he will be missing something or offended? God is not lacking in anything. There is worship around his throne continually throughout time. And he deserves our worship. We can and should worship him all day, every day.

The Counterfeit Kingdom of Outside In

I am not saying that coming together to worship God is wrong or a mistake. Not at all. I believe it pleases him when we do, but I also think we can please him as much (if not more) by interacting with one another intimately and personally. I am not against worship services; I am against giving biblical authority to a practice that is not in the Bible. It may be wise and even beneficial to do it, but it is not *biblical* to do it. In New Testament times the church had no buildings where they could meet. They gathered as small spiritual families in homes (see Rom. 16:5; 1 Cor. 16:19; Col. 4:15; Philem. 2).

Do We Need It?

Do we feel we must have services every week because if we do not, we Christians will start to fall away from God? Are we that weak in faith and anemic? Do we need to hear a sermon to make it through one more week? Do we really think that sermons keep Christians holy? If that were true, why wouldn't the Bible say as much? Or why aren't our churches holier, for that matter? Will we lose a blessing from God if we do not attend a worship service? Of course not, this idea would be superstitious and would convey to the worship service the power of a sacrament.

The Bible does say that we need God's Word to keep us from sin. It is true that God's Word sanctifies us and fuels our faith and growth (see John 17:17; Rom. 10:17; 1 Thess. 2:13), but do we receive the Word only through sermons? No, of course not. Most of the verses in the New Testament that tell us to preach the Word can really be understood in an evangelism context and certainly do not imply a pulpit, pews, and a poem at the end.

Is This What Church Is?

Perhaps the reason we feel the need to have worship services every single week and treat them as if they were the most important function of church life is because we have come to believe they constitute church. (I address this notion thoroughly in my book *Organic Church*.) The power of Christ's kingdom is not found in buildings or religious ceremonies. It is found in a transformed heart. The power is in the rule of Christ within us.

We have passed on the traditions of religious ceremony for so many centuries that we have come to believe that Sunday morning worship services are synonymous with church. To many, if you do not come to the Sunday service, you are abandoning church. But that is not the truth. No one in the Bible attended such a church. Church is much more than a once-a-week service.

Do We Need the Money?

Finally, I must ask, do we feel the need to perpetuate worship services because if we do away with them, many pastors and worship leaders will be out of work? As bad as that may sound, it is not far from the truth.

A friend of mine went to a new city to start a church made up of small groups. At the beginning he had full support as a church planter, but each year his support level would diminish, so that at the end of three years he would no longer be supported. This is a common scenario. The problem is that the pressure of a decreasing support level forced him to begin having worship services earlier than was prudent just so he could take offerings that could be used for his support. The result was that the focus of the church became Sunday services and not the cell groups, much to the pastor's dismay. Even in good circumstances finances dictate our practices more than we care to admit.

As my friend moved the church in a more organic direction, he had to make some decisions about the Sunday morning services. The church still gathers together weekly, but not only for worship services. One weekend they will worship together. Another weekend they will paint an elderly woman's house and mow her lawn. Another Sunday they will have a picnic in the park. Occasionally they organize a prayer walk as a church in the downtown area. In making these adjustments, they have been able to maintain a weekly church activity while at the same time pursue what a church is to do and be together from a New Testament point of view.

Another pastor friend from my denomination responded when tornadoes destroyed homes of people in Indiana. He and his leaders chose not to have a worship service but instead to go to the devastated neighborhood and help hurting people. The whole community noticed their love and compassion, and other churches were inspired to love and good deeds. Isn't this closer to what the New Testament describes church as being?

I asked the pastor how much they may have missed in the offering that week, and I was proud of his response. He said, "That doesn't matter at all. What matters is that people experienced the love of Christ through God's family."

While needing to collect the offerings and tithes is a logical reason for gathering the saints from a business point of view, it also brings us painfully close to the same thinking that confronted Luther. Offering religious services for the sake of financial benefit is never a good idea.

Defining Pharisaism

Jesus had these harsh words for religious leaders:

> Rightly did Isaiah prophesy of you hypocrites, as it is written: "This people honors Me with their lips, but their heart is far away from Me. But in vain do they worship Me, teaching as doctrines the precepts of men." Neglecting the commandment of God, you hold to the tradition of men. . . . You are experts at setting aside the commandment of God in order to keep your tradition. . . . invalidating the word of God by your tradition which you have handed down; and you do many things such as that.
>
> Mark 7:6–9, 13

Pharisaism is when nonbiblical religious traditions, upheld by professional religious leaders, become at least as important as scriptural commands and practices. Friends, I think we are unintentionally there. We have religious practices, which are not wrong in themselves (perhaps even good), but when we attribute to them the authority of the Scriptures, we cross a line that puts us in a dangerous place.

We cannot add to God's Word and expect good results. If almighty God had intended the practices we have elevated in importance to be biblically binding, he would have made it clear in Scripture. When we give biblical authority to nonbiblical practices, we face two lethal problems. First, these practices that are not authoritative become authoritative, which is a form of legalism. Those who practice legalism take for themselves God's place of authority, which is not just wrong, it is idolatrous—even blasphemous.

Second, such practices begin to supplant the important ones that the Bible does prescribe. As Jesus said, in following such practices, we neglect the commandment of God. We end up filtering out a gnat while swallowing a camel. Like a foreign infection in the body, traditions invade the church and try to take the place of biblical teachings. We cannot submit to two lords. Either God's Word is our truth or our traditions are; we cannot meld the two and expect a healthy outcome.

Now, to be fair, there are some "Christian" sects and denominations that actually make their traditions part of the sacred canon, giving them as much authority as Scripture. At least these groups are being logically consistent with their abuses, rather than acting as though they are biblical. On the other hand, I cannot find biblical precedent for making tradition authoritative and I find tons of reasons to reject the practice. Basically this is just an attempt to be consistent and justify religious practices that are not found in the Bible.

Let me reiterate. There is nothing wrong with worship services, sacraments, or abstaining from heavy lifting on the Sabbath. It is not how we observe the Sabbath that is wrong, but the spiritual significance and value we place on the man-made edict that is the problem.

Along the same line, the church has laid down what it considers healthy constraints to safeguard the righteous standards of God's people. Directives such as go to church, don't listen to secular music, stay away from R-rated movies, and abstain from all alcohol are not bad ideas for some people and may even be wise suggestions given the right context. Unfortunately, what begins as suggestion soon attains the clout of holy writ, especially when religious leaders pronounce them with authority and support them with Scripture verses ripped violently out of context. In little time we find ourselves functioning in a religious culture that has biblical principles intertwined with man-made injunctions, and few can distinguish between them. In fact we are certain to mix up the two, and spiritual priorities get messed up.

Beware of the Poison of the Pharisees

In Paul's writing, it is legalism that receives the harshest, unapologetic rebuke. His words to the Corinthians reproaching gross immorality, division, and selfishness were not nearly as harsh as his words to the Galatians for promoting a legalistic view of spiritual life. Think about it for a minute. The church where a man is sleeping with his father's wife (1 Cor. 5:1) is not as harshly criticized as the church that is working very hard to do everything right. It almost sounds unfair, doesn't it? To Paul, however, legalism was the very worst false doctrine one could promote (Gal. 1:6–9). It was a doctrine that put a spell on the Christian (3:1) and attempted to discredit Christ's redemptive work (2:21).

Paul even gets biting and sarcastic when confronting legalism. Concerning the idea of mandatory circumcision, he suggests that they not

The Counterfeit Kingdom of Outside In

stop with the foreskin but cut the whole thing off (5:12)! With a tongue in cheek he implies that if cutting off a little makes you more holy, cutting off the whole thing will make you superspiritual. To the Philippians, Paul warns that we should "beware" of the pitfalls of legalism (Phil. 3:2). He sums up his own self-righteousness legalism with a curse word that our Bible publishers have a hard time translating. The word is *skubala* (v. 8)—a slang term for excrement! My point is that when it comes to legalism, the Bible holds nothing back in its condemnation. It is not treated with gentle suggestions.

There is nothing that raised Christ's ire more than legalism. He turned over the tables in the temple and beat off sellers of religious wares and services with a whip. His words to the legalists were beyond harsh; they were outright contemptuous and (like Paul) often sarcastic and biting. He called them "hypocrites," "a son of hell," "whitewashed tombs," "blind guides of the blind" (Matt. 23:15, 27; 15:14).

Jesus knew the dangers of legalism to the body of believers. He knew it could be a subtle evil that gradually gained control. That is why he said, "Watch out! Beware of the leaven of the Pharisees" (Mark 8:15). He knew a venomous snake when he saw one. But we think that because traditional practices are not evil in themselves, and can actually be beneficial, we don't have to beware of their influence on us. We treat legalism like a donut, just empty calories, more than like the poison that it really is. In the New Testament legalism is never tolerated for one second. It is so bad that both Jesus and the apostle Paul mocked and ridiculed it in the harshest tones possible.

The Priesthood of All Believers

With the Reformation came a new theological understanding: the priesthood of all believers. This became a statement the church embraced but has not practiced. Despite the concept of the priesthood of all believers, the church continued to maintain a clergy class of Christians. The clergy, professional Christian leaders, have held all the power in the church. When professional positions within the church are invested with power, the common Christian, whom we call "laity," are divested of value and significance. The old joke goes: Do you know the difference between clergy and laity? The clergy are paid to be good, and the laity are good for nothing. But nothing could be farther from the truth.

In the church we must have a revolution of heart and mind so that we remember that people are more important than property and life together is more important than simply singing together. We must value God's Word applied in a family setting more than any sermon from a pulpit. We must allow the power of the kingdom of God to be released to ordinary Christ-followers and not monopolized by the clergy.

The Leaders Must Lead the Way

My friend John White once said, "My aim is not to do away with the clergy. I want to do away with the laity and make everyone a priest before God!" Clergy people need to take the first step; usually the laity will not. But the problem is that when people hold positions of power, they want to hold on to them to protect themselves. So they use their power to maintain their position. This is a vicious circle that prolongs an unhealthy environment.

Let's look at another scene from the film *Braveheart*. William Wallace is dialoguing with Robert the Bruce about leadership functions and moral authority. They have just left a room full of the princes of Scotland who are divided against themselves and unable to lead the Scots to freedom from British tyranny.

Robert the Bruce is the true heir to the throne of Scotland. Wallace has no position at all but has all the authority because the people respect his courageous leadership. Their conversation begins with Robert the Bruce saying, "I understand what you said in there, but these men have titles, estates, castles; it is much to risk."

To which Wallace remarks, "And the man who bleeds on the battlefield, does he risk less?"

People who are in positions of power stand to lose much if the church reverts back to the way it was meant to be. Just as Rome was threatened by Luther, many will lose their honored status and monopolized power if we give the reign of God's kingdom its rightful place in the lives of his subjects.

Unfortunately, those who are in a position to make changes are those who will be the least motivated to do so and this perpetuates the power struggle. If we are to turn things around, leaders must be willing to sacrifice power, prestige, and perhaps even profession, all for the sake of the kingdom of God.

The Counterfeit Kingdom of Outside In

I am not suggesting that we simply eliminate a Sunday morning service in a church building and meet instead in a home. All the arguments in this chapter can be applied to a house church gathering. The point is that church is shared life together, not an event, no matter how good the event is, whether a traditional worship service or a house church gathering. If we place importance on the event at the expense of shared life together, we have missed the point entirely.

A Stark Contrast of Powers

The religious leaders Jesus confronted were much like the Roman Catholic authorities Martin Luther confronted with his 95 Theses. They were leaders who were invested in the programs of the institution, and likewise, the institution invested power in them. In each case, because they were the protectors of doctrine, they were threatened by any who would challenge the status quo and allow ordinary people the authority of God's Word.

Jesus confronted these people with another kind of power. Luther also unleashed a force that threatened the established institution. In a sense there was a clash of powers. But the unleashed power of God's kingdom is far superior to any other, and this increases the fear of those who are part of the institution.

If you think you have authority because the system grants you position, you have not yet tasted true power. True power cannot be contained by programs, organizations, or human systems. It is found in God's own voice and presence.

I often mention that Martin Luther had two important goals for his life. They were to translate the Scriptures into the common language of the everyday man, and to compile a hymnal of praise songs for the people to sing. He said of these two ambitions: "Set them loose and the flame will spread on its own." That flame can be an unstoppable force consuming darkness and leaving transformation in its path in ways that our traditions and programs can never do. I believe we have yet to see the true unbridled power of the kingdom of God because we have been too satisfied for far too long with lesser power.

As leaders, we must decide if we will hold on to the Scriptures or let them loose. Will we continue to oblige our people to look to us as the only ones who truly understand God's Word? In the next chapter we will address this more fully.

4
STILL IN THE DARK AGES

Contributing to Ignorance
in the Name of Scholarship

A teacher is one who makes himself progressively unnecessary.

Thomas Carruthers

Education's purpose is to replace an empty mind with an open one.

Malcolm Forbes

John Cleese is the tall, gangly actor and comedian with a distinctively upper-class British accent who is one of the comedic troupe known as Monty Python. Once he was asked what his favorite act or scene was from all of his work. He mentioned a scene from the movie *The Life of Brian*, which is one of my own favorites too because, while performed with over-the-top exaggeration, it hits close to home.

The Life of Brian is an irreverent look at Christendom seen through the eyes of some unbelieving comedians. Many people would find the film offensive and perhaps even blasphemous. It is easy to think that the film mocks Christ, but, more than anything, it mocks Christians. I do not recommend it to everybody, but if you would like to see what we Christians look like to the world, through the humorous minds of a team of funny British comedians, you may want to rent this film.

The Life of Brian is the story of a somewhat slow man named Brian living in Jerusalem at the time of Christ. Due to some strange happenstance, a multitude begins to consider him the Messiah. He is reluctant to accept their adulation and tries to get away from them, but no matter what he does, they will not stop following him and worshiping him.

In the scene that Cleese speaks of, Brian is in his mother's apartment, and the crowd of foolish followers is outside the window waiting for him to come and speak words of divine wisdom. Instead, they hear from his mother. She tries to chase them all away. But refusing to go, they negotiate for one minute with Brian. So she drags Brian to face the crowd.

Brian hopes to convince the crowd not to follow him around anymore. Standing before them he says, "Please, please listen. I've got one or two things to say."

In complete unison, the entire mass speaks: "Tell us, tell us both of them."

He says, "Look, you've got it all wrong. You don't need to follow me. You don't need to follow anyone. You've got to think for yourselves. You're all individuals."

With perfect timing, the crowd, speaking as one, responds, "Yes, we're all individuals."

Sensing that maybe he is getting through, Brian goes on: "You're all different."

"Yes," they all say in perfect unison, "we're all different."

Adding irony to irony, one man in the crowd stands alone and confesses, "I'm not."

All the rest turn and shush him into submission.

The one man who claims not to be different is the only one who breaks from the others, only to be knocked back into place by them. British humor can often be silly and ironic, and this is no exception.

Brian continues, "You've all got to work it out for yourselves."

And the crowd repeats, "Yes, we've got to work it out for ourselves."

"Exactly!" finishes Brian, thinking he has finally accomplished what he set out to do.

But to Brian's chagrin, the voice of the crowd says, "Tell us more!"

"No," Brian counters. "That's the point. Don't let anyone tell you what to do. Otherwise . . ."

Brian's mother interrupts and pulls him away, announcing, "That's enough. That's enough."

Still in unison, the crowd complains, "Hey, that wasn't a minute."

"Oh, yes it was."

"Oh, no it wasn't," comes the united rebuttal.

Finally, Brian's mother demands, "Now stop that and go away."

Brokers of Truth

Good comedians are observant and are able to find humor in the real world. Good comedy is very close to reality, exaggerating it just enough to expose the foolishness that would otherwise go unnoticed. This scene is a prime example. What is the reality that makes this scene humorous? This silly clip from an insightful movie reveals a flaw in our Christian worldview. The multitudes of Christ-followers are always looking for someone else to tell them what to think.

And certain Christian leaders oblige. They feel called to think on behalf of the rest of the church, though they wouldn't say so. Usually they are heresy hunters, letting others know which leaders are "ortho-dox" and which are heretical. To an extent, most pastors consider this one of their roles.

There are monthly magazines and daily radio programs that scruti-nize all possible leaders and announce those who may be questionable and those who are acceptable. Shelves of books are dedicated to keep-ing us informed of whom we can trust and whom we can't. With every release of a new hit movie, bestselling novel, or successful personality, scores of books come out that vilify or verify the validity of each, all written by "trusted" scholars who are employed by the church to think on behalf of the rest of us poor ignorant souls who aren't qualified to figure these things out for ourselves.

Some of these brokers of truth come out with study Bibles so that when we read the Bible, we read it through their notes and observa-tions—as though God needs their help. The goal is that we don't make the mistake of thinking wrongly. Otherwise we too could end up identi-fied on a radio program as another heretic.

Once I was speaking with a veteran pastor and seminary professor about the way students are evaluated for ordination as pastors. He believed that each candidate for licensure should be scrutinized by a panel of professional pastors and seminary professors to be licensed for ministry. He was convinced that the church needs a higher level of scholastic scrutiny.

I suggested that churches should appoint their leaders based on the qualities they've observed day in and day out, rather than a committee of men who do not know the guy. He was not in favor of this because he felt that average churchgoers, without a theological education, would not have the astuteness to evaluate a candidate properly.

I asked the man how many years he had been pastor of the same church, and he answered proudly, "Twenty years now."

After a slight pause I said, "So you have been teaching the same people every week for twenty years (over a thousand sermons), and they do not know enough of the Bible to discern sound doctrine? What's wrong with your teaching?"

There was a stunned silence, and he looked like a deer caught in the headlights.

I asked, "If twenty years is not enough, how many more years of your teaching do you think it would take before they would be able to tell the difference between good teaching and bad?"

More silence followed.

I continued, "Would you call that *good* preaching if over twenty years your listeners are still unable to discern *good* teaching? Is that what qualifies you to scrutinize the ability of others to teach? Maybe we all need to reevaluate what good teaching truly is."

Perhaps I was a little too pointed and aggressive, but I do think this is a serious blind spot for most Christian leaders today. Christian leadership has kept believers in the dark, rather than enlightening them. There was a day when an elite group of educated leaders, the clergy, held on to the Scriptures, and the rest of the people could hear from God only through the clergy's teachings. We called that period the Dark Ages, and in some respects we are still groping in the dark.

Six Ways Leaders Mistakenly Keep Christians in the Dark

It's All Greek to Me: Preaching from the Original Languages

For a long time teachers of Scripture have used the original Greek and Hebrew languages in their study and this has been seen as a helpful and responsible method. It is not a bad thing at all for teachers to study the text from the original languages and learn some of the subtle nuances of a passage. The problem surfaces when we bring that study into the pulpit. By expounding on how the original languages unlock the true meaning of the Scriptures, teachers make the common people think a straight-up reading of the English Bible is insufficient to understand truth. Probably pastors never intend for this to happen, but what is communicated through this type of preaching is that only those who can read Greek and Hebrew can really understand the Bible. Occasionally it may be fine to bring in a nuance that comes from such a study, but to do so weekly, as many preachers do, leaves the listeners thinking they might as well leave Bible study to the expert.

I suggest that 95 percent of the time the pastor should leave the original languages in the study and use them occasionally to illustrate a point that the English Bible also makes clear. In other words, when the language adds nuance to what the reader can find simply by reading the text in English, this is better than coming up with interpretations and ideas that an ordinary Christian could never discover with only an English Bible. Even in the pages of this book, I will occasionally shed light on a portion of Scripture, using the original languages. I believe this is fine when it reinforces what is plain in the English or helps to underline the meaning that is easily understood. In some cases, if the meaning in English is not clear, the fault lies with the translators. I believe that we all have access to enough English translations to navigate such problems without needing to thrust doubt on God's Word in the eyes of the common Christian. Ironically, by attempting to preserve the Bible's authoritative message, we have unwittingly reduced the extent of its voice.

Often this practice hides what pastors truly want: increased authority as a teacher. They use the original languages because this makes them seem more scholarly and thoughtful. The result is that men steal the authority of God's Word, and of course this is completely wrong. The Scriptures alone are all the authority that is needed. Teachers do not need to be exalted.

Heresy Hunters: Publicly Denouncing Other Bible Teachers

Most pastors feel strongly that part of their role is to protect their sheep from false teachers. And of course this is true. Paul did so in many of his letters, and even Jesus did so in the letters he wrote to the churches of Asia Minor in Revelation 2 and 3.

Unfortunately, some pastors go too far. It is one thing to expose a false doctrine or a false teacher by name, but to publicly ridicule a person for laughs is a grave mistake. Many people have built entire ministries on this practice. When they run out of legitimate cultists and false teachers, they end up going after good brothers and sisters in the Lord who happen to see things differently than they do. Such pastors assume they will gain authority and respect if they knock someone who, from their perspective, is less "orthodox."

The challenge is that the average Christian listening to these heresy hunters can easily feel intimidated and begin to believe that he or she could also easily misinterpret Scripture and be susceptible to humiliation. Because of this, many stop thinking on their own and depend entirely on their pastor to tell them what to think.

Pastors must teach the truth straight up, without feeling the need to attack others. Occasionally we need to expose false teachers, even by name (Paul did so), but we must do so humbly, being careful to avoid trying to gain respect at the expense of someone else.

The goal should always be to get congregants to think for themselves by simply teaching the truth and letting them draw conclusions with the help of the Holy Spirit.

Gatekeepers for God: Protecting God's Word from His People

Closely related to the heresy hunters are the gatekeepers for God. They believe their role is to protect God's Word from false interpretation. This means tight control must be maintained over the official, sanctioned interpretation. While the heresy hunters feel they must protect God's people from false teaching, the gatekeepers believe their mission is to protect God's Word from abuse by his people. They see the people of God as dumb sheep who will go off on unhealthy tangents if they are entrusted with studying the Bible on their own. Educated teachers must be responsible for all interpretation in their eyes.

Safeguards for the Bible are what theologians call a proper hermeneutic. That is a ten-dollar theological word that means a system of interpretation. The idea behind this system is that men are incapable of interpreting the Scriptures correctly without an objective and universal approach.

There is nothing wrong with good Bible interpretation skills, but this perception does not allow for varying opinions. When someone comes up with a different view of a passage, he or she is said to have a different (implied, *wrong*) hermeneutic.

Often when teaching on this subject, I ask those in the audience to raise their hands if they have ever misinterpreted the Scriptures. Inevitably nearly 100 percent of the audience raise their hands. Usually I make some wisecrack about burning all the heretics at the stake. The point is that everybody makes mistakes, and that is how we learn. I like to remind such an audience that they were given room to learn and they should allow others the same privilege.

That said, I do teach sound interpretation skills to those who are beginning to teach others. I first encourage people to read and study God's Word without helps. I believe that our man-made systems, no matter how helpful or sound, must ultimately submit to God's Word—not the other way around. Unfortunately, the way many people approach the Bible leaves Scripture subject to our systems, and this is wrong.

John writes that we have no need for anyone to be seen as our official teacher because all of us have an anointing from God (1 John 2:27). The Holy Spirit is the author of the Scriptures and is resident in each one who follows Christ. It seems to me that this is a better source of interpretation than any man-made system. I realize that it leaves room for mistakes and different views but I am not so sure that isn't a good thing in most cases.

The fact remains that God's Word does not need to be protected. It has survived for thousands of years. It has withstood abuse for millennia and still stands true. It can survive this generation without my help, but I cannot survive this life without it.

Truth Translators: Depending on Scholarly Notes

We live in a day of privilege, which includes our ability to study Scripture. Today there are more scholars to bring light to the Scriptures than in any previous generation. We have tools available at the touch of a button that can shed light on the entire Bible. This is a good thing, but there is a shadow that this privilege casts on us. Now, having grown accustomed to scholarly help, many people have grown dependent on it, feeling unable to open the Bible and just read it with understanding. We need someone to interpret it for us. Many Christians have their favorite teacher of God's Word, often the only one whose interpretations they trust.

It used to offend me when I saw study Bibles with some teacher's name on the cover as if he wrote the book. Then I opened one and realized he did write half of it! Maybe he deserves coauthorship with God! It used to be that when you opened to the middle of the Bible, you would be in Proverbs, but if you open a study Bible, you are in Leviticus, because there are so many preliminary notes. Often these Bibles have half a page of Scripture and half a page of the teacher's notes, explaining all that God really meant by what he said.

I am not against study Bibles or helps of any sort, but I am concerned about the message such Bibles send about God and his Word. All the notes and tools tell people that the Bible is hard or nearly impossible for ordinary people to read and understand without help, and that God is incapable of communicating his truth to ordinary folk. This creates a dependency on scholarly teachers more than on the Bible's Author.

God is fully capable of speaking clearly without help. The Scriptures are not so far removed from our understanding as people seem to think, and the Holy Spirit, who is called the Helper, is very adept at guiding people in their understanding and application. He will give insight to all people who seek it. The Word of God is powerful and does not need people to make it better.

Bottle-Fed Babies: Feeding the Flock

A common complaint heard from parishioners who walk out the door of churches never to return is that they weren't fed by the pastor's teaching. What are they saying? It is commonly understood that the pastor is supposed to "feed the sheep" or deliver such an inspiring message each week that the entire congregation leaves with an increased understanding of and a deep commitment to God and his Word. But is this understanding biblical?[1] I see this attitude as an infantile and self-righteous excuse for lack of spiritual growth. Such people are blaming the teacher rather than assuming responsibility for their own faith.

Granted, having grown up on the beaches of Southern California, I am not much of an expert on raising sheep, but I know that rarely do shepherds actually feed their sheep. Shepherds do not pull up the grass, shove it in the sheep's mouth, and force their jaws up and down. No, the shepherd leads the sheep to grass and they feed themselves. One exception to this is when a lamb is orphaned and unable to feed itself. In this case a shepherd will feed the baby with a bottle of milk.

The writer of Hebrews rebukes the recipients of the letter because of their callous hearts and dull senses when it comes to hearing the voice of God. He writes: "Though by this time you ought to be teachers, you have need again for someone to teach you the elementary principles of the oracles of God, and you have come to need milk and not solid food" (Heb. 5:12). Like orphaned lambs they were not growing and could handle only a bottle of milk.

Welcome to the church of America! For many the only consumption of God's Word they receive is milk passed on to them from the bottle of a pulpit. It is predigested food, delivered to babes. Our churches are full of spiritual infants who are stuck in a baby state of maturity because they have grown dependent on milk from the pulpit. The Hebrews passage goes on to say, "For everyone who partakes only of milk is not accustomed to the word of righteousness, for he is an infant" (v. 13).

Many think this passage refers to deeper teaching as opposed to the basics, but while this is possible, the main idea is that the people of God should be maturing beyond a dependency on teachers, so they can study on their own and be a source of nourishment to others. Personally, I do not think that any teaching from the pulpit can be labeled meat. As long as it is predigested by someone else and then spoon-fed to others, it is milk. We eat meat when we consume the Word ourselves.

"Solid food," according to the passage, "is for the mature, who because of practice [habit] have their senses trained to discern good and evil" (v. 14). Maturity, then, is attained by repetitive practice in God's Word so that one is habitually hearing God's voice. When this occurs, discernment is the result.

Could it be that in our desire to prevent false teaching, we have in reality dulled the senses of God's people and kept them immature? In this case they are more susceptible to bad teaching because they do not "have their senses trained to discern good and evil." The solution is not more teaching on deeper subjects but getting the saints habitually reading God's Word! Of course, we risk that, as they read on their own, they may make some mistakes, but that indeed is how they learn to discern right from wrong, as opposed to simply taking their leader's word for it.

Pastors would do well to see their responsibility not as feeding the sheep but as leading them to the green pastures of God's Word. This is a pastor's role (Ps. 23:1–2). Then the people can feed themselves and ultimately mature to the place where they can feed other babes, perhaps even their own spiritual children. Reproduction comes with a level of maturing. As long as the vast majority of Christians remain immature and dependent on the milk of the pulpits of America, we will not reproduce disciples, leaders, churches, and movements. We all need to become self-feeders.

My book *Search & Rescue* presents a useful tool for getting ordinary Christians started in the practice of hearing God's voice in Scripture.

The Counterfeit Kingdom of Outside In

The Junk Food Diet: Daily Devotional Readings

I have met many Christians who have a daily devotional time, but not in God's Word. They read from a book with thoughts for each day. I assume that the authors of these books would be appalled to learn that many people read their book faithfully but never open the Word of God.

Usually devotional books offer a single verse, a homespun homily, and a catchy slogan. All can be read in just five minutes to start your day off with a godly thought. This can all be done in the short time one spends in the bathroom, which is why I find so many of these little devotional booklets in bathrooms across America.

Some people spend even less than five minutes a day reading their devotional thought. A desk calendar with a single verse for each day provides their daily intake from God's Word.

A verse a day does not keep the devil away! There is no substitute for God's Word. It is the only reading that has substantial nourishment for your soul; all the rest is spiritual junk food. Empty calories without any spiritual nutrition is what these devotionals are to a soul. They produce fat, lazy Christians who are out of shape and incapable of resisting temptation. The devotional thoughts are not bad or wrong; they simply cannot replace the substance of God's Word.

Now these devotional readings are a problem only when they take the place of reading God's Word. To add them to the steady diet of truth found only in the Scriptures is fine, but when they take the place of Scripture, we are left with anemic, malnourished Christians.

Building on a True Foundation

It may seem that I am attacking every channel people commonly use to receive God's message today. After reading this chapter you could think that I am against solid teaching, accurate Bible interpretation, or study helps. This would be a wrong assumption. What I am against is keeping God's people in a perpetual state of immaturity and ignorance. I am against their depending on scholars more than on God and his Word. I feel this state of affairs is so rampant in the Western church that I have made it a consistent theme in all of my writings. Most Christians are able to hear God's message only through the voice, mannerisms, and expressions of their favorite Bible teacher. Because their ears are so full of the preacher's voice, cadence, and accent, they cannot even recognize the Holy Spirit's voice. The Holy Spirit should not have to compete with leaders for the attention of God's people.

So what place do study helps have in a balanced approach to studying the Word? Christians need to digest a steady diet of God's Word, minus the intrusion of human teachers, their insights, and their lessons. When people are reading God's Word regularly, I have no problem with their beginning to use study tools and helps that may increase their understanding. I find that after people have been reading God's Word steadily, not only are the principles of Bible interpretation received well, they are actually found to reinforce lessons the Holy Spirit has already taught. Ultimately, of course, the goal is for the student to become obedient to the Word, not just knowledgeable of it (see Matt. 7:24–27).

Once people are familiar with God's voice, study tools will be helpful; but the foundation of God's Word must be laid first. Instead, people are trying to build on their human teachers' lessons about the Bible—a weak foundation in comparison that ultimately collapses. When there is a layer of teachers between God and his people, the teachers filter, translate, and apply the voice of God. This is an unholy priesthood that must be removed.

A caution to pastors and teachers: be careful about using intellect and scholarship as a means to establish your own authority in the body of Christ. This is a subtle temptation to which I fear most leaders have easily fallen victim. It always feels good to be thought of highly, but the truth is that the authority should be God's Word, not our scholarship.

Jesus tells us plainly that the seed of God's kingdom is the Word of God (Mark 4:14). There is no substitute for God's Word planted in the good soil of an open heart. You cannot grow God's kingdom by planting a seed substitute.

If people are to grow, mature, and ultimately reproduce the kingdom in others, they must be allowed to come out of the dark and receive the light of God's Word directly. It is time to leave the Dark Ages and move into a new enlightenment. Only fungus grows in the dark.

5

BOUND BY THE CHAIN OF COMMAND

Messed Up from Top to Bottom

People who look down on other people don't end up being looked up to.

Robert Half

Man's rank is his power to uplift.

George MacDonald

It was time to make a move. For three whole years they had heard every day about the coming kingdom of God. They were getting anxious to finally see it and felt that the time was getting closer. Hadn't their leader spoken about marching into Jerusalem?

It was obvious that they were favored, so why not expect a special assignment? After all, they had been with this band from the very first day and had given up as much as anyone. They had been invited into the inner conversations, and everyone seemed to recognize their special abilities. Why wouldn't they get high positions? Their only real competition was Simon, so they had to move fast before he got one of the positions they wanted. Both brothers deserved a high position in the kingdom.

But how could they make it happen? It didn't seem right to lobby for positions. And obviously the other members of the team were jealous, so they wouldn't suggest it. The Sons of Thunder couldn't appear weak. They needed someone to speak on their behalf. How about their mother? Okay, so maybe in hindsight, it didn't go over as well as they'd hoped.

The mother of James and John asked Jesus if her sons could sit on Jesus's right and left when his kingdom was established (see Matt. 20:20–28). What a mom! They were called the Sons of Thunder. I wonder if their mother was Mrs. Thunder herself! Of course thunder sounds real threatening but it is really just a lot of noise.

I imagine that there was tension between the brothers. John may have been younger, but certainly Jesus loved him in a special way, and often in the Old Testament writings, the younger son received preference. James was probably not so secure in his place.

Jesus responded to their mother with grace and kindness but he took the opportunity to let James and John know just what they were asking for and that his kingdom would not be like the kingdoms of the world. In the world such positions are for the posh and privileged, but in Jesus's upside-down and inside-out kingdom, these seats were reserved for those who gave up the most in service to others. And he told them that the greatest in the kingdom would have to endure the very worst of the world. Jesus asked the brothers if they were willing to suffer what he himself would undergo.

In perhaps the most ignorant and naive statement in the Bible, the Sons of Thunder replied, "Yes, we are able." I suspect they were expecting a coronation right there on the spot. They were probably standing tall at that moment. Each was probably wondering which of the two would get the higher place in the chain of command in Christ's kingdom.

Appearing to be disappointed that he was unable to fulfill Mrs. Zebedee's request, Jesus told the brothers that this choice was not his to make.

Of course, the other disciples did not take this political maneuver sitting down. How audacious of the Zebedee boys! And knowing their mother asked for them must have unleashed days of sarcastic mockery from their peers. But in reality, their own jealousy revealed that they were all thinking the same way, but the others just hadn't had the guts to act on it.

The Counterfeit Kingdom of Outside In

Seeing that division and spite were developing in his band of disciples, Jesus stepped in and said these profound words:

> You know that the rulers of the Gentiles lord it over them, and their great men exercise authority over them. It is not this way among you, but whoever wishes to become great among you shall be your servant, and whoever wishes to be first among you shall be your slave; just as the Son of Man did not come to be served, but to serve, and to give His life a ransom for many.
>
> Matthew 20:25–28

Jesus's Form of Governance

Jesus's words are potent and they are important and pertinent to us two thousand years later. They make clear one key difference between the kingdoms of the world and the kingdom of God. In the world we have our important men at the top and the rest follow on down the chain of command. John, James, and Mrs. Zebedee all thought this would be true in Jesus's kingdom as well. But Jesus corrects them and us.

The truth is that the world still functions as it did in the days of Christ. We still see the same top-down chain of authority in about every domain of life (see image below). It is still the way of the world. Every army in history and in our day is formed with the same structure of command. Every government, every business, and every educational institution runs the same way. You may have a king, a CEO, a president, a principal, or even a senior pastor in the top spot, but it is still the same structure.

**The Chain of Command
or Pyramid of Power**

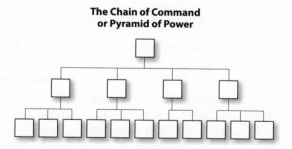

Many people feel that the world cannot operate without this structure, and perhaps this is so. It seems that the military needs such a chain of command to operate effectively, but the church, or the kingdom of God, does not. In the kingdom there are no people who lord it over others. In fact Jesus clearly states, "It is not this way among you" (Matt. 20:26). It is not an option. It is *not* to be so among us.

This flow of authority is all we really know, having never experienced anything else. But the true kingdom of God is revolutionary. It is countercultural. It is upside-down from what we normally expect. Jesus is introducing a whole new form of governance. It is not a new idea for Jesus, but it is for us.

This debate has plagued God's people nearly from the beginning. The people of God wanted a king like the other nations (1 Sam. 8:1–22). Though God wanted to be King of his people, the nation of Israel wasn't satisfied with that. They wanted the same chain of command that the other nations had.

With God as our head, the church can operate well without the top-down hierarchical structure that the world is unable to operate without. God is all-knowing, all-powerful, and everywhere present. He can speak directly to each and every member of his body without getting confused or being distracted. Only because of who God is are we, his body, able to function with order in a flat structure.

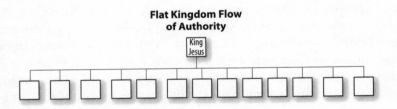

**Flat Kingdom Flow
of Authority**

Consistently the New Testament uses the analogy of a body to explain our relational connections to one another and to Jesus. Your own body is a remarkable expression of how we are to function in the kingdom of God. Every part of your body is connected directly to your brain. Your mind can send instant impulses to your body and it will immediately obey. The body of a top athlete functioning in masterful coordination is a beautiful thing to behold. Each part is hearing from the brain simultaneously and functioning as one. In much the same way, the church is intended to function as one coordinated body. Every part is connected directly to Christ, our Head, and his commands make it possible for us to function as one.

The Counterfeit Kingdom of Outside In

Who's in Charge Here?

Why are we afraid of the flat structure of the body of Christ? I believe it is because we are so used to a hierarchical structure we cannot imagine that any other system could work, and without our usual structure everything would fall apart, chaos would ensue, and we would have anarchy, as each part does its own thing.

There are three common concerns people have when considering life without the typical top-down structure.

Anarchy

The first thought people have when they try to imagine a nonhierarchical governance is that it will cause anarchy. People point to the dark days of the judges of Israel when "everyone did what was right in his own eyes" (Judg. 17:6; 21:25).

If we all operate independently and have no direction, chaos will occur. But that is not what I am suggesting. Jesus is at the top and all follow him. Without Christ in people's hearts and his leadership in their lives, there would be anarchy unless someone is in charge, keeping order.

In Christ's kingdom, however, there is a Head. It is Christ himself. He is at the top and all follow him. Jesus has authority and power. He is capable of communicating and leading, but we must follow him.

I am not suggesting that we all be in charge. I am suggesting that none of us be in charge. Jesus has earned the right to sit at the top, and all of us should be under his command. He is in charge. If everyone does what is right in their Lord's eyes, we will not have anarchy but a perfectly balanced and coordinated body acting as one.

The problem may be that often Christ-followers place more faith in their own ability to lead than in Jesus's leading. This is a serious problem.

A Lack of Leadership

When a nonhierarchical structure is suggested, people fear a lack of leadership. For some reason, we have tied leadership only to a position in a structure, but this is a shallow view of leadership, as we will discover in later chapters.

Leadership is not bound to an organizational chart but is, in a word, influence. One can influence from *any* position on the chart, or from *no* position on the chart. Jesus operated completely outside of the formal organizational structure of his day yet he was a strong leader.

Often people assume that I am ignoring examples of New Testament leadership when I suggest a nonhierarchical church structure. The assumption is that where there are leaders, they must be over others. This is not a valid assumption. Yes, there are to be elders and deacons. Yes, there are apostles, prophets, evangelists, shepherds, and teachers in the New Testament, and these people should be among the churches as well. But this does not mean we must assume a top-down structure. *Overseer* does not mean the person is over the others looking down; it means he is among the others looking over (1 Tim. 3:1–7; Titus 1:7–9). Leaders are to "keep watch [looking out] over your souls" (Heb. 13:17). It is as though they are scanning the skies, watching for incoming missiles, and at the same time searching for new directions they can head in service of the King. This is what I believe an overseer is responsible to do as a leader. Leadership in the New Testament, as Peter puts it so well, is always "among," not "over," the rest of the flock, leading by going before them in example (1 Peter 5:1–4).

In 1 Thessalonians 5:12 Paul says, "Appreciate those who diligently labor among you, and have charge over you in the Lord and give you instruction." This seems to imply a hierarchal leadership structure. The actual meaning, however, is not to be "over" but to "go before" the flock. That is, in essence, what leadership is to be—leading from among the flock by going first. When people follow you, it means you are leading; if no one is following, you're just out taking a walk.

The term *office* (1 Tim. 3:1), referring to eldership, never actually appears in the original writings of the New Testament. It is simply supplied by the translators, who, like us, cannot imagine church leadership void of a chain of command. But we must let our imaginations rise to the level of Christ's competence as a leader. He does not need our help.

A Lack of Order

We are so afraid of all hell breaking loose that we do everything we can to keep things in control and maintain order. The result is that heaven never breaks loose. Unfortunately, we have mistaken order for control. Order is not the same as control and not necessarily the outcome of it either. Who was in control in the book of Acts? It is called the Acts of the Apostles as if they were in control, but of course they were not. By my count the Holy Spirit is referred to fifty-seven times in the book, and

The Counterfeit Kingdom of Outside In

it should be called the Acts of the Holy Spirit. Rapid expansion was taking place in the church, but the Holy Spirit was maintaining order. He is the leader we all need so badly, and he is ready to help us; in fact he is called the Helper (John 14:16–17, 25–26; 15:26–27; 16:6–7)! We need to get back to the place where we truly believe he is a better help for us than the human leaders we have appointed.

Thus it is possible to have an out-of-control kingdom that maintains order, and I am convinced that the nonhierarchical life of the kingdom can have much greater order than the measly structures we create to keep things under control.

When every part of the body is submissive to the impulse of the Head, the body is unified, functional, and coordinated. There is order. The key of course is to let each part be directly connected to the Head, as opposed to being under the direct control of some lesser part of the body.

There is a DNA to God's organic kingdom that is simple, uncluttered, and powerful. This DNA keeps the constantly expanding, ever-multiplying kingdom under the Spirit's control. It is:

Divine truth
Nurturing relationships
Apostolic mission

This DNA must make up every single cell of Christ's body.

When reduced to the smallest possible unit, the church is two or three disciples in relation to God, in relation to one another, and on mission. Healthy and whole DNA must be intact in this tiny cell of Christ's body. Then when these small units are gathered together into one larger movement, the DNA will be maintained, as long as it is maintained in the smallest unit. My book *Search & Rescue* articulates how and why disciples should live together in connection with God's Word and one another and be on mission together in units I call Life Transformation Groups.

I am so committed to this idea that I have yet to write a book that does not mention it. The purpose of *Raising Leaders for the Harvest* is to train leaders to form these groups. *Beyond Church Planting* was written for missionaries, church planters, and denominational leaders about this kind of disciple making. In *Cultivating a Life for God* I write to pastors and lay leaders about how to make and multiply healthy disciples.[1] And in *Organic Church* I have explained the reason this is important in the life of the church. *Search & Rescue* was written to ordinary Christians to inspire and challenge them to live as radical disciples in such a missional community. Now I am writing briefly about it in this book, *Organic Leadership*, because if we do not grasp the importance of making healthy disciples, we will not be able to become the expression of Christ's body necessary in this world.

Some people may wonder why I write so many books about such a simple idea. It is the most basic idea. It is as basic as planting good seed in good soil, which Jesus says is so foundational that if you do not get this idea, you will not understand the rest of the ideas of God's kingdom (see Mark 4:13). I am convinced that we must see health in every cell of Christ's body, and this is not possible without every disciple following Christ fully. This, in fact, is a cause I have found worth giving my life for.

When we are assured that every part of Christ's body is connected to the Head and hearing clearly from Jesus as Lord, we know there will be order and unity. We will be of one mind, one purpose with one Lord. This is as it should be. This is what Jesus died for. To be content with less than this is sin. To support something opposed to this ideal is adulterous. It is sleeping with the enemy. It is not to be so among you.

Worldly Woes Disabling the Church

The church today is like the nation of Israel who wanted a king like all the surrounding nations. We emulate the structures in our world—businesses and governments that have a hierarchical organization. But what is there to emulate? The governing of every culture, group, and tribe has failed in some way. Power is usurped, elections corrupted, whole groups of people killed or enslaved. Simply perusing the global news any day of the week will expose the crumbling nature of hierarchical leadership and the weight it leaves on the shoulders of its citizens.

Jesus said that the great men who want to exercise authority over the rest must dominate (lord it over) those under them (Matt. 20:25). In time, the oppressed will rise up and topple the previous regime and exact vengeance, and we have blood running down the streets once again.

In view of this, it is puzzling why we have adopted a similar system in the church, but we have, and the same sort of domination, revolution, and retaliation regularly occur in our congregations—of all

The Counterfeit Kingdom of Outside In

types in every culture and country. Whether it's a strong-armed pastor, unaccountable leadership that wastes money on personal luxuries, a deacon board that harasses a pastor until he leaves, or a congregation that bestows authority on the wealthy, we are following the ways of the world and its structures.

To establish order and control, we have erected structures that not only oppose the unity and order that Jesus wants, but prevent us from ever having it. Our structures have enslaved us. The chain of command that we have established is the chain that holds us in bondage.

It is time to repent. We have rebelled against our King for far too long. We will never see a radical, spontaneous expansion of the kingdom that multiplies to all the nations and the ends of the earth with a top-down hierarchical structure in which the leadership must give a green light to every decision. If every person on the field has to report back to headquarters rather than to the Head, we will stay stuck in the cycle of feud, rebel, dominate, and retaliate, and nothing of significance will occur. It may be the way the world operates, but there is no reason for it to be a part of the church.

That said, I believe that even though the structures we employ in the church are from the world rather than from the Lord, a direct assault to try to change things will greatly disrupt the church and may not be necessary. In a sense, we must not break the old wineskins or we may lose the precious wine. There is, perhaps, a better way in which subtle changes are made within that lead to a new way of operating in submission to the King rather than through the chain of command. This may bring about subtle change, but I think this change can occur rapidly.

Many, of course, will launch out to establish a healthier and more connected expression of God's kingdom as the New Testament describes. But some are to bring that same life back to the people who are still stuck in the old regime. I will attempt to unwrap this idea in this next section.

Reforming the People, Not the Structure

Some will think I am an idealist without any grasp of reality. Perhaps, but I think Jesus died for more than the status quo. I am ready and willing to commit my whole life to this ideal of the church operating without a hierarchical structure. If we are unwilling to take risks to see what can be, we will always be enslaved to what is. The chain of command in the church is keeping us from becoming a living, thriving, functioning spiritual body that has arms to reach out and embrace the lost and broken and feet that move at the impulse of the Head's compassion.

Again I ask, Who's in charge here? It is either Jesus or it is not. It cannot be Jesus *and* our designated leaders. You cannot serve two masters (Matt. 6:24). A body with multiple heads may be a great idea for a horror movie and is even described in apocalyptic writings in Scripture (see Dan. 7:6; Rev. 12:3; 13:1), but it is not the way Christ intended your body to work—or his.

If Jesus is indeed telling us that we cannot operate with him as Head and remain in the old structure, would we be willing to trust him and let go of the old to embrace the new? It is not a question of what structure we use, but the base of authority from which we operate. If we utilize a top-down structure for our advantage (even with good motives), we are helping to perpetuate a corrupt system. If we choose to function only on the relational and spiritual authority that Christ gives us, rather than through the authority of our position, we can work effectively in any environment.

In chapter 12 we will look more closely at the varieties of authority available to us as leaders and what channels our authority can take to get Christ's work done. I suggest strongly that leaders never capitalize on their position in the system. They should not exploit the system to get good things done, because there is not any good reason to do so. We can and should accomplish the mission Christ has given us without needing the top-down structure to do so.

The Headship of Christ

I have already said that we do not need to get rid of the old wineskins to have new life in the church. We can birth new wineskins and even bring health back to the old ones. Leaders who are high up the chain of command in these Christian institutions do not have to resign their positions to turn things around. But they do need to stop using the authority of their position in the hierarchy to get things done. When we start leading from spiritual and moral authority and release others to do the same, a healthy process begins that may turn some things around.

We need to stop reinforcing the hierarchical structure in the church and start reinforcing Christ's headship. We need to empower every person in the body to do God's work, not just the leaders. If leaders simply

The Counterfeit Kingdom of Outside In

ignored their positions and titles and functioned out of the authority Christ gives to all of us, we would not only still be leaders, we'd be better ones. I believe that if we began to do this, we would not need to dismantle the old structure immediately but would, instead, transform the true church from a relational point of view. We will simply infuse the body with the life of Christ, and the old structure will not be as relevant and important as it once was.

Many who, like me, espouse a nonhierarchical kingdom perspective believe that the structure itself is evil and cannot be reformed. They would say that it is the source of all our evils and must be eliminated or the kingdom will not be allowed to prevail. While I have stated clearly that I think the hierarchical structure is indeed contrary to God's kingdom, I am not as hopeless as some.

I believe that if we all began to function according to the New Testament pattern—every believer directly connected and submissive to the Head—and no longer gave recognition to the illegitimate hierarchical forms forced on us, we would see change. In other words, if leaders no longer exercised authority because of their title and position but rather spiritually and relationally connected everyone to the headship of Christ, we would see health in the body. If the people no longer looked to their leaders for their order but to the Head, we would be operating in the New Testament pattern. My hope is that if we do this, the old structure will become irrelevant and easily replaced. This is not reform of the structure but of the people within the structure.

If we could learn to ignore the chain of command and begin to function as Christ intended, the structure would fade into irrelevance. It is amazing how patient God is with our foolish attempts to establish his kingdom here on earth. He continues to work faithfully even in the midst of some pretty odd contexts that we have created for ourselves. In doing so, God isn't sanctioning or sponsoring the artificial structure; he is simply extending his grace to us in spite of it.

We do not need to be afraid of the structure, for when we are, we empower it. Instead we need to work to change it by functioning correctly rather than giving credence to an illegitimate organization. Rather than a violent revolution that seizes control to overthrow the old, I suggest that we simply live the kingdom life within our hearts and learn to recognize that true authority is in Christ and all whom he redeems. If we all just listened to his voice and followed his lead, we would ultimately replace invalid forms with true obedience and connectedness—to the Head and to the rest of the body.

Submission to Christ

Rather than a call to rebellion, I suggest a call to submission, not to titles, offices, or positions of power, but to Christ and everyone for whom he died. We do not need a revolution of the structure but a revolution of how we relate to Christ and his people. How many countries have thrown out the old regime only to be plagued by an equally abusive new regime? Socialist systems, democracies, and monarchies all end in the same abuse if the people do not change from within. We all need to solidify our submission to Christ and in love submit to one another—leaders and nonleaders alike. In this way we will be functioning in a flat kingdom orientation rather than the hierarchical one imposed on us.

I believe that we will be better at eliminating this unhealthy weed in God's garden by simply replacing it with right relationships to one another and the Head than by trying to uproot it in a more direct assault. In itself, structure is neither good nor bad. It is not the solution for the kingdom of God and it is not of the devil either. We should not give structure such power. It is the people that make up the good and the bad of an organization. If we all change for the better, the way we relate to the whole will also change.

All of us are reborn to live a life that is empowered in the bleakest and darkest of environments; therefore we can certainly shine brightly even in a religious hierarchical institution. To do so, we must all be directly connected to Jesus—the Head—and not expect to get his command passed down through the chain of command that once had us bound and gagged.

The Counterfeit Kingdom of Outside In

6

VIEWING LIFE THROUGH FAULTY LENSES

False Dichotomies That Obscure Our Vision of Reality

What we see depends mainly on what we look for.

John Lubbock

From the sublime to the ridiculous there is but one step.

Napoleon

Buzzzzzz. How annoying the alarm is, especially when it's still dark out and you've barely had any sleep! All of us have to go through this at times, but for three years this was my *daily* experience.

Still foggy in my brain, but awake enough to slap the alarm clock across the room, I forced my body out of bed. It was 2:45 a.m., and I was already running late for my job. There was no time for a wake-up shower—not that I needed to look good for the people I worked with. I was on my way to a warehouse where I would fold, bag, and band 750 newspapers, load them in my car, and toss them out the window to 750 homes. I would be done by 6:00 a.m., just in time to shower and get dressed for my next job.

Some lessons are learned in the midst of pain. Some are learned with very little sleep, lots of hard work, and some needed attitude adjustment. I want to share with you one such lesson I learned.

I was fresh out of seminary and had taken my first "full-time" position in ministry—the senior pastor of a small suburban church in Southern California. Dana and I moved about fifty miles east, and I felt like it was a dream come true. This church was going to pay me almost three times as much as my previous ministry position, and I would be able to lead a church to growth.

We spent eight years there and it was a wonderful time. But sometimes the dream seemed more like a nightmare. Shortly after our arrival it became clear that the promised salary was just not possible. We had moved into a rental house based on the expected income, but our real income would be about ten thousand dollars less and there was no health insurance. I tried to get out of the lease to take a cheaper apartment, but the landlord wouldn't help us. Then Dana became pregnant with our son Zachary. We were learning a lot about God's call and provision that would shape the rest of our lives, but at the time all the problems just felt like horrible trials that served no other purpose than to toughen us.

I went in search of additional employment and landed a couple of jobs. They were not glamorous, but they provided additional income and the hours let me work full-time for the church. I was a pastor, a paperboy, and a property manager.

Sundays became the best and the worst days. I loved being with my church on Sundays, but on that day the paper route was always a nightmare. The paper is two to three times bigger and heavier on Sunday than the rest of the week—full of ads and weekly sections. Often the papers arrived at the warehouse late, which would make me scramble the rest of my day to get everything done.

One early Sunday morning I had loaded all the papers into my car. The good news was that it wasn't raining, so I hadn't had to bag the papers, an extra step that takes time. Every space in the car was full, leaving only enough room for me to sit and drive, barely able to see out the window. Off I went, tossing paper after paper.

On these mornings I remember having long dialogues with the Lord (which, in hindsight, made these times more beneficial than I thought at the time). This morning I started off with complaints. "Oh, Lord,

The Counterfeit Kingdom of Outside In

why am I doing this? I have a bachelor's degree and a master's degree and here I am doing the job of a junior high school kid! Why? What could possibly be more humiliating than this?"

The following week the Lord showed me what was more humbling than having a paper route. I was fired. Somehow an address didn't get on my list and they were not receiving their paper, so I was let go. I couldn't keep a job that a junior high school kid could do! Now that is humiliating! Thankfully, after the initial humiliation, the paper decided to give me a second chance, which I took with much more seriousness. I stayed there for a few years.

But I digress. Getting back to that special morning. In the midst of my complaining to the Lord I threw the heavy paper to a house and in midflight the rubber band broke, spilling the paper and ads all over the front lawn. It was like pouring salt in an already throbbing wound.

I decided to just keep driving. I was already late as it was. As that thought was taking form in my mind, my right foot slowly lifted off the brake and started pressing on the gas pedal and I looked straight ahead. Just then I sensed Jesus was saying something to me. All he said was, "I live at that house."

Yikes! That was enough. I stepped on the brake, put the car in park, got out of the stuffed car, and gathered up all the loose papers. Tossing them in the back of my car, I picked up a fresh, nicely folded paper and placed it on the front doorstep.

In my mind I could hear the Scripture, "Do your work heartily, as for the Lord" (Col. 3:23). I heard the Holy Spirit say to me, "This job you are doing now is as sacred as the pastorate. You are serving me here and there equally, and I expect you to do so well." This idea radically transformed my whole view of life as well as my own identity. For years later I would continue to discover the significance found in this moment, because I had been deceived into thinking that the world was divided up into some categories that do not really exist.

A Paper Route Pastor

I always saw myself as a delivery boy, but in my mind it was the Good News not the bad news that I was to deliver. I was delivering both. As a pastor I had assumed that my job, my vocation, was indeed a holy calling. But being a paperboy, that couldn't be a holy calling, could it?

If only my job as a pastor was a holy calling, the jobs the other people in the church were fulfilling were not holy callings. If this was the case, more was expected of me than of them in the church. This lets them off the hook with the responsibility of the kingdom of God, something Jesus never intended.

Through these challenging events the Lord was instructing me to reevaluate my identity and profession. I realized my calling was not to a career but to a life of service that even included doing a job once relegated to junior high school boys on bicycles.

I began to view my job at the paper as more than just part-time employment to help pay the rent and doctor's bills; it was also a call. I went to the warehouse believing that God wanted me there. I began to see the people next to me at the tables folding papers as a mission field. We had a good hour together every day, and we talked about life and occasionally would have a rubber band shooting war when the manager wasn't looking. They even started calling me "Rev," much to my chagrin. I became the paper route pastor.

Before long I was helping people through difficult problems by listening and praying. I would meet some of the other "paper chuckers" for breakfast after our routes were finished. The manager and I spent lots of hours talking about Jesus, family, and life. We would often have lunch, then pray and play basketball together. Some of them started coming to my church on Sunday, and a few from my church even started working at the same warehouse when they needed some extra income. I had two churches that were starting to blend together.

The lines between what was sacred and what was secular became blurred. I began to learn that a job is a job, but I am a disciple of Christ no matter where I work. Kingdom fruit was not restricted to what happened as a result of church ministry or even my professional clergy status. The divisions, which once were so obvious to me, I began to suspect were illegitimate.

There are many different false dichotomies that affect the way we view life. For some reason, we Christians want to find a nice category for everything. We're experts at this. The problem is that the world does not always go along with our labels.

When we label everything, we are able to see life only through the lenses of our artificially framed categories. This forces us to live our lives submitting to false ideas that do not represent real life and we become more and more removed from what is indeed true. And worse, we do not even know it.

The Counterfeit Kingdom of Outside In

False Dichotomies

Secular versus Sacred

The first false lens we must remove to see life correctly is the division between the secular and the sacred. This is what I was having removed from my eyes with God's laser beam every day at 3:00 a.m., while I was folding hundreds of newspapers.

HOLY AND UNHOLY

Paul writes, "To the pure, all things are pure" (Titus 1:15). When Jesus redeemed you and me, he made us holy. We are no longer *striving* to be holy; in actuality we are *already* holy.

I know that our life experience doesn't seem to reflect this truth, but it is true nonetheless. From God's point of view we are already redeemed, cleaned, and esteemed in the high courts in heaven. Now from your spouse's point of view, this may not be as clear! But one of our problems is that we do not respect that God's point of view is more true and real than our own.

There is indeed a struggle we face in seeing the reality of our position in Christ actualized in our lives. Our holiness is in process. We are holy and we are becoming holy. Theologians refer to this as the sanctification process. It is a big word for being set apart, which is what *holy* really means. The way I see it: holiness is already ours, and we are learning to become at home in it as we mature in Christ. We are learning to lay aside old destructive patterns and live out a life that reflects Christ's beauty and transcendence. This will not be accomplished in the seventy to one hundred years we have to live, so none of us ever totally arrives at holiness in this life. We always have some of the crusty residue of the flesh. But trust me, if you are in Christ, Christ is in you, and therefore you are holy—right now.

That crusty residue doesn't make you unclean. The atoning sacrifice of Christ has cleansed you wholly and made you holy. It covers every flaw, every mistake, and every blemish—past, present, and future. Its redeeming power doesn't change. Christ's work is eternal, powerful, and stable. As he said on the cross, "It is finished."

In the New Testament there is not a single church that struggled more obviously with immorality and carnality than the Corinthians. They were wrestling with all sorts of evil—divisions (1 Cor. 1:10–11), pride issues (3:18), and even gross sexual immorality (5:1). Yet when writing to them, Paul says they are "saints" (1:2). Wow, there's a word we don't understand after centuries of reinforcing false ideas about what a saint is. Literally *saint* means a "holy one" and can be used to refer to all who are in Christ. Paul calls the carnal Corinthians "holy ones." He remarks in chapter 3, verse 17, that the temple of God is holy and that they are indeed "holy"! How remarkable this is!

SAFE AND UNSAFE

The idea that there are secular things and sacred things for the Christian is just plain wrong. This is an idea we have carried over from the false religious viewpoint of the Middle Ages. But let's not blame the Catholics, it was also found in the early church. In fact it is addressed in the New Testament as an issue. So if we want to blame anyone, let's blame Gnosticism that taught the same sort of viewpoint (see 1 Tim. 4:1–5; 6:20–21).

There isn't secular music and sacred music, there is just music. There aren't secular movies and Christian movies, there are just movies. There are not secular schools and sacred schools, just schools. Labeling things secular or sacred gives them a moral quality, but things have no moral capacity. Only people with souls and the freedom to make conscious choices have moral qualities.

You can judge a book by its cover, but it has no soul, so you cannot judge it as "Christian." It is simply a book written by someone who has a soul and views life through a Christian mind-set. You can judge a song as good or bad but not as guilty of sin. I have no problem with calling a song *bad*, just don't call it secular. A song does not have a soul, unless of course it is performed by James Brown or Aretha Franklin, but that is an entirely different sort of "soul."

People are able to make moral choices and are therefore good or bad. The fruit of their lives reflect what is within, so bad people produce bad fruit.

When we call the things Christians produce *sacred*, we are assuming they are good, and this is definitely an incorrect assumption. A lot of the works Christians produce are less than stellar in quality. We may do Christ a favor by removing his name from some of the things we call "Christian."

This false dichotomy, deciding whether something is sacred or secular, has wreaked havoc on the kingdom of God in multitudes of ways. We start assuming that the sacred is safe and the secular is unsafe. Often it may be the other way around. It is common for something labeled "Christian" or "sacred" to be indeed toxic, legalistic, and unsafe. Many churches, schools, and even families are this way.

The Counterfeit Kingdom of Outside In

Some believe that the spiritual can be contaminated by coming in contact with the secular. The truth is that we simply cannot be removed from contact with the world. Paul states that it would be virtually impossible to be removed from the sin of the world (1 Cor. 5:9–11). But of course we can carefully choose those with whom we share our intimate lives. Paul states, "All things are lawful for me, but not all things are profitable. All things are lawful for me, but I will not be mastered by anything" (1 Cor. 6:12). It would be far better if we called things "healthy" or "unhealthy" rather than "secular" or "sacred."

There were laws in the Old Testament that seem to imply the secular is unsafe. When you touch something unclean, it rubs off, and you become unclean. This implies that godliness comes from the outside in, rather than the other way around. Jesus changed all the rules when he came and established the new covenant, which places God's pure law in our hearts. Spirituality was no longer conditioned on people staying away from the unclean but comes from within and is worked out in any and all environments.

Inside and Out

It is interesting that whenever Jesus wanted to heal someone of leprosy, he did so by laying his hand on the person. We know from reading the Gospel accounts that he didn't have to heal this way. Jesus healed people he never touched (see, for instance, John 4:46–54). According to the law, someone with leprosy was unclean; to touch him or her meant you would become unclean. Lepers had to shout, "Unclean," whenever people came by so they would avoid any contact.

Jesus did not avoid contact; he initiated it. And it's remarkable that he didn't become unclean. Instead, the leper became clean! This is a new spirituality. It is more powerful than the dirty world around us. We can actually have a sanctifying effect on the people around us as we walk in the power of God's Spirit within us. We rub off on others, not the other way around.

There is an interesting story in the book of Acts. Peter is hungry, waiting on a roof in Joppa for a meal. He falls into a trance and sees the sky open up and the Lord drop a sheet full of unclean animals. He tells Peter to kill and eat them. Peter refuses, stating that he would never eat anything unholy. Then the Lord announces, "What God has cleansed, no longer consider unholy" (Acts 10:15). This happens three times to verify that it is the Lord who is speaking to Peter.

You have in this story a hungry and devout Jewish man, some Old Testament laws, a herd of unkosher animals, and God. Something changes here that is profound, but what is it? Are the previous laws no longer any good? Did God change his mind about pork? Or did God suddenly run all these particular animals through a carwash?

It is Peter who changed, not God, not the Old Testament, and not the animals. Once he was unclean, but then he was clean (John 13:10). Jesus's death, burial, resurrection, and ascension and the indwelling Holy Spirit had altered Peter forever. His life was no longer subject to the damaging effects of mixing it up with unclean animals or people. He was no longer affected by touching something unclean, because his holiness was not subject to what surrounded him. He was so changed from the inside out that he could become a change agent to those around him, including Gentiles, which is really what the vision was about.

Before Christ's atoning work, being married to an unbeliever was condemned because God's people were incapable of withstanding the influence of false gods. But all of that has changed, so Paul writes that the believing spouse should stay with an unbeliever because he or she will have a sanctifying effect on the one who is not yet a Christian (1 Cor. 7:12–14).[1] This shows us that our salvation in Christ is more powerful than the darkness in the world around us. We are holy and nothing can change that.

Now to us, all things are lawful but not necessarily profitable (1 Cor. 10:23). It is now a question of what is beneficial, not what is secular and what is sacred.

Clergy versus Laity

It did not take long in church history before a special class of Christians developed that was professional. The idea that there should be a class of professional Christians has plagued Christianity for almost two thousand years, but is just not biblical.

The idea that special people are set apart and called to serve the Lord "full-time" is a cracked lens that distorts our view of everything and we have developed language that supports our view. Those who serve as professional pastors are "called." Those who fold and throw papers are just working.

ACCOUNTABILITY

The distinction is not biblical. As I read and reread the New Testament without this lens, I find that all are called to follow. It is not the

The Counterfeit Kingdom of Outside In

destination of the following that indicates the calling; the calling is the following. So if God calls you to serve as a pastor, your calling is fulfilled among a flock. If you are called to be a contractor, your calling is fulfilled at the contractor's worksite. Whatever your calling, you are to serve your Master well.

The problems with seeing some people as called into special roles are profound. Those who serve the church professionally are seen as more holy than those who do not. Expectations are placed on them that are not placed on other Christians. And as I said earlier, this lowers the bar for those who are not pursuing a ministry vocation, with the result that average Christians do not bear the responsibility of following God fully. They are simply the drones who work hard to finance the real workers who carry the weight of the kingdom. The lives of those who serve professionally are held to higher account. We have a whole list of traits that we must check off before someone is allowed to serve in such a high position.

I do not see this in the New Testament. Jesus calls all of us to surrender our whole lives to follow him. This is not a call into a career but into a kingdom. All citizens of Christ's kingdom are called to serve fully. No Christian is held to a higher level of accountability for his or her character than another. Jesus bled so that all of us could be holy and set apart, not just a few.

Now it is true that leaders are held to a stricter accountability, but that is true whether they are paid to lead or not. And regardless of accountability, each of us is called to a holy life. None is called to a more holy life than another.

THE RISE OF THE CLERGY

I started this section saying that it didn't take long for the institutionalization of Christian leadership to take root in the church. I believe it began before the New Testament was even completed.

The apostle John lived longer than the other eleven disciples. Later in his life, one of his greatest battles was against this separation between Christian leaders and the rest of God's people.

He wrote of one such skirmish in 3 John when he said:

I wrote something to the church; but Diotrephes, who loves to be first among them, does not accept what we say. For this reason, if I come, I will call attention to his deeds which he does, unjustly accusing us with wicked words; and not satisfied with this, he himself does not receive the brethren, either, and he forbids those who desire to do so and puts them out of the church.

3 John 9–10

Apparently an insecure leader, who wanted to be exalted above the rest, seized control of a church and censured input from anyone else. This contrasts with other leaders who remain anonymous out of respect for their servants' hearts and are mentioned in verse 8. John writes of these heroes with flattering terms, encouraging the church to support such men who "went out for the sake of the Name [of Christ], accepting nothing from the Gentiles" (v. 7).

The issue is not receiving support for ministry. The issue is in developing a separate class of Christians who are elevated to a higher stature. It is becoming professional Christian leaders who have seemingly greater responsibility and therefore more privilege and respect than other Christians that is the problem. I believe that Diotrephes is not the only one who is such a threat at this time.

In John's last writing, the Revelation of Jesus Christ, he addresses the seven churches of Asia Minor. In a few of the churches the rise of the clergy is addressed. It is called the deeds of the Nicolaitans. Scholars disagree over what this group is. Some believe it is a band following some false teaching of Nicholas, but the only Nicholas that they can point to is the one mentioned in Acts 6:5. This is one viewpoint, but I see another view that is probably more consistent with the whole of Scripture.

Nike, a word made famous by athletic shoes, means "victory." It comes from the word *nicos*, which means "to conquer" and is the prefix in the word *Nicolaitans*. *Laos* is the Greek word for "people" and is the term from which we get the word *laity*. I believe the Nicolaitans were an emerging professional class who ruled over God's people in the church. From their name we can say they were the ones who "conquered the people." And Revelation 2:6 says that Jesus hates "the deeds of the Nicolaitans."

To the church in Pergamum, Jesus writes that the Nicolaitans were guilty in the same way as Balaam, a professional prophet for hire, whom Balak bought (the highest bidder) and sent to curse God's people with his special spiritual authority (vv. 14–15). It is interesting that the name Balaam in Hebrew is made up essentially of the same combined words as Nicolaitan in Greek—meaning to conquer or destroy the people.

Our very language betrays that we have fallen victim to the deeds of the Nicolaitans—those who would "conquer the people." Some people have a special "call to ministry." We refer to them as "ministers." They are "ordained for ministry." We even call them "reverend" as though they are more holy than the rest and deserving reverential respect. The New Testament does not use language like this, in fact, quite the opposite. Leaders in the church are not to *do* the work of the ministry, but to equip the ordinary saints to do the work of the ministry (Eph. 4:11–16). The ministers in the New Testament are all those who are of the family of God. No one but God is to be revered.

Jesus took this idea way beyond our comfort zone. He said we should not call anyone our leader, our father, or even our teacher, because God is all of these things for us (Matt. 23:8–12). God is the only one to be revered or worshiped. To do otherwise is clearly blasphemous. The idea that some people are more holy than others is not found in the New Testament. The people, whom the leaders are supposed to equip, are called "the saints," which, as we have seen, means "holy ones." They are the ministers—the ones "called to the ministry." These ordinary Christians are set apart, called to be holy and to serve.

The idea of professional Christians who are for hire is something that Jesus hates. He refers to leaders who are for hire as hirelings (John 10:12). They are not only "for hire" but, like Diotrephes, they have ambitions to *be higher* than the rest. This is what Jesus says clearly that he hates, and so should we.

Local Church versus Universal Church

Another false dichotomy we have created is the local church versus a universal church. You can find these terms in most theological textbooks, documenting their statements with verses from the New Testament, thus assuming biblical authority. But in reality these words are not used in the Bible in this way.

Church is both universal and local, hence the labels, but I have to wonder if Jesus sees his church through this same broken lens. Or does he just see the church? Are we all members of one another at both the local level and the universal level, even throughout history? Yes, I think we are, and while this false viewpoint may not be as harmful as the previous two, it does excuse a whole lot of foolish polarization in the church.

When we allow for a "local" church, we give credence to separation and noncooperation among the members of Jesus's body. We have defined church as a local group of people who are committed to an organization and usually to some property in a neighborhood. We do not see "church" as all of Christ's church in that locale, just the one group with whom we happen to associate. And we think this is biblical, because we are convinced that the idea of a "local" church is in the New Testament.

But when the authors of the many New Testament letters wrote to local churches, they were writing to all the Christians in a given geographical region.

Today we are separated by minor differences over doctrines that were not even a passing thought in New Testament times. The Thessalonians had two competing views of eschatology. They didn't have some dispensational churches in Thessalonica and some who were not. Rather than forming separate local churches they were still one family. The Corinthian church was divided over spiritual gifts and especially speaking in tongues but were still one church. They didn't become two local churches, one that was charismatic and one that was not. The church in Thyatira had some who followed one leader's attempt to contextualize, which led to some serious compromise. Others, who did not follow them into worldliness, were still part of the same church according to Jesus. They didn't have some who were the liberal church and others who were not.

We use the theological justification of a "local church" doctrine to maintain space between family members. This division keeps us weaker and is a poor witness to the community around us. We cannot really change the situation we find ourselves in now, but justifying it with false distinctions doesn't help our cause and will lead us down an even more dysfunctional path.

To maintain this false distinction, we have instituted something called "church membership" and then established hoops for people to jump through to be called "members." In a church you can have some Christians who are "members" and others who are not. This is a secondary dichotomy that is built on the first, but both are unbiblical viewpoints. There is no distinction in the New Testament between the disciples who were "members" of a specific church and those who were not "members." We are all members of Christ's body (see 1 Cor. 12:12–13, 27).

The idea of a new members class is foreign to the New Testament. The idea of dividing God's people according to those who are "members" and those who are not, and having such membership based upon who took a class or was baptized in a certain manner is absolutely foreign to the Bible. Having part of Christ's body able to voice an opinion and

The Counterfeit Kingdom of Outside In

cast a vote, and others remain silent because they are not "members" is foolishness. This sort of distinction is not the kingdom of God; it sounds a lot more like a country club, with certain rites and card-carrying members. All this is built on a false view of the church.

Parachurch versus Local Church

A final false division I want to discuss is the separation of the parachurch from the local church. This is very prevalent today. Again this label is not found in the Bible but is used to categorize a segment of the church, and the label has an effect on us that is both subtle and subversive.

This false dichotomy is relatively new and was born out of function rather than doctrine. It has become such a prevalent way of viewing ministry that I will give the attention of the next chapter to it.

The prefix *para* has the idea of coming alongside something. So a "parachurch" ministry is a ministry that comes alongside the church to help her fulfill her mission. So now in our thinking there is the church and there is an auxiliary ministry that is not the church but functions alongside the church. If Jesus saw this as a need, why didn't he create the church and the parachurch from the beginning? Why did it take eighteen hundred years before parachurches were formed?

An Unbiblical Distinction

Once we view the world through these illegitimate lenses, we start to live accordingly and end up making some foolish decisions. For instance, one parachurch ministry exists to reach college students. They insist on being in the parachurch camp for many reasons. Since they need to raise their support from the church and exist to serve the church, they never want to be seen as competing with the church. Because they are "parachurch," they do not start churches (unless it happens to be overseas where the new churches wouldn't be seen as competitive with their support base), so this organization does not function as a church (at least according to a very limited understanding of what makes a church a church). They are also a streamlined business that is not bogged down with the bureaucracy that is found in many churches.

For these reasons this group works hard to maintain a parachurch status. The problem is that they are making decisions based on understandings and distinctions that are not in the Bible. In their eyes (much as it is in the eyes of the U.S. government) a church is defined as fulfilling certain sacerdotal duties, such as baptism and communion. But simply dunking people in a pool or dunking bread in a glass of wine is not what defines the church.

In a staunch effort not to be a church, this group refuses to practice these specific duties, thus maintaining their parachurch status. They evangelize but do not start churches. They make disciples but do not baptize them. Doing all they can to keep their mission focused, they make every attempt not to threaten the local church in any way, and they encourage their people to attend a local church and maintain membership there.

STRANGE PRACTICES

The reality is that starting churches is the by-product of evangelizing and fellowshiping with one another on mission together. By living within the false boundaries these faulty lenses have created, Christians are actually instructed to disobey Jesus when they are told not to baptize their disciples. The practice of baptism is not something Christ gave to the church organization but to all disciples. One of the sayings in our own church-planting movement is "The Bible doesn't command us to be baptized but to be baptizers" (Matt. 28:19–20). There is absolutely no biblical support for the idea that only the clergy in the local church can baptize (another false view discussed above). Though our traditions and experience may reinforce these standards, the Bible does not.

It is amazing how much damage the simple idea of baptizing another has caused through church history. People have been killed, cults have been initiated, denominations started and split, heretics burned at the stake, and parachurch organizations have been formed—all because we view baptism in a strange, unbiblical fashion. If we would only read the Bible and take it for what it says literally, rather than defend our "sacred" traditions, the church would be healthier. Both sides of the church aisle are guilty of this.

Boundaries may start as helpful language to manage our understanding of things, but soon they disrupt our spiritual lives and divide the body of Christ illegitimately. When false boundaries begin to take on a biblical sense of authority, they are quite insidious. We accept them as truth and even rise to defend them as though they come from the Bible, when they do not. Unfortunately, we are willing to submit to these false divisions more than to Scripture itself. This is how the subversive strategy of the Enemy causes much damage. Because we have allowed artificial boundaries to separate Christian groups, based on illegitimate organizational differences, weird things happen.

For instance, one motto for the parachurch ministry discussed above has been: "To fulfill the Great Commission in this generation." This seems honorable, except that they have rules in place that prevent them from ever fulfilling the Great Commission in any place. Right in the middle of the Great Commission is the command to baptize disciples, which they strictly forbid.

I want to raise awareness of the weird, almost schizophrenic policies we have made in the church. Whether it is separating a spiritual family into voting "members" and silent "nonmembers" or telling Christians to fulfill the Great Commission by disobeying it, false and artificial divisions have caused some strange practices to be established.

The purpose of all the categories we have created was to make life better, but they have had the opposite effect. We have limited God and his kingdom because the views developed through false understandings have kept us bound. We must shed the lenses that cause our distorted vision and enjoy a more holistic and healthy view of the church.

Delivering the Good News with the Bad

I learned a lot through my venture into the paper delivery business. Some lessons came unexpectedly. One morning I was delivering a paper and noticed that the house had a small Buddha idol on the front porch. The Holy Spirit whispered to me to pray for the people there. I did. Then as I went to the next house, he whispered the same thing. As it turned out, he told me to pray for every house where I delivered a paper.

At first, with my small faith, I couldn't simply obey, I had to question. My assumptions were still trapped in small boxes, divided into manageable categories that limit the kingdom. So I questioned God. I stated plainly: "There is no way all these people are going to come to Christ. It would be nice, but I just can't believe it."

The Lord patiently replied, "I didn't ask you to save them all, just pray for them all."

Oh, okay, I can do that. So when I threw out a paper, I also threw up a prayer.

After finishing the route that day, I went up to my office at the church and sat down to work on some stuff at my desk. Later that morning the phone rang. I could sense some desperation in the voice on the other end. He said his name was Steve and he was a truck driver. He had found the church's phone number in the yellow pages because he was lonely and lost and was overwhelmed with the pain of being separated from his wife and the Lord. We talked a little and prayed on the phone. I asked him if he would like to have coffee with me the next morning and start meeting together. He said he would like to but that all he had was his work truck so he couldn't drive to the coffee shop very easily. I told him I could pick him up and asked where he lived. He gave me his address, and I had one of those holy moments, with goose bumps and hair standing up on the back of my neck.

Then I told Steve I had already prayed for him that morning before the sun rose. He asked how it was possible since we'd never met. I told him I was his paperboy and had delivered his paper that very morning and had prayed for him.

That was enough to convince him. He and I started meeting and we met together for several years in a discipleship relationship. The Lord was showing me that my paper route was as much a holy calling and spiritual opportunity as my pastorate. I also came to understand that Steve's truck driving job was a holy calling as well.

Lenses that once defined my view of the world were removed, and I saw the kingdom in a new way. Even the Bible came alive for me in a fresh way. Using the Scriptures, I began to question the categories that defined my worldview, categories that had been passed down through the generations. I refused to accept them as real just because they had been labeled as such.

What was once either secular or sacred was suddenly only sacred to me. There was no longer a difference between the clergy and the laity. I realized that all Christians are called to the ministry, serving Christ in their life and work. The church is the church, whether it meets in a warehouse at 3:00 a.m.—fellowshiping while folding newspapers—or at 10:00 a.m. on Sunday morning in a building designed for religious activities. And God's people are God's people and part of his body whether they are serving in a focused and more mission-exclusive ministry or a general all-inclusive church ministry. For me life became more beautiful because I could see all the rich colors and variations, unclouded by rigid, unforgiving boundaries.

7

PARASITES ON THE BODY OF CHRIST

Why Some Ministries Suck . . . Literally!

An expert is one who knows more and more about less and less.

Nicholas Murray Butle

It's not what we eat but what we digest that makes us strong; not what we gain but what we save that makes us rich; not what we read but what we remember that makes us learned; and not what we profess but what we practice that gives us integrity.

Francis Bacon

A warden meets an incoming inmate for questioning, as he does with every inmate who comes to the prison known as the Castle. This is no ordinary inmate and no ordinary prison. The Castle is a penitentiary for military convicts. And the incoming inmate is a former general, convicted of negligence while on command, which led to the death of some of his men.

In the movie *The Last Castle*, Robert Redford is inmate Irwin, a leader of men who had a distinguished career that ended in disgrace. The warden he meets, played by James Gandolfini, is a very different kind of military leader. These two present a sharp contrast. One is a con with no authority or rights. The other is the chief commander of the prison with troops of soldiers under his authority. One has been through the experience of war and the other has only read of it.

When the two meet, the warden asks if inmate Irwin will sign a copy of his book *The Burden of Command*, which the warden has on his shelf. This odd little scene reveals much. In a moment of irony an inmate without any rights, title, or authority is asked by the one who holds all the authority of the prison to sign his book for him. This is a revealing moment, setting a thematic contrast that will play out in the remainder of the film.

While the warden searches for the book in his library, he leaves the new prisoner under the care of one of his captains. Irwin notices a collection of war memorabilia and looks it over. "Impressive," he remarks. As Irwin holds a minié ball (a bullet used with musket rifles in the Civil War) from the battle of Shiloh, where Grant lost thirteen thousand men, Captain Peretz asks him if he has a collection himself. Irwin says he doesn't and that he doesn't have a taste for it. Then he adds, and the warden overhears him, "Any man with a collection like this is a man who never set foot on a battlefield. To him a minié ball from Shiloh is just an artifact. To a combat vet it is a hunk of metal that caused some poor bastard a world of pain."

Hearing this and feeling both embarrassed and disrespected, the warden tosses the book back on the shelf and returns to say he couldn't find it.

Irwin returns to his cell, and the warden settles into his elaborate office full of artifacts and seminal books about war—wars he has read of but never seen.

In the film the two end up squaring off against one another. After much conflict and a prison revolution led by ex-general Irwin, it is evident that one man has all the position and none of the authority. The other has all the authority and no position. The prisoners are not even allowed to salute him. In the end, the warden has become so abusive that the prison guards will not carry out his orders. Finally, his actions catch up with him and the warden is taken away to become a prisoner himself.

The film makes clear that there is a stark difference between a warrior who has been on the battlefield and a soldier who is an expert on war but not experienced in battle. Experience changes your way of viewing things. You may have read books about a subject but you are not an expert until you have tasted it.

The Counterfeit Kingdom of Outside In

There are many soldiers of Christ who are experts on the battle but who have never tasted it. They have read books, built reputations, and become men of authority but they have never been on the field of war. Their expertise is flawed because it is shallow and unrealistic, lacking in the wisdom acquired from experience.

Parasitic "Ministries"

There are entire organizations that are built by people who have never been on the battlefield. Though they offer services to the church on how to do church better, they've never led a church to health.

As we saw in the last chapter, parachurch ministries are a relatively new phenomenon in the scope of church history. Of course there have always been auxiliary ministries that exist to accomplish specific tasks, but in the past they were usually part of a denomination, so they were considered part of the church. They would not have called themselves parachurch, because they considered themselves a ministry of the church.

In the last one hundred years some organizations have sprung up that are not connected to the church. They are Christian organizations and usually have a unique purpose, which will help the church accomplish her mission. Often these organizations become profitable, nonprofit, religious businesses.

While many of these organizations are helpful and have respect and credibility, I am afraid some are not healthy for the church at all and are actually parasitic.

A parasite attaches itself to an organism and feeds off it for its own survival. Parasites can cause some severe health problems for the host, because they take nourishment from it and often give nothing back in return. In essence, parasites suck.

Here are a few ways that *some* parachurch ministries are parasitic: they feed off the church's resources, off the church's purposes, and off the church's experience.

Feeding Off the Church's Resources

So many churches are weak and anemic because they have lost valuable resources—to ministries that were originally started to *help* the church! Valuable leaders, often the best, are recruited away from churches. Then those same leaders are sent back to the church to raise their financial support so they can serve in the parachurch ministry.

Feeding Off the Church's Purposes

Often parachurches exist to fulfill the mission that was clearly given to the church. Whether it is evangelism and church planting or equipping and training leaders, the churches of America are forfeiting the role they should have, so other ministries, which are supposedly not the church, can step in the gap. The church has outsourced much of the work that she is called to do.

This is an unfortunate reality today. The church has become irrelevant and out of touch in our world, mostly because she has surrendered her God-given role in society and culture. Often the church is a feeble corporation incapable of contributing anything of substance to a lost world. In many cases, she has farmed out the most important tasks:

- Her leadership development has been assumed by colleges, seminaries, and Bible institutes.
- Her compassion and social justice have been given over to nonprofit charitable organizations.
- Her global mission has been relinquished to mission agencies and evangelistic ministries.
- Church government and decision making have often been forfeited to denominational offices.
- Her prophetic voice has been replaced by publishing houses, self-help gurus, and futurist authors.
- Her emotional and spiritual healing has been taken over by psychologists, psychiatrists, and family counseling services.

The essence of the church is lost when she farms out her responsibilities to other organizations. The world today looks at the church wondering what relevance she has. The only use they see for the church is performing the sacerdotal duties of preaching, marrying, burying, baptizing, and passing around wafers and grape juice. How sad! The church was once a catalyst for artistic expression, social change, and the founding of hospitals, schools, and missionary enterprise, but today she has settled for providing a one-hour-a-week worship concert, an offering plate, and a sermon.

Feeding Off the Church's Experience

There are a growing number of experts on church health, growth, and multiplication that have not ever done any of the things they teach.

Instead, they observe closely what others have done, write it out in a workbook, and offer seminars and consulting on how other churches can see the same success. In these cases, they use the fruit of a successful church or two to gain information that they can sell back to the rest of the churches. I know of some organizations whose leaders are supported as missionaries to do this work. So they double dip into the resources of the churches via financial support and the added cost of the seminar or consultation. This is parasitic. It is feeding off the church's resources and experience and then selling it back to the church!

Putting Experience Back into Expertise

One organization recruited me to develop a training resource. I will not name this organization because it is full of good people whom I respect to this day. They had me raise part-time ministry support so I could accomplish the project. After working a couple of years for them, I decided that their ministry was not for me, and our contract ended. Not only did they get a 15 percent commission from the money I raised, they also got the resource that I developed from my own church experience. That was the deal and I can live with it. I am happy that the lessons we learned are having a broader influence. But what happened next was alarming.

They gave the training materials I had developed to some of the staff who had neither worked on them nor used them. These people went on the road offering this training to others for a high price. I can even handle that, though I would highly recommend a different path. To add insult to injury, they tried to sell the expertise to me! I looked at the guy who wanted me to sign up for a consultation on my own training with a look that must have said, *What kind of an idiot do you think I am?* Then he said, "Well, of course you may not need the training."

I am convinced that those who do this sort of thing are truly unaware of how far they have gone down the parasitic path. There is a sort of blindfold that covers their eyes and keeps them from recognizing their own actions. How else can you explain their trying to sell me, at a hefty cost, the material I had developed, after already having received money from me so that I could create it for them in the first place? I am confident they do not see it this way.

Today many who are consultants for the church started off doing ministry work. Then, encouraged by their success, they decided to expand their influence and offer their expertise to the greater body of Christ. This is fine and may be helpful—for about a year to a year and a half—the amount of time I figure someone can remain relevant and offer anything significant.

There is an increasingly small window of relevance for those who remove themselves from hands-on ministry experience. There once was a day when a ministry, built from the expertise won on the field, could have relevancy for years. Now life moves so fast, things are so global, and culture changes so quickly that what was expertise two years ago is now old news and hardly applicable. For the very sharp leader there are a few things that can prolong the relevance, but ultimately this reality will cause the leader's authority to evaporate.

So leaders who are not engaged in real life ministry and mission are out of touch in just a year to a year and a half, and I suspect that in a few years the time span could be even shorter, perhaps six months. Of course that depends somewhat on the area of expertise, but every area of expertise has a time limit, which continues to diminish. This makes the world ever more hostile to the ministry consultant.

As I have said, to try to stay relevant, a lot of these consultants have taken to using other people's experience on which to base their expertise. They become talent scouts, coming alongside someone who is out in the field of battle, watching what they do, and learning. Then they add this expertise to their own consulting work. When the people they train ask questions, these consultants have to try to guess the answers, because they haven't actually done any of the work themselves.

At times I have chosen to allow this to happen to me, because I have a true affection for some people who want to serve the church in this way. And I believe their work grants broader exposure to helpful information. But as a whole, this is not a healthy practice.

I develop ministry tools for others, but I do so while on the front lines and in the crosshairs of the Enemy. I have done this for two decades. For every resource we release for our leaders to use, there are three or four that we shelve because they didn't work during field-testing. Because we develop resources from our actual experience, the resources are more powerful. We have worked out bugs and have seen how they work and why. So our training and materials have an authority.

When people develop resources untested by life experience and sell them to the church, the results are pathetically weak. A good idea in your office does not always translate to a good idea in real life. Believe me, I have shelves of these ideas gathering dust. It is the reality of experience that sharpens us. Experience on the fields of battle refines us and our strategies. There is no substitute for this.

Christian Business versus the Business of Christians

Like it or not, there are "Christian businesses." If you read the previous chapter, you know that I do not believe there are Christian businesses and secular ones. Business is business, neither secular nor sacred. There are, however, businesses that cater to a Christian market; some are exploitative; some offer good resources.

Because some offer good resources, I do not want to say all businesses that focus on the Christian market are evil, for that would be harsh and wrong. There are, however, many businesses that exploit the kingdom of God and do not really contribute much to it. Such exploitation is part of a free society, so this is to be expected. What bothers me is when such exploitative businesses are seen as a spiritual enterprise, such as a missionary endeavor. Those who adorn their business in such a guise will be held accountable.

Since a business does not have a soul, a business cannot be evil. Oil companies are not evil, as much as some of us would like to think they are. Exploitative, yes, but it is not the business that is evil. It is the people in the business that are either evil or good. I know for a fact that there are evil businessmen and businesswomen. There are also good people who are in business.

So, to make my point, let me push this a little. You may ask, "What about drug dealers, surely that is an evil business, right?" No, it is just business. It is the people who are selling the drugs illegally who are evil, not the function of exchanging product for currency. But what if the product is harmful? Isn't that evil? No, the product is neither spiritual nor unspiritual, it is material and incapable of having moral qualities. As you know, there are drug dealers who are not only legal but also needed for the health and betterment of society. They are called pharmacists. They may even sell the same product as the illegal drug dealers. To confuse you even more, there may be pharmacists who sell their product ethically, but who are still immoral people. This doesn't make their business evil; it makes *them* evil.

Now, there are businesses that are built on evil practices, such as prostitution or the slave trade. Again, it isn't the business (the sale of goods or services) that is evil, but the sinful practices of immoral men and women that are evil.

Separating the Business from the Church

Businesses and the church are not the same. The objectives of a business and the objectives of the church are two very distinct and competing propositions. What makes a church successful is far removed from what makes a business successful. I have seen businesses that try to sound almost churchlike in their mission. One business touts: "Our business is to serve people." But the reality is it exists to make a profit just like most other businesses. Even "nonprofit" businesses make a profit and cannot function if they lose money continually.

There are some businesses that have as a mission to resource the kingdom of God, and their purpose is not to make money. These businesspeople wrestle with the tension of serving the church and surviving at the same time. I know, because I am part of a team that leads such a resource business: CMAResources.

More than once we have made suicidal decisions for our business. I will elaborate more on this in a later chapter, but suffice it to say, our purpose is not self-preservation but kingdom expansion. That sounds very churchlike, doesn't it? Some would wonder why we would consider ourselves a business and not the church. CMAResources is a business in that we seek to resource the kingdom; we are not a church. We exchange goods and service for money and that puts us in the business category, even if we're intentionally not very good at it. Those of us who work with CMAResources are in fact a part of Christ's church, but the organization we serve in is a business.

I learned something a few years ago about all this. It is a simple two-point formula that seems to make sense and bring clarity.

1. Running a business like a church will kill it.
2. Running a church like a business will also kill it.

When this became clear to me, we decided to separate Church Multiplication Associates (CMA) from CMAResources so that we could view each differently and not unwittingly kill both of them.

CMA is pure kingdom, no employees, no job descriptions, no organizational flow charts, and no exchange of goods and services for financial remuneration. It is not a business and does not function like a business. CMA is like-minded servants of Jesus who are in relationship together while on mission for the King, and thus it is the church, expressed through a variety of people functioning together on their joint mission.[1]

CMAResources, however, does have employees (two of them). We exchange resources for money, and that alone puts us into a business category as far as I am concerned. We are an intentionally lean organization that tries hard not to be exploitative. We keep our prices lower than we have to so that our resources are more accessible to Christians and we give much away, intentionally. Our mission is to create resources that reproduce healthy disciples, leaders, churches, and movements. But we are a business, although not a profitable one.

We may be a business that functions like a church, but not the other way around. Now, I did say that such a proposition would kill the business, didn't I? Well, it can, and we're okay with that idea. We do not exist to make money but to further the kingdom. Still, we want to stay in the business category so that we do not assume the sacred trust of being a church and all that goes with it. We want to resource the church and not compete with it. If we go "out of business" in fulfilling our mission without exploiting the church, that is an acceptable risk. We would even view it as a success.

Running a Church like a Business

Unfortunately, there are a great many churches that function like a business. In my opinion this is a problem of epidemic proportions. Churches have become brokers of spiritual goods and services to Christian consumers. They have a board of directors and a CEO, and if they are large enough, they may even have a CFO (chief financial officer).

Running a church like a business is a far more dangerous proposition than running a business like a church. A business that runs like a church will just go out of business. Running a church like a business, however, will suck the life out of the church. The church will die, but unfortunately, the business may not—it may continue to thrive and remain a business that calls itself a church. This is the danger.

It is a very scary situation when, in the eyes of God's people, a business carries on with the authority of God's sacred church behind it. An exploitative company that profits from the "business of God," while enjoying tax-exempt benefits, is a dangerous entity if you ask me.

We all seem to understand the principle of the separation of church and state. Perhaps we should start understanding the wisdom of the separation of church and corporate business. Everyone who knows me or has read any of my previous work would know I am not saying that church should be removed from the marketplace. No, I am suggesting that the marketplace be removed from the church. Perhaps we should overturn the money tables again.

Modalities versus Sodalities

Ralph Winter, the missiologist who established the U.S. Center for World Missions, has done much to influence our way of thinking about global missions. He has raised our awareness of unreached people groups. He has also influenced how we think of missional ministries and their relation to the church. In an article written years ago, "The Two Structures of God's Redemptive Mission," he describes two structural entities that are both the church. One he terms as a *modality* and the other as a *sodality*. A modality is inclusive of all and concerned with meeting the needs of all in the group. It tends to be more managerial and less missional, though that is not exclusively true. The sodality is a more exclusive group formed around mission with those who are selected for a missional task. It requires a decision on the part of some who are part of the modality to move out to accomplish a purpose.

Winter uses Paul's missionary band as an example of the sodality and the "local church" as an example of the modality. Both are necessary and both are valuable. Unfortunately, some people have separated the two to the detriment of both.

Some leaders of parachurch organizations, in defense of their ministry, quote Winter as if they are quoting the Bible. Winter's idea, however, is not that a ministry is either a church or not a church; both the modality and the sodality are part of God's redemptive purpose. Both are the church in the eyes of Paul. As Paul wrote Ephesians and described the "body of Christ," I do not think he saw himself as at all separate from the church, even though he was functioning in a sodalist missionary band. His entire purpose was the expansion and health of the church.

Our problem is not the use of Winter's terms, but our own misunderstanding of church itself. We have constricted ideas of church because we define it by our experience and tradition rather than simply through a straightforward reading of the New Testament. Then we coin words to describe what we do and we find ourselves trapped in boxes that should not exist (as described in the previous chapter).

Often parachurch ministries are developed because people feel called to fulfill Christ's purpose and move out to do so without the bureaucratic red tape of the church to slow them down. There is no doubt that the church has a tendency to slow down missional works, and a gifted team of people who are called and sent specifically to get a job done is indeed valuable, but I have difficulty when the gifted team and the church are separated. To disconnect the church from her mission is perhaps the most devious strategy Satan has ever devised. Like two wings of an airplane, both structural entities are needed and valued in the church, and both are the body of Christ. To separate them is to crash and burn. We must recognize the unity of Christ's body and accept all the beauty of its various parts.

When we form organizations to fulfill the mission of the church so the church doesn't have to, there is a serious breakdown in God's kingdom. Paul never saw himself as separate from the church. The church was not simply a source for his financial needs. Nor did he see himself as all that was necessary for the church to accomplish her mission. He argued that when he was unable to get around, the church rose up to do the work, and that was better (Phil. 1:12–18).

The church expresses herself both modally (the local expression of a church family) and sodally (smaller apostolic band sent by the church). But Jesus did not establish an entity beyond the church to get his work done.

Seeing the kingdom of God as a business opportunity is parasitic. It is also the reality of a free trade economy in a capitalistic culture. We can live with consumerism without embracing it. We can survive it without letting it invade us. The church is the body of Christ, not a target market or a client base.

The gospel of the kingdom should be countercultural, not conforming to our culture. In our capitalistic society the church has allowed way too many cultural values to shape who we are, how we function, and what we think is valuable. Consumerism, commercialization, and opportunistic profiteering have invaded the church, and we must break free from these weeds so we can be healthy and fruitful and transform our world.

SECTION TWO

THE INSIDE-OUT KINGDOM

Growing
Leadership
from Within

Jesus used many agricultural analogies to describe his kingdom. He said, "The kingdom of heaven is like a mustard seed" (Matt. 13:31). He also said, "The kingdom of heaven may be compared to a man who sowed good seed in his field" (v. 24).

To understand leadership emergence in God's kingdom, we must take into account the essence of the kingdom itself. The kingdom is like a field of wheat. It involves soil, seeds, natural processes, and fruit. In this section we will address these areas of concern. We must allow the DNA within to generate the life, growth, and ultimate fruit of God's leader.

Within every seed is the life of the future plant. The plant bears fruit, and the fruit contains the seeds of the next generation. The seed that gives birth to the plant also has within it the idea of a seed for the future generations of the same plant. All is contained within, and the life starts there.

The overarching theme of leadership emergence in God's kingdom is that it grows from the inside out. Like the seed, if leadership is not planted in good soil, it doesn't matter how much effort, resources, and programs we invest from the outside—the leadership seed will not bear fruit in the end.

Chapter 8 will address the soil, or source, for God's kingdom leaders. If you are a pastor or other church leader and want to know the secret to having more than enough leaders around you, you do not want to skip over this chapter.

Chapter 9 focuses on the organic process that unleashes the life of God's kingdom in a leader. If we want success, we must understand where it comes from. We must abide in the vine if we want fruit.

Chapter 10 redefines what success is for an organic-church leader in the context of today's false ideas of success. It is all about the end product—the fruit. What do we want to see in the end? What is the fruit of one who abides for a lifetime and what does it take to finish strong?

8
THE SECRET SOURCE OF LEADERS

Or, Where We Start Makes All the Difference

The most dangerous leadership myth is that leaders are born—that's nonsense. In fact the opposite is true. Leaders are made.

Warren Bennis

I start with the premise that the function of leadership is to produce more leaders, not more followers.

Ralph Nader

As word spread of an underground resistance forming against the oppression of the English, more and more Scots rallied to join William Wallace and his band. In an insightful and lighthearted scene of the film *Braveheart*, two such recruits come to the camp to pledge their allegiance to the cause.

One is a Scot; the other is Irish. The Scot seems bright and devoted. The Irishman does not. He actually seems a little off in the head and somewhat hostile.

While the Scot presents Wallace with a gift, the Irishman starts laughing and conversing with God—and he believes God is talking back.

His name is Stephen. He wants to fight the British alongside the famous Wallace and his band. Introducing himself, he says he is the most wanted man on his island. "But of course, I'm not on my island. More's the pity."

"Your island? You mean Ireland?" one of Wallace's lieutenants enquires.

"Yeah. It's mine," comes the reply.

Another of the men retorts: "Insane Irish." To which the Irishman quickly draws a dagger, which is instantly at the throat of the one who insulted his people. Of course, just as quickly everyone else has their blade strategically placed on various parts of the Irishman's body.

In this precarious standoff, Stephen says to the one who called him insane, "Smart enough to get a dagger past your guards, old man."

Calmly Wallace diffuses the situation by affirming that if Stephen fought beside him, he would get the chance to fight the Brits. All the blades drop. "Excellent!" remarks the stranger.

Wallace's friend looks at the Irishman and remarks, "You're a madman."

As if to prove the point, Stephen starts laughing, nodding his head with shifty eyes. Soon everyone else is laughing too.

At the end of the scene Stephen remarks, "I've come to the right place then."

The next scene reveals the true nature of the two new recruits. The bright and devoted Scot is really an assassin sent to kill William, and the insane Irishman saves Wallace's life, proving to be a loyal and devoted associate, ultimately becoming one of the most respected of the soldiers.

More men join the resistance. Momentum builds and explodes in a crescendo on the battlefield of Stirling, where the Scots win a battle the first time any can remember. From there, more battles and more victories come. Eventually Scotland wins her freedom.

Movements are like this. They are grassroots, often underground, and they start with crazy people who are willing to believe in the impossible. Movements never start in corporate offices with executives drawing up a master plan. Looking for the best and brightest and recruiting them to the work is not how world-changing movements start.

If we truly want to see the world changed, we must begin as a band of madmen, welcoming other crazy people who want to be part of something bigger than themselves.

Psst! Want to Hear a Secret?

Perhaps the single most consistent need in our churches today is for leaders of ministries. The vast majority of churches I have encountered in my travels could use more leaders to maintain their ministries. So many churches have more children than child workers and more students than student workers and everyone could use more musicians.

There are always a few churches, however, that do not have this struggle. At least one church in every city seems to have all the leaders they need and more.

Why is that? Why do some churches have more leaders than they need, while the rest are struggling in manpower poverty? We may be tempted to think the difference is in the charismatic personality of the pastor who is able to attract more leaders than other pastors. Or we may conclude that the programs in these churches have an edge over the programs in other churches. Or we may decide to just attribute it to the blessing of God.

These are all interesting theories. Perhaps each has some degree of truth, especially the last one. I do not think any one of these reasons alone is sufficient to explain this phenomenon. I know the secret and in this chapter I will share it with you, so you too can have more than enough leaders and resources to accomplish all the work God has called you to do.

The Problem with Recruitment

The churches that have the most leaders do not recruit leaders at all, and this is why they have enough. The churches that recruit can never find enough leaders. Here are some of the reasons for this.

Seen as the Only Option

In most churches, when there is a need for ministry, the leaders begin immediately to recruit. Recruitment is when we search for a leader from the outside to fill a need on the inside. We take on a headhunter role and search for the best leader we can find for the task at hand. Almost always, there are some ministries that go a long time without any real leadership, or worse, the pastor does it all. Sometimes we get lucky and find a great match; at other times we have to settle for whatever we get. Occasionally a leader is found, and he or she works well for a while but then is recruited somewhere else. Like some cruel joke, we get to keep the less successful leaders. In most churches, there is always more ministry than leaders. That just seems to be the way it is.

The recruitment approach is very common in the kingdom of God. It really has become an epidemic. For most pastoral staff, it is the only way they know to find more leaders. Most of Christendom is set up for this method.

Never Satisfied

There are never enough leaders for all the demand, and plugging in new people to work in established ministries is a challenge in the best cases, because matching the right people to the right task is such a hit-or-miss proposition. In this world there are not enough leaders to fill the gaps let alone start anything new.

In organic terms, this approach is like grafting in leadership. It is slow, awkward, and only successful on occasion. The church is left constantly hungry for more leaders and seems to have to compromise quality on a regular basis.

The way recruitment works is backwards. We start with a ministry need, and then work to find someone to match the task. Often, when we start with our eyes on our needs, we are never able to see anything else. Starting down the recruitment path seems only to make us acutely aware of all that we do not have.

It Sucks!

I used to think that recruitment was a strategy that could only add leaders to the kingdom and could never multiply leaders. I have come to see that recruitment is not even an addition strategy. It is a *subtraction* strategy. It doesn't *add* anything to the kingdom. It simply takes from it. It is a strategy that uses the kingdom for its own good rather than contributing to the good of the kingdom.

When everyone is taking and no one is contributing, soon the pool is dry and we are all left with nothing. The vast majority of churches are sucking up what little resources are left in the kingdom and contributing nothing back. The results are that we are in a leadership drought. Our pool is shrinking daily and in the end all we have left to us is the muck at the bottom of the pond.

This explains why so many churches are dying of thirst. Quality diminishes. Needs are left unfilled. Our thirst for more resources increases. Our churches are left weakened.

There is a solution, however. There is an oasis available to all our churches with enough resources for everyone. We can learn this solution by a quick analysis of how leaders are found in the book of Acts.

Lessons in Recruitment

Surprisingly, there isn't a whole lot of information in the Bible on the practice of recruitment. It is almost as though it wasn't even on the radar in the New Testament. And for the most part, it wasn't. In the New Testament we do not see established ministry needing to find leaders to fill the gaps. The only examples are perhaps Acts 6 when the seven are chosen to serve the Jerusalem church, but these were selected from among those in the ministry already; they were raised from within. You have the selection of Matthias in Acts 1:26, but of course he was already in the thick of it all; that is what qualified him, so he wasn't coming from the outside to fill a spot. He was already a proven insider.

Barnabas recruited Saul to come to Antioch (11:22–26). That is the best example of the practice that I can find, and it seems to have been successful.

The Holy Spirit set apart Barnabas and Saul for the first missionary trip (13:2). Scripture says they were busy ministering to the Lord when it occurred, so, even in this case, they were leaders from within, sent to start new ministry, not to fill existing holes. Their leaving may have created holes for others to fill.

The only real case I see of recruitment as we practice it is when Paul went on his second missionary journey. Learning from his first enterprise, he decided to take along a larger team, twice the size in fact. Paul, Silas, Timothy, and Luke head out to Macedonia on Paul's second missionary journey. Paul recognized that the new churches from the previous journey were weak without leadership, so on this trip he recruits a team that will try to fill in the void. He leaves Luke behind in Philippi. Silas and Timothy are left behind in some of the next church plants. Suddenly Paul realizes the folly of his recruitment strategy when he lands alone in Athens. Alone and provoked by the idolatry there, he is uncomfortable and leaves for Corinth. In Corinth, the sin capital of the world, Paul is frightened. Jesus comes to him in a vision and tells him, "Do not be afraid . . . I have many people in this city" (18:9–10).

From Recruitment to Reproduction

Christ's words to Paul are more than comforting; they are a lesson in strategy. Jesus is telling Paul, you don't need to recruit a team; you can find them in the harvest fields. All the leaders you need are available; you just have to farm them from the soil. With this new strategy, Paul would never be alone and never lack for leaders.

Jesus is teaching Paul, and us, the difference between recruiting leaders and reproducing them. Paul is a quick study and adapts everything he does from that point on in all his work. Paul stayed in Corinth for a year and a half, which indicates a dramatic shift in his methods.

He had gone to work immediately, making tents for a living. In the workplace, he met Aquila and Priscilla, who decided to follow Christ and become part of Paul's team. The story line of Acts departs from Paul and stays with this couple as they find Apollos and lead him to Jesus. In the next few verses Apollos is found reasoning with the Jews in the same way Paul had been doing (Acts 18:24–28). Luke, the author of Acts, is not on a tangent, away from Paul's ministry. This information about Apollos is a magnifying glass to reveal how Paul's strategy had shifted and suddenly become more effective. Ministry leadership was being reproduced to the third generation in a short period of time.

From this point on, Paul raised all his new leaders from the harvest rather than recruiting them from other churches. He never lacked for leaders again. On his third missionary journey he went to Ephesus and stayed there for almost three years. He never left Ephesus in that time, yet all of Asia heard the word of the Lord (19:10). It is clear that Jesus showed Paul a better way. He taught Paul to reproduce leaders rather than recruit them.

This is a lesson we need to learn today. Recruitment is a practice in subtraction—taking people from one ministry to work in another. Reproducing leaders from the harvest and for the harvest is a practice of multiplication. The end results of these two methods are as far apart as the east is from the west.

The Inside-out Kingdom

Farming for Leaders

Recruitment is much like picking out produce at the grocery store. Someone else has done all the hard work of cultivating soil, planting seeds, growing the crop, and harvesting the fruit so that you can conveniently pick it up and take it home. If everybody was only consuming the fruit, and no one was farming, we would quickly have a problem on our hands. That describes the stark and desolate drought we are experiencing now in the kingdom. Having too many consumers and not enough producers has created a shortage of fruit. We all want fruit, but Jesus wants us to *bear* fruit, not just *buy* it.

It is not enough that a few churches or ministries increase the production of workers for the rest of us. We need to increase the capacity for production.[1] Churches need to start farming, producing leaders, and contributing to the kingdom rather than simply consuming. So many Christian leaders are more enamored with finding golden eggs than with finding the goose that lays them. Having a golden egg is a nice treat for a time, but soon you want and need more of them. Having a goose that lays golden eggs means you will never want for more.

The few churches that do not lack for leaders have adopted a harvesting mentality. They are doing the things God told them to do. They are making disciples, which is more than merely teaching the saints. Making disciples starts with the lost.

You see, there are untapped and almost limitless leaders all around your church. As Jesus said, "I have many people in this place." These future leaders are not in the kingdom of light yet, so there is a simple formula Jesus gives us that is necessary to discover the rich wealth of workers all around.

More than Enough Leaders

Jesus said, "The harvest is plentiful." This is the good news you have been waiting for. While the harvest is indeed plentiful, Jesus also adds: "but the laborers are few" (Luke 10:2). Yes, I'm sure you can relate to the latter part of the verse. What he says next, however, is crucial to our topic. He tells us where to find workers and then shows us where they will come from. He has a plan. He is the Lord of the harvest. His plan is probably better than yours and mine. We should pay close attention.

Beg the Master of the Harvest for Workers

Jesus says, "Therefore beseech the Lord of the harvest to send out workers into His harvest." We need to go to the Lord of the harvest on our knees and beg him for workers. The word translated "beseech" means to beg as if your life depends on it.

Why must we beg? Why such a strong word? I believe God wants us to want it that much.

Any who have had small children know about this kind of begging. A simple trip to the grocery store with small children is a lesson in the fine art of begging. My kids could find something in almost every aisle to beg for, and each item was worthy of pleading as if their life depended on it. We had to master the problem early on. But even now, in their early twenties and late teens, they can occasionally drift back to the old habits of begging, only now it's for the car keys and some gas money. Whether they're tots or teens, they know how to beg for something they really want.

And this is what Jesus tells us to do—beg our Father. I guarantee you; if you beg God for a harvest of souls for his kingdom, he will grant your request with joy. It is what he wants—*even more than you do!* It is his idea. He is the *Lord* of the harvest. He has a vested interest in seeing it happen. If it doesn't happen, it will be his loss more than yours. So join him in his concern. Want it like he does.

As I mentioned in *Organic Church*, I have actually set my mobile phone alarm to go off at 10:02 every morning to remind me of this verse in Luke so that I can remember to beg for workers. In fact I spread the practice wherever I go. We call this the 10:2b virus, based on the reference Luke 10:2b, which commands us to beg for workers for the harvest. Go ahead and put the book down at this point, get out your cell phone or PDA, and program the alarm to go off at 10:02. Join the movement. Spread the virus.

When my alarm goes off, whomever I am with and whatever I am doing, I stop and explain what the alarm means, and we pray. I also have those with me set their alarms.

As I travel around the globe, I spread the virus to each time zone. Cell phones are ringing every day, all day, all over the planet. Prayers are going up every hour of every day begging for the Lord of the harvest to do something miraculous in our day. How could we not see a global harvest when we are all obediently doing exactly what he told us to do?

This is Jesus's solution to our predicament, and it starts with going to the Lord of the harvest in prayer.

Find Workers in the Harvest Fields

I am confident that most of the leaders who stare at the empty leadership roles in their church have turned to God and prayed for workers, perhaps even begged for them. This is a start, but we must shift our thinking as well. Our expectations are misplaced. Jesus knows where to find the workers.

When he tells the disciples to pray for workers, where do you think they were expecting these leaders to come from? Seminary or Bible colleges? Of course not. Other churches? None existed. The passage is about farming leaders, not robbing other ministries of them. No, there is no other solution than that the leaders for the harvest must come from the harvest itself. We must farm our leaders, not recruit them. The new disciples *are* the new workers, and the seed of the next generation is found in the fruit of the current one. This is farming, and it is the way God created the world to work. Farming, or harvesting, leaders is a long-term solution. Recruitment is a short answer to a long problem.

When my children were quite small, if someone asked them, "Where does an apple come from?" they might have said Ralph's grocery store. Of course now they know that the apple they eat was grown on a tree in an orchard. We must have a similar shift in our thinking and realize that the fruit we need for the church should be grown, not just bought.

After Jesus told the disciples to beg for workers for the harvest, he instructed them how to find the workers. This is exactly what Luke 10:3–20 goes on to teach us.[2] If we all started simply to obey what Jesus says in this pivotal passage, we would begin to see a great harvest. We would find the fruit we long for out in the fields, not in the barns or produce departments.

Jesus will never ask you to do something and then not provide you with the resources you need to get it done. When Jesus places the order, he pays the bill. So if you find you do not have enough resources for what you are doing, first, you need to ask yourself if you are doing what he wants you to do. Second, you have to look for the resources in the very places he has clearly laid out in Scripture.

If we are going to see a harvest, all the resources we need will be found in the harvest. If we never venture out into the fields, we will not discover the abundant resources God has for us, and we will remain in the state of poverty we have experienced for too long.

In another passage about a harvest Jesus said, "Lift up your eyes and look on the fields, that they are white for harvest" (John 4:35). Open your eyes and look at the fields around you, they are ripe for a harvest. There are more than enough leaders if you know where to look and whom to ask. Don't look for them in other churches. Look to the fields for leaders and ask the Lord of the harvest for them.

Most leadership development and deployment strategies begin with already committed Christians. While training should lead to this place and beyond, it is the wrong place to start. I believe that if your leadership development strategy doesn't begin with lost people, you are starting in the wrong place. We must expand our strategies to begin in the fields. We must shift from a consumer posture to a contributor posture.

I am convinced that God is going to do something incredible in our day. This will be something on a global scale. It will be unlike anything the church has seen before. It is a privilege to live at this time.

The kingdom heroes who will carry the day in this near future may have awakened this morning with a hangover—*in the wrong person's bed*! They are stuck in a cycle of darkness and their lives are rapidly circling the drain. When someone reaches out to them with hope, help, and life, they will take hold and never look back. Perhaps instead of looking only at the local Bible institute for future leaders, we should look at the local bar with more interest.

Transformation the Key

Transformation is the key to leaders who turn the world upside down. This means we need to start with madmen outside of the church. We need to be a band of madmen who welcome other madmen who need to belong to something that gives them purpose and makes them better for it.

The impetus of a changed life provides the momentum of a movement. The transformed life is contagious, drawing others in and keeping us holding tightly to Jesus through thick and thin. Our changed life validates the movement, for without transformation, we are just a religious club.

When churches reach new people, the changed lives infuse the whole congregation with energy. But it isn't only the new followers who should have changed lives. As Jesus lives in us, our lives are in process. Transformation should be a constant for us all. When we are stagnant as a people, the movement stops dead in its tracks. When we are doing the work God has called us to do, we must step out in faith in God and walk in his power, because the work is bigger than we are.

If your ministry is struggling without leaders, do not reevaluate your leadership development program. It is time to reevaluate your disciple-making system.[3] If you are doing next to nothing to reach lost and broken people, your leadership development system will yield very few results. A lack of leaders is a symptom of a much greater problem—the lack of transformation in people's souls. Do not mourn your lack of leaders; mourn your lack of changed lives. If you have changed lives, the leaders you need will emerge with some simple mentoring (which we will look at in section 4 of this book).

It all starts with someone transformed from the kingdom of darkness into the kingdom of light (Col. 1:13–14). This is the fodder for the flames of a movement. If this is happening, our churches are surrounded with the fuel for a true movement. All the resources for the harvest are found in the harvest. We do not need to feel impoverished or desperate. We simply need to do what Jesus instructed us to do. It can be scary, but the risk we take is the place for faith, and with faith we will see the fruit we need.

9
ORGANICALLY GROWN LEADERS

Healthy Leadership Emergence

> When the effective leader is finished with his work, the people say it happened naturally.
>
> Lao Tse

> Character is not made in a crisis, it is only exhibited.
>
> Robert Freeman

The Big Kahuna is a movie about three salesmen. It is a comedic drama that exposes the outlook of people in different stages of their lives. The whole movie takes place in a hotel room in Kansas City where the three men are setting up a party for attendees of a convention.

One of the three salesmen, Phil (played by Danny DeVito), is old and over-the-hill but he is a sage. Larry (played by Kevin Spacey) is the man at the top of his game, and the rookie, Bob (played by Peter Facinelli), is on his first sales trip.

The men are industrial lubricant salesmen and they are hoping to make one important sale—to the big kahuna. In the course of the evening, the rookie strikes up a relationship with the sales target. The young salesman is a committed Baptist, however, and is more concerned with winning a soul than a client. This does not sit well with the hotshot Larry, so they argue and eventually even tussle for a moment in a heated exchange. After the exchange, Larry goes to bed, leaving Phil and Bob to figure out what just happened.

Phil breaks the silence: "There's something I want to say to you and I want you to listen very closely, because it's very important."

After comparing selling Jesus to selling lubricants, he goes on to say, "We were talking before about character. You were asking me about character. We were speaking about faces, but the question is much deeper than that. The question is, Do you have any character at all? And if you want my honest opinion, Bob, you do not; for the simple reason that you don't regret anything yet."

Bob responds in disbelief, "Are you saying I won't have any character unless I do something I regret?"

"No, Bob," continues the older sage, "I'm saying that you've already done plenty of things to regret; you just don't know what they are."

With a faraway look in his eyes, as he numbers the scars of his own life, he comments further: "It's when you discover them, when you see the folly in something you've done, and you wish that you had it to do over but you know you can't 'cause it's too late. So you pick that thing up and you carry it with you to remind you that life goes on. The world will spin without you. You really don't matter in the end. Then you will attain character, because honesty will reach out from inside and tattoo itself all across your face. Until that day, however, you cannot expect to go beyond a certain point."

Character from the Inside Out

Character is not something that comes cheap. It is expensive. It will cost you years of hardship and struggle if you choose to pay for it. It is worth the cost, but you will have to count the cost often if you are to attain solid character.

Unlike the false sense of righteousness that comes from the outside in, true character in God's kingdom grows from the inside out. In essence, character is unearthing what Christ has already planted within you. It is a becoming. It is your being.

Jesus said, "Listen and understand." When Jesus starts off with these words, we should definitely pay attention. He continues, "What goes into a man's mouth does not make him 'unclean.' . . . Don't you see that whatever enters the mouth goes into his stomach and then out of the body? But the things that come out of the mouth come from the heart, and these make a man 'unclean.' For out of the heart come evil thoughts, murder, adultery, sexual immorality, theft, false testimony, slander. These are what make a man 'unclean'; but eating with unwashed hands does not make him 'unclean'" (Matt. 15:11, 17–20 NIV).

Character is within. Who you are will determine what you do and what you say. Who you are is more important than anything else, for from it flows all else (Prov. 4:23).

Jesus also said, "Make a tree good and its fruit will be good, or make a tree bad and its fruit will be bad, for a tree is recognized by its fruit. . . . The good man brings good things out of the good stored up in him, and the evil man brings evil things out of the evil stored up in him" (Matt. 12:33, 35 NIV).

Once I was at a Promise Keepers rally with some men from my church. I was sharing a hotel room with a man for whom I have great respect. We were tired after a long day in the sun listening to preachers. It was time to hit the sheets and get some badly needed sleep if we were to enjoy the next day.

Carlos went into the bathroom to brush his teeth. Suddenly I heard a muffled shout and a moan as if he had hurt himself. I asked him what was wrong as I rushed in to see if he was hurt. He was okay but washing his mouth with cool water.

Apparently, in his fatigue, he reached into his toiletry bag, grabbed a tube, and squeezed it on his toothbrush. He was in for a big surprise when he brushed his teeth with mentholated rub—not toothpaste! *Yikes!*

This got me thinking. What if an accident happened at the factory that made both toothpaste as well as mentholated rub and the labels were mixed up on a batch of tubes sent out to the retail stores? It doesn't really matter what label is on the outside, what matters is what is on the inside.

When life squeezes you, what will come out? You cannot change what squeaks out under life's pressure simply by changing the outside label. Whatever is on the inside is what will come out under the pressure of life.

Nancy Reagan once said women are like tea bags; you find out what they are made of when they are placed in hot water. This is true for all

The Inside-out Kingdom

of us. The hot water of life will draw out whatever is within us, good or bad.

If Jesus has placed his love in you, that love will come out in the decisions you make. It will also be evident in the regrets you have for poorly made decisions. His love redeems all of our good choices as well as our bad.

The Key

Skill is a wonderful thing. Education and great knowledge are advantages. Charm and personality as well as good looks can get you farther in life than they should. Money can buy a lot of things and open many doors. Power can get things done. But none of these things is as valuable as good character.

One day, all the other things mentioned above will be gone and your soul is all that will be left. Your character, good or bad, measures the health of your soul. Your soul is all you will have in the end, and if it is broken and crooked, you will have nothing.

In choosing leaders we must look for character—not doctrinal integrity, preaching style, or managerial skills. Character is so important because it defines who you are. Character is your whole being. Jesus asks us, "What good will it be for a man if he gains the whole world, yet forfeits his soul? Or what can a man give in exchange for his soul?" (Matt. 16:26 NIV).

It has been pointed out that who you are when no one's looking is important—this reveals your character. We are truly ourselves when we are all alone. When we know that there is no one to impress, we tend to behave more naturally and honestly. If you knew that no one but God would know what you did in isolation and that you could never be caught by anyone else, what would you do? This is the true test of your character.

It's also important to see who you are when everyone is looking. Do you cave in to peer pressure? Are you the same person when everyone is watching as you are when no one is watching? Our behavior should not depend on whether others are present, but unfortunately it often does.

We each have a choice regarding how we will live our lives. Life is essentially a stream of conscious decisions that we make, which eventually make up who we are. This is our character and is the most important thing in life. Who we are is more important than what we do or what we know, because who we are will determine everything else.

Refined in the Furnace of Life

Character does not come from reading a book about it. You cannot learn character in a class or from a teacher.

How do we learn character? Character is first placed in us from our Redeemer, well before we ever deserved it or even knew that it was there. Character, your character, was first purchased by Jesus and deposited in your account when your spiritual life began. His righteousness was imputed to your spiritual account, and in exchange, Jesus took your sinful character and paid its penalty in full on the cross (Rom. 4:22–25; 2 Cor. 5:21).

The problem is that the new character you received was only a seed, planted in the old you. Two things are necessary for your character to emerge strong: the old you must be chiseled away, and your new character muscles must be exercised. There must be a lessening of your old self and a growth of the new you. As John once said, "He must increase, but I must decrease" (John 3:30).

1. *Peeling away the old you.* This is a stripping of the old, carnal self. It is painful, hard, and always a good thing. The reason it is painful is it requires a cutting away of your flesh.
2. *Building up the new you.* This is like a constant workout. It is getting your inner self in good shape. There are two exercises to build up the new you: sound decisions when faced with temptations and regular spiritual disciplines. Each wise choice and every investment in spiritual discipline yield a stronger and more vital character within you. Paul says that physical exercise is of little profit, but spiritual exercise is of great profit (1 Tim. 4:8).

J. Robert Clinton, in his excellent book *The Making of a Leader*, identifies eleven process items that God uses to strip us down and to build the character of our lives. He discovered these items by studying the lives of Christian leaders (more than seven hundred at the time of the book's publication) who finished with strong character. These are the tools that God uses to chip off the hard shell of our old self and carve the intricate beauty of the marble that is our new self. He uses tools such as isolation, integrity checks, obedience tests, unusual revelations of our destiny, a divine contact (the right person who comes at the right moment), faith challenges to overcome, negative preparation for what is to come, a life crisis, ministry conflict, the

The Inside-out Kingdom

backlash of others against our leadership, and listening checks to see if we are paying attention to his leading.[1]

All of these process items involve circumstances or people that God allows to test, refine, and build our character. Each test and every difficult person we face make up part of an overriding purpose to develop character in us. Character is built in the fires of pain, conflict, temptation, difficult decisions, loneliness, and fear. You cannot learn character any other way. There is no shortcut to a strong finish.

Developed over a Lifetime

Clinton also marks out the typical life phases of leaders who finish well. He presents six phases of maturity in the leadership development process. They are sovereign foundations, inner-life growth, ministry maturing, life maturing, convergence, and finally for a few, afterglow.[2] These are not static. We cannot pigeonhole people into these categories, but it does help to understand that we do pass through phases of development in our path to maturity.

The apostle John laid out three phases of maturing that are helpful to our understanding. He refers to little children, young men, and fathers (1 John 2:12–14). These broad categories can help us see what the maturing process is like. Please excuse the masculine exclusivity, but I am merely following the pattern put forth by the apostle John to discover the maturing process.

1. *Little children* cannot help themselves but are consumed with their own needs. That is the nature of immaturity and is true of the spiritual life. Young believers are focused on themselves and their own spiritual needs. I find that typically they are wracked with shame over their sin. The good news for them, according to John, is, "Your sins have been forgiven" (v. 12). The child is set free from his or her sins, and most of childhood is about coming to realize this.
2. *Young men* are warriors who finally venture out into adulthood. This phase of development is when leaders begin to emerge and deal with the issues of life. A young man is interested mostly in winning the battle, wooing the girl, and making a name for himself. Therefore he is no longer thinking only of himself but is now facing an enemy. The good news for young men, according to John, is, "You have overcome the evil one" (v. 13). The strength of faith in God is the protection of a person in this stage of life.

3. *Fathers* identifies a phase of reproduction. It is a time of maturing when you now are more concerned with the success of your children than your own success. Your legacy and the inheritance passed on to the next generation become the greater concern for this stage of maturity. Your life, at this point, is spent to help others grow and bear fruit. No longer are fathers the ones taking on the Enemy with a full frontal assault; instead, they are training the new, young warriors with their own rich experience and mature, paternal heart. It's unfortunate that not enough Christian leaders ever reach this phase. In my opinion this is when we become equippers of others. Too many stay in the less mature levels and never give birth to the next generation. The good news for these leaders is, "You know Him who has been from the beginning." Intimacy with God is the reward of maturity. You can get there only through the path of difficulties, challenges, and multiple times of being rescued from your mistakes and having them redeemed.

One of the best lessons I gained from reading Clinton's book is that earlier phases are not about getting stuff out of you as much as putting stuff in you for the future. In the earlier phases of growth, God is less concerned with using you to gain results as he is in investing in you for future yield. This is helpful to know when you are younger.

As Jesus said, if we are faithful in the small things, we will prove faithful with more as we grow (see Matt. 25:21). God first *tests* us and then *trusts* us. As we prove faithful at the less influential, earlier stages of life, we will be blessed with greater fruitfulness later in the maturing process. If you are not seeing the fruit you wish you would see, it may be a good thing. It could very well mean that you have a long life yet ahead of you. I am always reminding young leaders who are frustrated with less than stellar progress early in their life that they have time yet to grow. If you are still wrestling with your youth, it is a good thing; you have longer to live.

As some leaders mature to a father stage of influence, it is common for them to find themselves surrounded by an abundance of better quality emerging leaders. There are a number of reasons for this, but perhaps one that is above all others—God trusts this leader with his truest treasure. He understands that a mature person will be concerned with the other leaders' success more than with his or her own success, and this is the primary difference between a leader who does the work

The Inside-out Kingdom

and one who is able to equip others to do the work. There is a big difference between a young man and a father.

Grown on the Vine

Jesus, who likes to use organic language to describe the most important aspects of the Christian life and the kingdom of God, talks about character being the fruit of living on the vine. In John 15:4–5 he says, "Abide in Me, and I in you. As the branch cannot bear fruit of itself unless it abides in the vine, so neither can you unless you abide in Me. I am the vine, you are the branches; he who abides in Me and I in him, he bears much fruit, for apart from Me you can do nothing."

Character is the fruit of abiding in Christ. Like a branch that is connected to the vine, we bear fruit only as long as we are attached and the life of the vine is flowing through us. Our role is to cling to the vine with everything we've got and let Christ's life flow through us. When we abide in him and his Word abides in us, character is the fruit.

When we are attached to this vine, fruit is not optional. It is essential. Not to bear fruit is to be useless, cut off, and torched. In the next chapter we will look more closely at the fruit of a leader.

Jesus also says, "Every branch in Me that does not bear fruit, [My Father] takes away; and every branch that bears fruit, He prunes it so that it may bear more fruit. . . . My Father is glorified by this, that you bear much fruit, and so prove to be My disciples" (vv. 2, 8).

Today's Forecast for Tomorrow

Picture this from the film *The Weatherman*. It's pouring, but many people are standing out in the rain. Holding umbrellas and dressed in dark overcoats, they are all at a funeral, standing at a gravesite. It is Robert King Spritzel's memorial service.

Robert was well loved by countless people, so it makes sense that so many would come out on such a dark and dreary day to pay their respects. Robert (played by Michael Caine) was a Pulitzer Prize–winning author. He is well known around the world as a man of great character. His life, his reputation, and his accomplishments will live beyond this day of remembrance. As his son David describes him, "He was a great writer and a great dad."

As many people pay their respects, David (played by Nicolas Cage) tries to figure out why he is not as good a man as his father. David may be as famous as his father but he is not known for his strong character. David is a weatherman at a local Chicago station and has received lots of rewards for two hours of easy work each day reading prompts in front of a green screen.

As he reaches midlife, David begins to question himself. Living in the shadow of his father was never easy. He made a name for himself and has a respectable income, but he also has a failed marriage, kids who are not perfect, and nothing of substance for which to be remembered. This has him thinking.

Prior to his death, Robert Spritzel had given sage advice to his struggling son. He said, "Do you know that the harder thing to do and the right thing to do are usually the same thing? Easy doesn't enter into grown-up life. To get anything of value you have to sacrifice."

In the movie we fade from the funeral with David's voice narrating, and we see David walking through a busy Chicago street full of traffic and pedestrians. It is snowing lightly while a strong Chicago breeze is blowing. As the narration continues, all the people and cars move from the street until David stands alone on a street corner with the realization of who he has become.

The narration is as follows:

I remember, once, imagining what my life would be like. What I'd be like. I pictured having all these qualities, strong, positive qualities that people could pick up on from across the room. But as time passed, few ever became any qualities I actually had. And all the possibilities I faced, and the sorts of people I could be, all of them got reduced every year to fewer and fewer, until finally they got reduced to one—to who I am. And that's who I am, the weatherman.

As we live it, life strips away all we once hoped to be and reveals who we truly are on the inside. The furnace of life either melts away any supposed good in our lives or refines what is truly good. The same sun that melts the wax hardens the clay. Either you become a softer, more pliable, and pure person from the fire of life, or life makes you hard and bitter and ultimately breaks you into pieces. It isn't the fire that makes you that way; the fire only reveals what is already there.

Life is the test of the measure of your leadership. Do not fail this test; you get only one chance at it.

The Inside-out Kingdom

10
LEADERSHIP SUCCESS
Goals of Organic Leadership

The only place where success comes before work is a dictionary.

Vidal Sassoon

If my life is fruitless, it doesn't matter who praises me, and if my life is fruitful, it doesn't matter who criticizes me.

John Bunyan

Every year I watch a movie that always warms my heart. I am not alone in this tradition because the same movie plays multiple times during the Christmas season. It's Frank Capra's film *It's a Wonderful Life*, starring Jimmy Stewart.

The reason I like this movie so much is I can really relate to the character of George Bailey. He is a man who has vision beyond his life, but his values keep him fighting the same battles all the time. He never gets to leave the small rural town of Bedford Falls and doesn't realize he's living a wonderful life there. He bought into an idea of what success is, and his life wasn't it. An angel named Clarence, and a revelation of what the world would look like without George, reveals how much George has already.

Clarence shows George a town called Potterville, named after the evil Mr. Potter who wants to consume all of the town through his own greed. It's the dark world the town of Bedford Falls would be like if not for the goodness in the daily life of faithful George.

I think a lot of us suffer from the George Bailey syndrome. We are convinced that something else would make our lives meaningful if we could only grasp it, whatever it is.

Our view and heaven's view of the wonderful life are often two very different pictures. The sooner we experience a transformative conversion to heaven's true values, the better off we will be.

The problem is that, unlike George Bailey, some of us do not have the value system that keeps us focused on the important stuff. Often we are ruled by our desires for lesser things, and our choices take us to Potterville.

What do you live for? What gets you up in the morning and keeps you up at night? When your life is over and its true meaning is revealed, who will be better off for your having been here? These are important questions.

The Importance of the Leader's Goals

I have read a lot of books on leadership, and almost all of them tell us that good leaders set goals for themselves. These good leaders must also have a vision that is compelling and will cause people to want to follow them.

The goals you have can define who you are, or at least who you will become. Goals can help define your objectives, values, and beliefs. Some people go through life without goals. Remember, the person who has no goal usually hits it.

What Is Not Success

Before we can understand what success truly is for a leader, it would be very helpful to understand what it is not. There are a great many counterfeit goals that are dangled in front of leaders today. These beautiful baubles are enticing and seduce leaders into thinking, *These are the things that would finally verify for me, my family, and the world that I am a success.*

Determining success can be very personal and is influenced by our culture, which has its own values that establish what is important, and therefore, what is success. So the idea of identifying for all Christians what is success and what is not is a rather precarious proposition. Of course it would be absurd for me to define what you should set as your goals and what success should be for you. That would actually go against all that I have given my own life to and therefore would discredit my own goals and mean my own failure.

So personally and culturally, we must all find our own way to what is success. But in God's kingdom there is a call that supersedes our own desires and values. There are values inherent within God's revealed truth about the kingdom that inform us regarding our work. One day we will all stand before Jesus and give account of how we invested the few years we received.

What does Jesus think is worth the commitment of your life? What can we say about our current culture regarding the values of God's kingdom? Here are a few thoughts about what does *not* define success as a leader.

Lots of Church Members

Having lots of people in your church does not make you a success. This is quite clear in Scripture. Often Jesus withdrew from the crowds to invest in the few. He said things like, "The way is broad that leads to destruction, and there are many who enter through it. For the gate is small and the way is narrow that leads to life, and there are few who find it" (Matt. 7:13–14). "Many are called, but few are chosen" (22:14).

In today's Christendom, however, we have made large attendance a barometer of successful ministry. Those who are able to attract a large number of members are usually given all the accolades of success. Why is that? I think a simple equation provides us with the answer:

- The gospel mandate is to see people saved.
- The more saved the better.
- Saved people go to church.
- Church growth is important.
- My church measures only those who come on Sundays.
- The size of our attendance is an indication of our success or failure.

It's the last line of the equation that really betrays our misguided direction. It is there that we find practices like raffling off cars or paying people to attend, as we compete with other churches for the attendance of the Christians in town.

There are thousands of pastors of smaller congregations across the country who live with a feeling that they are failures because their church isn't as big as the megaplex congregation down the street. This is sad and should not be the case.

A global survey conducted by Christian Schwartz found that smaller churches consistently scored higher than large churches in seven out of eight qualitative characteristics of a healthy church.[1] A more recent study of churches in America, conducted by Ed Stetzer and Leadership Network, revealed that churches of two hundred or less are four times more likely to plant a daughter church than churches of one thousand or more.[2] It may be that the smaller a church gets, the more reproductive it actually is.

It pains me that so many churches and leaders suffer from an inferiority complex when in fact they could very well be more healthy and fruitful than larger churches and just what God wants them to be.

LOTS OF MONEY

Having lots of money is not success. Many believe that financial prosperity is indeed a sign of God's blessing, and therefore, not having money is a sign of God's curse. This is especially true in America. We see it in the name-it-claim-it culture of Christianity, but not exclusively there. It is also inherent in just about every other part of American Christendom.

The Scriptures are clear that living a humble and simple life is of great value. There is clear evidence in Scripture that having lots of money is dangerous to the soul and often ends in God's condemnation.

One sobering thought is that the churches that were poorest in the New Testament are most commended (Rev. 2:8–11; 2 Cor. 8:1–5), and those that are wealthiest receive the worst rebuke (Rev. 3:1–6, 14–22).

For those who want to make a difference in the world, it is tempting to think that we must have an abundance of resources. I have found from experience, however, that with great surplus comes great waste and greater demand. The smaller congregation around the corner from the huge megachurch complex may think that, if they only had the same sort of resources, they could do such good work. But the reality is that when you have greater resources, you also have more obligations and greater expense. Most churches believe they do not have enough money. In reality, though, "enough" always seems to be "more."

The Inside-out Kingdom

LOTS OF BUILDINGS

Having lots of buildings is not success. It is hard to walk through the state-of-the-art facility of some churches today and not feel a sense of awe and desire as a Christian leader. This is true for almost all of us. It's the sense of awe that the disciples felt when they passed by the temple that Herod the Great built. They were amazed at the sheer size of the cut stones. But Jesus made it clear that the building they were drooling over would not last even through their own lifetime (Mark 13:1–2).

It is hard to walk through a beautiful facility and not assume that the church is successful, because our culture, which sets our values, tells us that a large, beautiful facility indicates success. Jesus and his will for us, however, are not subject to our cultural values.

LOTS OF PROGRAMS

Having lots of programs is not success. For many years now, churches have assumed that the key to developing solid disciples is having quality programs. This is very modern and very American, but again it is a faulty assumption. The Bible never mentions a single program, not once, because it is not programs that make disciples.

No church has had as much invested in their programs as Willow Creek Community Church near Chicago. Recently they did a study to see how well their top-shelf programs were doing at making quality followers. The answers were shocking.

Greg Hawkins, a staff member who led the team that did the study (now called *Reveal*), said afterward: "Participation is a big deal. We believe the more people participating in these sets of activities, with higher levels of frequency, it will produce disciples of Christ." With great honesty he continues: "I know it might sound crazy but that's how we do it in churches. We measure levels of participation."[3]

Their own research revealed, however: "Increasing levels of participation in these sets of activities does *not* predict whether someone's becoming more of a disciple of Christ. It does *not* predict whether they love God more or they love people more."

Speaking at the Leadership Summit, Bill Hybels, pastor of Willow Creek, summarized the findings this way: "Some of the stuff that we have put millions of dollars into, thinking it would really help our people grow and develop spiritually, when the data actually came back, it wasn't helping people that much. Other things that we didn't put that much money into and didn't put much staff against is stuff our people are crying out for."[4]

Hybels called this research "the wake-up call" of his adult life. He confesses:

> We made a mistake. What we should have done when people crossed the line of faith and became Christians, we should have started telling people and teaching people that they have to take responsibility to become 'self feeders.' We should have gotten people, taught people, how to read their Bible between services, how to do the spiritual practices much more aggressively on their own.[5]

Defining Success

So if the above are not indicators of success, what is? What does the New Testament define as success for a follower of Jesus? When it is all over and we stand alone before him, what are the standards by which we are judged by our Lord?

Personally, I find that having multitudes of goals is about as useful as having no goals at all. When you have only so many arrows in the quiver, a multitude of targets is a nightmare. I prefer a few goals to which I will give my whole self. I find it very challenging but helpful to narrow my goals down to three.

As I read the New Testament, I have found three things that Jesus views as crucial to the success of his followers. They are faithfulness, fruitfulness, and finishing well.

FAITHFULNESS

The first indicator of success is faithfulness (Matt. 25:21; Heb. 11:6). Jesus asked, "When the Son of Man comes, will He find faith on the earth?" (Luke 18:8). A common refrain from Jesus's mouth is "You of little faith!" (see Matt. 6:30). Jesus seemed pleasantly surprised when a Gentile showed his faith in Matthew 8:10: "He marveled and said to those who were following, 'Truly I say to you, I have not found such great faith with anyone in Israel.'" One thing we know: Jesus is looking for faith in us. It doesn't even have to be a whole lot of it, just a mustard seed's size is enough.

FRUITFULNESS

Often Jesus spoke of fruit as the evidence that someone is indeed one of his disciples. In John 15:8 he says clearly: "My Father is glorified

The Inside-out Kingdom

by this, that you bear much fruit, and so prove to be My disciples." At one point, to demonstrate how he feels about fruitfulness, he cursed a fig tree because there was no fruit on it; it shriveled and died. He also told a parable about a fig tree that didn't bear fruit. It was given a brief reprieve before it would be dug up as worthless (Luke 13:6–9). There is no doubt that Jesus is looking for fruitfulness in his disciples.

In the New Testament, bearing fruit is natural to who you are or what you do. It was not unusual for Jesus to refer to actual fruit, such as grapes or figs, when he taught (Mark 11:13–14): a child is the fruit of the womb (Luke 1:42); good deeds are fruit (3:8–14); godly character qualities are fruit of the Spirit (Gal. 5:22–23); and when we reproduce in others the life of the kingdom, we are bearing fruit (Mark 4:20).

Finishing Well

The third indicator of success is finishing well (2 Tim. 4:6–8). In the context of being a follower of Christ, Jesus instructed us to count the cost before we start something so that we will be sure to finish it (Luke 14:25–35). The reward for life comes at the end, not at the beginning or middle. This is true for us all. How you live your life is important. How you finish your life is most important. There are some in the Bible who lived their whole life in crime but at the end found redemption and paradise (23:41–43). There are others who committed themselves to live a good life every single day, but in the end found they had nothing to show for it (Matt. 7:21–22).

Jesus finished all that he had been given to do (John 17:4). In the end he declared, "It is finished" (19:30). At the end of Paul's life, he said, "I have fought the good fight, I have finished the course, I have kept the faith" (2 Tim. 4:7). As I serve the Lord, I am finding that there are fewer people than you would imagine who, at the end of their life, are able to say words like these.

The Only Applause That Counts

In any competition, the number of those who start the race is always greater than the number of those who finish. And of course the number who win the race is far smaller—only one in fact. Everyone gets a T-shirt; only one gets the gold medal.

In the spiritual race that is our life, we do not compete with one another. Instead, we push ourselves to better our own previous best.

Every year we are to work hard to improve so that in the end we win. To finish well is success. It means that when we cross the finish line, we have a vital and growing spiritual life.

It's alarming how many Christian leaders do not finish well. Author J. Robert Clinton has found that fewer than a third of the leaders in the Bible finished strong. After studying thirteen hundred historical and contemporary leaders, he estimates that the percentage of those who finished strong is also about a third.[6] This is startling. If this holds true, two out of three Christian leaders today will not finish well. When I share this with an audience, I usually have everybody look to the person on his or her left and then on the right. Then I say only one of the three of them will finish well if these findings are true. Usually this puts the statistics in perspective and drives the truth home.

What derails so many Christian leaders? Well, a good many are disqualified spiritually because of failure in one of the areas discussed in chapter 2: power, possessions, or pleasure. Even more leaders simply plateau in their spiritual growth (see Introduction). Two out of three leaders today will not finish strong.

Clinton's research has yielded lots of helpful information about what goes into making a leader who finishes strong. After all of his study, he has identified the following five factors that enhance the probability of a leader's finishing well.[7]

1. *Perspective:* Usually a leader who finishes well has a perspective that focuses his or her energies on ministry strengths over the course of a lifetime. Seeing the whole picture gives a person the type of perspective that sees beyond the immediate and helps him or her invest in the long haul. It is common for such a leader to take stock regularly by asking, *What would be left if I were to die today?* This is not a morbid interest in death but a perspective on what it will take to finish well over a lifetime.

2. *Renewal:* A leader who finishes well enjoys repeated times of spiritual renewal. It is not enough that the leader has had an experience of renewal in the past. A leader who finishes well sees his or her life as a stream of such moments connected together by the valley times through which a leader must occasionally pass. Many leaders who finish strong recognize this need in their life and schedule times alone with God for renewal purposes—not vacations as much as retreats for listening and waiting. Even Jesus needed times such as this; how much more you and I?

3. *Discipline:* A leader who finishes well has learned to discipline his or her spiritual formation. People don't just spontaneously enter a marathon and run it if they haven't invested the time necessary in training to complete such a race. Finishing well over the course of a lifetime is not accidental but intentional. If you do not choose to take the steps necessary to discipline your development, you will more than likely land in the two-thirds group who do not finish well.

4. *Learning:* A leader who finishes well maintains a learning posture throughout life. There is an insatiable hunger to learn, an untamed curiosity, that carries the leader through life. These are not the leaders who become experts in some area and then never learn again. Those who finish well enjoy launching out into unexplored territory to discover new things. It is easy to find older people who haven't grown or changed since they were young. It is rare to find in an older person the vitality of life that keeps him or her learning until death, but that is what separates the winners from the losers and determines who will finish well. The leaders who last are leaders who learn.

5. *Mentoring:* Relationships are vital to life. One who finishes well has recognized that such a feat does not come about through going it alone. Leaders who finish well mentor others and are also mentored. They do not restrict themselves to a single mentor, as if one person can provide them with all they need. Usually these people have many voices that speak into their lives and hold them accountable to what is truly important. We need this to finish well. More than that, we need also to invest it in the next generation. The very definition of finishing well requires that we leave this planet in the care of the next generation of leaders. Unlike the Dead Sea, which receives water from many tributaries but contributes to none and is therefore stagnant and dead, the leader who finishes well is constantly growing because he or she is always giving and receiving.

Leadership Instruction

Paul wrote to the Corinthian church about leadership, using himself and Barnabas as examples (1 Corinthians 9). This passage deals with the Christian leader's "right" to be supported for the ministry, but also the heart of those who choose not to exercise that right. In Christ we have certain liberties but we must learn how to live in them with freedom and responsibility. At the end of the chapter, Paul shares with us his own life perspective, which kept him focused and moving forward (vv. 24–27).

The Desire and Discipline to Win

Paul writes, "Do you not know that those who run in a race all run, but only one receives the prize? Run in such a way that you may win. Everyone who competes in the games exercises self-control in all things. They do it to receive a perishable wreath, but we an imperishable" (1 Cor. 9:24–25).

Any great athlete, whether it is Michael Jordan, Wayne Gretzky, or Tiger Woods, will tell you that skill and physical ability are not enough to reach the top. It takes heart. Those who become champions at the highest level do so because they want it more than anything else, more than anyone else. This separates them from the rest of the pack—*they want it more*!

One NBA team was in Boston to play the notorious Boston Celtics in the eighties. The coach had the team come unusually early to the Boston Garden. They were expecting to run some drills or practice or maybe have an early shoot around, but the coach had them sit high up in the stands. They asked why, but he wouldn't answer them; he just told them to be quiet and sit still. Then they heard a solo ball dribbling—*bounce, bounce, bounce*. They looked in the direction of the sound—a dark hall that led into the court. There was Larry Bird, several hours before the game, coming alone into the gym. Unaware of his audience, he started shooting. He took hundreds of shots from all over the court, while the other team's players sat silently watching. Finally the coach turned to the men sitting in the uncomfortable seats of the nosebleed section and said, "I just wanted you guys to see what you're up against tonight."

Desire leads to discipline. It is not enough to just want it; you have to want it enough to work hard for it. The more you want to win, the more you have to work. In high school I used to wake up early and swim thousands of yards each day before school. I was tired, the water was cold, but I swam. From the pool, with my red eyes, I would go to school, smelling all day of chlorine. When school ended, I went right back to the pool and swam several more thousand yards. Did I do this because I liked swimming? *No way!* I hated it! I swam hard every day because I loved winning in water polo. I knew that to be able to win, I would have to log in my time disciplining my body until I was able to perform at a much higher level than others. My work paid off. We won the LA city championship in water polo every year I was in high school because we wanted it enough to work hard for it. I was recognized on the all-city first team for two of those years. I tied a goal-scoring record as well.

Shortly after I graduated, the LA City Section CIF (California Interscholastic Federation) shut down men's water polo. While this was disappointing at first, it did assure that my records would last! A little more than a year ago, I read an article in the *LA Times* that LA City Section CIF was starting the water polo league back up after a hiatus of almost thirty years. In the article it mentioned that they used to have a water polo league many years ago in the seventies. Then it said they could not find any record of the results from those years!

I have boxes full of old rusted trophies and faded brown clippings in my attic that can shed some light on the subject, but the truth is no one really cares who won the championship in the seventies! Paul says that athletes work hard for a perishable wreath, and it's true. Over time even the glory of gold medals fades.

You are probably not a world-class athlete that competes at the highest level. You may not even have been a semi-good high school athlete. But when it comes to your spiritual life, you need to have the drive of a world-class athlete, because it's a race worthy of the investment. It can't be just a secondary commitment tagged on to your other priorities. This is your *life*! This is who you are. This is what will make it all meaningful or meaningless in the end. Don't just sail through this life on a smile and some charm. These will not always get you by. If you want to win, you will have to work at it. The reward you will receive for winning this race will last for eternity and never fade or become old and irrelevant news.

Direction for the Duration

There is nothing sadder than intense effort invested in the wrong goals. Direction is important; you have to know where you are going. I'm not just talking about heaven; I mean you have to have direction to your spiritual workouts. We are all used to people telling us the importance of reading the Word and prayer, but do we have measurable goals? Most of us don't, except maybe the goal of reading through the Bible in a year.

Imagine an athlete who worked intensely at his or her special event to a level of world-class ability, but who never competed. Imagine if this athlete was never tested against the clock or against the competition. Though the athlete has medal-winning ability, without direction and goals, he or she is just investing time in a hobby.

The goal of our spiritual discipline is to get better at our spiritual life. Of course, it is foolish to see this as a competition with others; that is not it. We are competing with ourselves. Are you closer to Christ today than you were last year? Have you recorded your progress? This is one of the reasons I am so committed to journaling—so I can record the progress of my own spiritual life.

And the reason we need this direction is we need to have our eyes on the goal—the finish line. This is a race to the finish, and we need to invest spiritual discipline now so that we make it to the end. Personally I do not want to just glide in at the end, running on fumes. I want to finish stronger than when I started.

In 1 Corinthians Paul continues, "Therefore I run in such a way, as not without aim; I box in such a way, as not beating the air; but I discipline my body and make it my slave, so that, after I have preached to others, I myself will not be disqualified" (9:26–27).

In athletics you have a time limit for your peak performance. Your body changes and eventually even the champions have to retire and make room for the new studs. But in the spiritual race this is not true. You can get stronger with age. I am so sad when I hear people say, "Oh, if only I were as passionate as I was when I first became a Christian." Those are sad words to me. You have every reason to be at least as passionate as you were when you first committed yourself to Christ; in fact, you should be more passionate than you were then, because of the experiences you've had with Jesus! He hasn't changed, and the world is still in need of your passionate ministry. Don't quit until you win the prize. Make the last lap your best time.

Priorities of an Organic Leader

If Jesus is looking in us for faithfulness, fruitfulness, and finishing well, then perhaps our priorities should reflect these goals. Usually Christian leaders put more emphasis on tasks at the expense of relationships, but

The Inside-out Kingdom

actually it is our relationships that will ultimately reveal our success or failure.

The diagram below reflects a variety of roles that a typical Christian leader can feel obliged to fill. At the top of the chart are the roles and at the bottom are the number of people he or she can expect to influence in each of those roles.

Focus of Influence
The Roles and Influence of Christian Leadership

visionary teacher
shepherd
facilitator
discipler
mentor
the inner circle of 3
the 12
the 70
the 120
the multitudes

greatest demand, least significance

greatest significance, least demand

Never sacrifice the permanent on the altar of the urgent.

The chart reflects Jesus's pattern of ministry; he fulfilled all the roles. He preached to, healed, and fed the multitudes (Matt. 13:1–34; 14:13–21). He shepherded a congregation of disciples that, we are told in Acts, numbered 120 (1:15). He coached and facilitated the training of 70 (Luke 10:1). He discipled 12 (Matt. 10:1) and of those 12 he invested his most personal self in 3 to reproduce his leadership (Mark 5:37; 14:33; Luke 9:28). The 3 were part of the 12, who were numbered in the 70. The 70 were counted among the 120, and of course the 120 were part of the multitudes.

As you look at the circles in the chart, imagine them on a potter's wheel spinning fast. The Christian leader feels the pull of centrifugal force to the outer roles. The crowds beckon us. The demands of the immature call us to help them.

Leaders who perform well on the outside tasks get the most accolades and affirmation, but the tasks that fuel true success over the course of a lifetime are found at the center of the circles. The greatest demand and the least significance are found in the roles on the outside of the circles. The least demand on your time, yet the greatest significance for your life investment, is found in the center of the target.

Jesus was not enamored by large crowds. Though obviously he had the ability to draw tens of thousands, it was not his purpose to do so. He did not consider that success. Frequently he tried to get away from large crowds (Luke 5:14–16), and sometimes he intentionally offended them without worrying about losing his popularity (John 6:41–71).

We simply must realign our priorities to reflect what is valuable in God's kingdom. The greatest leaders are not those who win the most followers. The greatest leaders are the ones who produce other leaders.

It is the lives you touch, one at a time, that will be the fruit of your life. Like George Bailey, you may find that all the people you have influenced through your loving care will make the whole world a better place. Now that is success!

The Inside-out Kingdom

SECTION THREE
THE UPSIDE-DOWN KINGDOM

Navigating a Correct Leadership Trajectory

Leadership requires direction. One of the biggest problems leaders face in the church is that we want to lead, but we do not understand the basic tenets of God's kingdom and are unfortunately much more familiar with the way of the world. As a consequence we lead in the wrong way and to the wrong ends. Having momentum and velocity is not a good thing if your trajectory is off.

God's kingdom is counterintuitive. It is the opposite of what we see as normative. The problem is that we try to lead right side up in an upside-down kingdom, and this leads to warped leadership. Before we can understand how to lead in God's kingdom, of which we are a part, we must first understand the kingdom.

In this section we will examine how God's kingdom is the opposite of what we would think. We will discover that the new "up" is "down." This book is not specifically on the kingdom of God, so I will only lightly touch on the fact that the characteristics of the kingdom are contrary to the default mentality we have developed about life. Understanding this is essential if we want to provide leadership that flows in the kingdom direction.

In contrast to the world's leadership style, we will find that leaders are to lead, follow, *and* get out of the way. The authority needed to lead in God's upside-down kingdom is indeed more powerful and influential than what we typically expect. In chapter 12 we will examine five varieties of authority that are available and which are best for kingdom leadership. We will also look at the best channels for disseminating authority in God's kingdom.

In a reversal of the norm, we will discover how God's leaders are to be "downwardly mobile," following Christ's example. It is common to hear Christian leaders speak about servant leadership, but not common enough for us to see it. In Chapter 13 we will look at a critical passage that elaborates poetically on Christ's own leadership trajectory.

Those who allow Christ's Spirit to lead will in fact live as incarnational leaders and demonstrate Christ in a world that so badly needs to find him. Followers of Christ will find their path on the very same trajectory as Jesus's. Downwardly mobile leaders will demonstrate Christ's character in their lives at all levels. That is what it means to live with Christ within you as a follower, as a leader, and as an equipper of others.

Welcome to the upside-down kingdom, where the values, paths, and power are all backwards to our typical default mind-set.

11
THE NEW "UP" IS "DOWN"

The Paradoxical Kingdom

Everybody can be great because anybody can serve. . . . You only need a heart full of grace and soul generated by love.

Martin Luther King Jr.

Education is a progressive discovery of our own ignorance.

Will Durant

During a black-tie dinner at a New Year's Eve party, aboard a fancy cruise ship, all seems peaceful and glamorous. Suddenly and without warning, a rogue tidal wave strikes, knocking the *Poseidon* around. Finally it settles dead in the water, capsized. Remarkably many survive, only to find their lives still in great jeopardy.

Under the command of ship personnel, most of the passengers elect to stay where they are and wait for rescuers to come to them. They remain submerged deep under water in an upside-down ballroom where the pressure of tons of ocean water will eventually bust in and drown them all.

Against the objections of the established authorities, a spiritual leader in the movie, played by Gene Hackman, has to lead a small band of survivors against all intuition to the bottom of the boat where they will find they are actually at the top, near the surface and rescue. Here those who survive the journey will escape.

You may be familiar with this story from the original film *The Poseidon Adventure*. It came out in the seventies during a rash of what is now called disaster films. One of the things that captivated the audience was the idea that suddenly everything in their world was upside down. The way up was down. The ceiling was now the floor. Corridor stairs were now on the ceiling. Exit signs were at their feet. The world that was so glamorous and right a few hours earlier suddenly and completely turned upside down.

Like the *Poseidon*, the kingdom of God is upside down; at least it appears to be from our point of view. In God's kingdom, the basement is the penthouse. The first become last, and the last are first (Matt. 19:30). The humble are exalted, and the exalted are humbled (1 Peter 5:5–6). The weak are strong, and the strong are weak (2 Cor. 13:9). The rich are impoverished, and the poor are wealthy (8:9). The wise are foolish, and the foolish confound the wise (1 Cor. 1:27). Death comes from life, and holding on to life brings death (Matt. 10:39).

Are you seeing a pattern here? From our worldly perspective, the kingdom of God is backwards. It is upside down. In a sense, everything you think you know is wrong, and everything you think is wrong is right. Wow! That is how separate the kingdom of God is from this world.

As God says it: "'For My thoughts are not your thoughts, nor are your ways My ways,' declares the LORD. 'For as the heavens are higher than the earth, so are My ways higher than your ways and My thoughts than your thoughts" (Isa. 55:8–9). There is beauty in this, real poetry. But it is more than just a pretty poem; it is a staggering truth that we need to digest if we are to send people in the right direction. We must be careful that we are not like the officer on the ship who gave the wrong direction to the people on the capsized boat and led them to their demise. The kingdom of God is in all ways contrary to the kingdom of the world. In God's kingdom, like the capsized *Poseidon*, the way up is down.

The world will tell you to get ahead, climb the ladder, and step on people if that's what it takes. Jesus tells us otherwise. He says that to be exalted, we must first be humble. To go up, we must first go down—on our knees. The only way to get ahead in Christ's kingdom is to lift others up, not ourselves.

The Upside-down Kingdom

Reset the Default

We must readjust our entire navigation system—south is now north; up is now down. The kingdom is opposite from the way we normally see things. Much of what the world sees as good is in fact bad. What the world sees as great is not. What the world thinks is wise is indeed foolish.

Therefore, getting direction from the world system is a bad idea. Learning how to lead from successful businessmen, politicians, sports stars, or military leaders is not the best endeavor in God's kingdom. It can become a lethal direction, not only for the leader but for all who would follow. This, however, is what we have often done.

Albert Einstein once remarked, "The kind of thinking that will solve the world's problems will be of a different sort than the kind of thinking that created those problems in the first place." We must change our way of thinking. We must reset our default way of thinking about what is good (values), what is power (authority), and what is our path (direction) if we want to lead in an upside-down kingdom.

Henri Matisse said, "To look at something as though we had never seen it before requires great courage." It is time for us to show courage and look at God's kingdom with fresh eyes. Do not just accept what has been; look for what should be.

Learning to Lead from the World

In the world, leaders are usually considered the best when they are the cream of the crop. The strongest and most dynamic personality is the one we want at the top of the organization. We think we need a strong vision caster, a motivator, and a decisive manager. This is because so much of the success of the organization is placed squarely on the shoulders of its leader.

Whether it is a military command, a leader of a Fortune 500 company, or a presidential candidate, we want a strong leader at the top to infuse the whole organization with strength. This person will be the face of the institution, which will rest on his or her proven character, vision for the organization, and driven nature. These qualities will make good things happen.

Many churches and ministries have adopted the same mentality when it comes to leadership. Our church ministries have become high-profile organizations built on a business model. We have strong dynamic leaders at the top who are responsible to set the culture and direction of the ministry. The weight of the organization is placed on the leader, and unfortunately, little is placed on Jesus. In our eyes, a strong leader can make or break a church, and Jesus has little to do with it, except to bring us a real savior—a dynamic preacher/leader/CEO.

A Twisted and Painful Irony

In recent years some of the best nonfiction literature, written by those who are not in the church, reveals a painful irony. The truth is the business world is sometimes better at understanding kingdom dynamics than the church is. This is a bold statement, but look at the facts.

After studying the most wildly successful companies, Jim Collins has determined that the leaders who are most effective are not the most dynamic personalities but are those who are more quiet, less assuming, and humble. They are successful because they empower, release, and exalt others rather than themselves. Such leadership is less personality dependent, and the businesses flourish over the long haul because of it. Often this form of leadership makes the difference between a good company and one that is great. In his bestselling book *Good to Great*, Collins calls these humble and successful leaders "Level V Leaders."[1]

Sociologists have discovered the secrets of epidemic movements, and Malcolm Gladwell has articulated them with surprising clarity in his bestseller *The Tipping Point*.[2] This is a better book to read if you want to start a kingdom movement than the vast majority of books available on missions today.

On the cutting edge in business today are decentralized organizations that multiply influence rather than simply adding it. Dee Hock, founder of Visa, has written a few books that are insightful. Learning from the organic world of God's creation, he writes about how organizations can be value-led rather than personality-driven and how order can be maintained in the midst of a chaotic, out-of-control movement without a centralized command post.[3]

After studying how some of God's creation functions, Ori Brafman and Rod Beckstrom have written *The Starfish and the Spider*, an excellent book about the unstoppable nature of decentralized organizations.[4]

These books have more to do with the kingdom than do most of the organizational books and seminars available in Christendom. Could it be that God has found those in the church are more inclined to listen to the business world than the Bible, so he is now speaking to us through whatever medium will get our ear? These non-Christian authors have discovered that the new "up" is "down," while we are still stuck in the old way of thinking that the way "up" is to climb the ladder of success.

How do these authors come up with kingdom ideas without using the Bible? They study the creation and how it operates and learn from it. The books are chock-full of examples from nature and people movements. Any casual reader can see easily where the authors are gleaning these insights. They are studying the very concepts that Jesus told us to look at two thousand years ago. While we have been studying Fortune 500 companies, they have been studying nature and the dynamics of God's created order. They are discovering how the kingdom operates without even knowing or acknowledging that it exists. Jesus said, "Consider [study] the lilies of the field" (Matt. 6:28 KJV). Jesus was constantly telling us that we can learn about his kingdom by studying the way his creation works. His parables about his kingdom are constantly pointing us to the natural, organic world to find understanding.

This latest breed of authors has been accidentally obedient to Jesus's command—more than most Christian leaders are today. They are looking at God's creation for direction. I am not promoting the idea that we should look to unbelieving authors for how we should live and function as leaders. I am simply stating, to our shame, that they are doing better at learning kingdom principles by studying God's created order than we are. Though these authors lack a kingdom set of values by which they can fully understand the significance of their own discoveries, their findings are extremely insightful. How ironic that the church is looking for answers from the business world, while business leaders are looking at God's created order to find success!

Hank's Story: A True Agent of an Upside-down Kingdom

Perhaps Hank Montoya is the best example of God's kingdom leadership being the opposite of what we would expect. For a season Hank was our most prolific organic-church planter. He was a very unassuming and quiet man, inclined to stay behind the scenes and never longing for the attention of any group.

Hank worked for a local grocery store in the produce section. A middle-aged Latin American, he was divorced with grown children—

according to the thinking in Christendom today, not an ideal candidate for a church-planting leader. But he enjoyed playing the drums and had some percussion skills, so a church found a useful place for him behind the rest of the band, and for a time, Hank was content to stay there.

At this time Doug Lee launched out to start a network of organic churches called the Fountain. He asked Hank to come along, and he did. They began meeting in a Life Transformation Group (LTG)[5] and weekly were reading entire books of the Bible, confessing their sins one to another, and praying for the lost and broken people in each of their lives.

Hank sort of enjoyed the anonymity that he lived in at work and at church. All that changed when he began taking Jesus and his Word more seriously. The first thing he noticed was that people at work who had any real problems started coming to him for prayer, even though Hank knew there were more outspoken Christians working at the grocery store. He asked Doug what he should do with these increasing requests for prayer. Doug answered simply: "Pray." And he did, and his prayers were being answered. People started noticing that the Lord was using this humble, ordinary man.

Hank's mother saw the difference in him. She asked about his new church experience. After he described his organic church and LTG, she asked if he could start one in her house. He agreed and they began a church with all of her friends and associates.

At work a pallet of heavy items fell on Hank's foot, causing a serious work-related injury. Hank had to take a considerable amount of time off for the injury to heal. He was unable to walk and was in a wheelchair. Since he couldn't work, he decided to give his time to serving the Lord.

One of Hank's grown children asked if he would start an organic church in his home, and he did. Then another church started and then another. Soon the network of organic churches called the Fountain had churches across fifty miles of inland Southern California.

Hank's foot was not healing properly, and the doctors were baffled. In fact the foot seemed to be somewhat atrophied. They ran other tests and after considerable consultation they finally determined that Hank was suffering from Lou Gehrig's disease, a lethal condition that affects the nervous and muscular systems.

Hank would never leave the wheelchair. His disease would continue to eat away at his health until all of his independence and physical function were robbed from him. But his love of Jesus and usefulness in

God's upside-down kingdom would not diminish or atrophy. He would never turn his back on the kingdom of God in which he had discovered his gifts and usefulness.

Even in this state, up until the last year of his life, Hank was starting churches. For a period of a couple of years, this quiet, unassuming man in a wheelchair was the most prolific church planter we could find in our movement.

In one of the churches in the Riverside area, there were friends of a young man who had tried to take his life with an overdose of drugs, and for all intents and purposes he had succeeded. His friends took Hank with them to the intensive care unit of the hospital to pray with the man, only to be told that he was all but gone. He had no more brain activity. He was being kept alive by machines so the doctors could harvest his organs for others who could be saved. Hank, from his wheelchair, placed his hand on the young man's arm and asked God to somehow be glorified in this situation.

Hank and the others hadn't eaten lunch, so they went downstairs to the cafeteria, which has easy wheelchair access, for a quick meal. Before leaving the hospital, they went up to say good-bye one last time. When they got back to the ICU, they found the young man very much alive, sitting up in his bed, eating a Popsicle! The doctors had no explanation. A true miracle had occurred. God's kingdom power had surged through the trembling hands of a man in a wheelchair who had a fatal disease.

After reading the book of Acts, church history, and accounts of kingdom movements in other parts of the world, many of us had been inquiring of the Lord why we were not seeing as many supernatural miracles as there had been in other movements. Since Hank's experience, we have seen more and more of the miraculous, not because we seek it, but because we seek Jesus Christ and his kingdom. The first miracle was when God used Hank to raise the all but dead.

It amazes me that a man who is dying can bring life to another. God delights to use the weak things of this world to confound the things that are strong. Even when Hank could no longer feed, bathe, or dress himself, he was still starting organic churches. Hank has been responsible for the start of six organic churches from Azusa to Moreno Valley (a fifty-mile distance) in just a couple years.

People would see him and think, *If he can do this, why can't I?* It wasn't because he had a strong and dynamic personality that he was able to lead others. His weakness was his strength. He was an upside-down leader in an upside-down kingdom.

This humble, quiet, ordinary produce grocer has led us in so many ways, and he is already missed. On Friday, December 28, 2007, Jesus finally welcomed this hero home.

12

LEAD, FOLLOW, AND GET OUT OF THE WAY

Authority Worth Following

I have as much authority as the Pope; I just don't have as many
people who believe it.

George Carlin

All authority belongs to the people.

Thomas Jefferson

William Wallace (played by Mel Gibson) in the film *Braveheart*
had true authority. He did not have any title or position and
couldn't have cared less for such things. What he did have was
an inspiring sense of obligation to fight for freedom at any
cost. Unlike those who had true position in Scotland but did not have
the hearts of the people and therefore did not have true authority,
Wallace had the ears and hearts of the people of Scotland. That is
real authority!

In one compelling scene Wallace is speaking with Robert the Bruce,
who is the true heir to the throne of Scotland. With passion he looks
into the Bruce's eyes and says, "If you will only *lead* them, they will
follow." Then, with a glimmer of hope, he adds an extra punch: "And

so would I." For a revealing moment, the prince of Scotland is envious of the authority of a no-name son of a peasant who displays true authority. He is visibly touched by the notion that this peasant warrior would follow him.

One man had all the position and title, but the other had the authority. Leadership that rests on title is weak. Leadership that rests in a cause and inspires others to follow is strong.

As the banditos said in the 1948 classic film *The Treasure of the Sierra Madre*—parodied in Mel Brooks's *Blazing Saddles*—"Badges? We don't need no stinking badges!"

Leadership is not about position but influence. "We don't need no stinking badges." We need something better. We need real authority.

Learning a Lesson from a Bloodless Coup

California was headed in the wrong direction. Because of exorbitant taxes and workers' compensation costs, small businesses were being forced to leave our state to survive. The hemorrhaging was so bad that extreme measures had to be taken. In a nonelection year, we Californians decided we didn't like our current governor and we forced a new election. With more than one hundred candidates, from porn stars to movie stars, we had the wildest election imaginable. We ended up selecting the Governator himself, Arnold Schwarzenegger. Isn't democracy great?

This was a bloodless coup. A governor was toppled in the middle of his term with no loss of life. And we can learn something from it about authority. Positional authority exists only as long as the people choose to salute the position. In a sense, your position is not what grants you authority, but the respect of the people for the position grants authority. If suddenly people choose not to respect the position you have, you have no authority, no matter what your job description or performance review says.

Authority, then, does not rest in the position but in the hearts and minds of those who choose to respect and follow the ones who are in a position of authority. In any governing system, as long as the people respect the position enough to follow, they will, but when they choose to rebel, the authority is no longer there. Fear and the threat of violence can solicit respect, but so can sound thinking and ideas. Every government is only as strong as the people's confidence in it.

The Upside-down Kingdom

The Nature of Authority

We tend to think that people are either leaders or followers, one or the other. This sort of polarized thinking can get us into deep problems. The reality is that a good leader begins by being a good follower. Before you can exert authority in a healthy manner, you must first respect it yourself. An un-submissive leader is a dangerous leader.

The better you are at following, the better you'll be at leading. Good leaders will be good followers all the days of their lives. And most important: a good leader must first and always be in submission to Christ.

Leadership is, in a sense, going first. It is starting out in a direction you want others to go. You cannot lead where you do not go. To move others, you must first be moved.

There are five kinds of authority I want to discuss.

1. *Positional authority:* This authority is based on the place you hold in a chain of command. The title that you hold grants you power to accomplish the role demanded of the position. Submitting to this authority means submitting to the system that empowers the position.
2. *Expertise authority:* This is the authority you gain when you have effective experience in a specific area and others seek out the wisdom gleaned from the experience. With this type of authority, your voice is respected because of your expertise. You may hold no actual position, but people see that you have the right solution.
3. *Relational authority:* This is the authority you have because you are loved and therefore respected by those with whom you are in close relationship. People respect you as a person, which grants you some degree of authority in their lives.
4. *Moral authority:* This is authority that comes from the substantive character of your life. People recognize the depth of your commitment and integrity and they respect you for it. This is not a self-righteous religious authority, but one gained when your character has been truly tested and found strong.
5. *Spiritual authority:* This is the authority that comes when God speaks through you and people recognize that it is God who is using you, not the other way around. There is a sense that you are merely a vessel God is using for the moment. Usually God is not constantly using you in this way, but at opportune times, your spiritual authority is noticed and respected. The response

to this authority is not a willingness to submit to the leader, but a willingness to submit to God, when we say, "Yes, Lord."

The weakest of all the authorities is *positional authority*. This authority has little to do with who you are but is more about your place in the organization. Granted, position is not given to just anyone; it usually has to be earned. But all of us have dealt with someone who would not be given respect if it were not for his or her position. Positional authority is easily removed or overcome. All it takes is a bribe or a deception.

The Chinese spent several centuries building, extending, and reinforcing a great wall to protect them from the threatening neighbors to the north. It is estimated that two to three million Chinese lost their lives building the wall. It is said that the Great Wall of China is the only man-made structure that can be seen from the moon, but this is an urban myth. It can be seen from space at a low orbit (but so can your own house now, thanks to Google Earth).

When the wall was finished, the Mongols faced a barrier that seemed insurmountable—except for the weakness of positional authority. Genghis Khan was able to pass right through the wall with very little trouble and conquer China—*by bribing the gatekeeper*. Now that presents a scary idea: your frontline defense against hostile terrorists is only as good as the guys working at the airport security for minimum wage! Ultimately, your hierarchical organization is only as strong as the integrity of your gatekeepers.

Expertise authority can be effective but is very limited. One can have expertise on one subject and be a total novice on most others. People listen only when your expertise is consistent with their own need and proves to be sound.

Relational authority is far superior to the other two, for it is based on who you are as a person and how you relate to the people around you. The more you are loved and respected, the more authority will be entrusted to you. Of course one can abuse and manipulate relational authority for personal gain.

Moral authority is also strong. People believe they can trust the word of those with moral authority because their reputation is sure, and it is evident in words that everyone accepts as right and true. Usually moral authority just makes sense to any thoughtful person. Your moral authority will remain as long as people believe they can trust your word and if your reputation remains true. Those who retain their moral authority

The Upside-down Kingdom

will have influence, and the respect of others can build over the years. Moral authority is hard to gain but easy to lose. You can spend a lifetime getting it and lose it in a few moments of weakness.

Spiritual authority is the strongest authority there is. It is the type of authority that can stand up to anyone or anything. Spiritual authority does not concern itself with position, titles, or the rules that men establish. It is only concerned with God and his will. While people hear God's voice through someone with moral authority, the person being used does not lose his or her own voice. We are not merely God's dictation machines or tape recorders. We are involved in the word that God is delivering, but the authority in what is being said is from God, though his thoughts and ours are joined as one.

Leaders do not seek spiritual, moral, or relational authority. This authority is bestowed on the one who leads well. People do not gain moral authority by doing good just so that they can have moral authority. It is because they live a life of goodness that they have moral authority, not the other way around.

When it comes to spiritual authority, the more you seek power, the less true power you will have. Those who hunger for power will get only positional power (and perhaps some expertise authority), because positional authority is the only type of authority to which one can aspire. The other forms of authority are simply granted because of who you are in relation to God and others. They cannot be bought or sold. Spiritual authority does not come from seeking power, but from seeking God, and one does not seek God from a position of strength but in weakness.

Misplaced authority is also a reality. Misplaced authority is granted without meaning or substance. Sometimes because a person has exceptional charisma, people will follow him or her to their own destruction. Being famous or just beautiful will often grant a person access and authority that are not earned. And of course there are many times when a person gains authority because he or she has deceptively put forward a false persona or credential. Unfortunately, simply being persuasive can gain authority even when it is based completely on delusion.

Ultimately it is not what authority you have that is important, but what you do with it. In God's kingdom, authority is not something to hold on to selfishly, but something to give away wisely. As an organic leader, you are not meant to be a cup but a channel for God's authority.

Delegated Authority versus Distributed Authority

There are two ways to channel authority from one person to another. These authority channels determine, in one sense, whether you are functioning in a hierarchical structure dependent on positional authority or in a multiplication movement that is out of control and unstoppable.

Delegated authority is when you merely lend authority to others down the chain of command to fulfill your own will. The authority doesn't actually leave the people above; it is simply lent downward.

Distributed authority is when power is given to others without regard to their position. They don't need permission from someone else to have it. They have access to the source itself, rather than simply from the next person above them.

In a top-down hierarchical structure, delegation of authority is important; it is nesessary for every action. Authority is recognized and granted by those who follow. Sometimes, however, someone takes authority through force or even the threat of violent enforcement, and in such cases delegated authority is pressed upon others. This is how the world operates, but the kingdom of God is not to be that way.

All authority comes from God, and there is a vast difference between *delegated* authority and *distributed* authority. When God distributes his authority to us, there is a freedom granted with power to accomplish all that Jesus asks of the follower—any follower.

Delegated Authority and Codependency

Speaking to his disgruntled disciples, each vying for a better position of authority, Jesus said:

> You know that those who are regarded as rulers of the Gentiles lord it over them, and their high officials exercise authority over them. Not so with you. Instead, whoever wants to become great among you must be your servant, and whoever wants to be first must be slave of all. For even the Son of Man did not come to be served, but to serve, and to give his life as a ransom for many.
>
> Mark 10:42–45 NIV

Many take Christ's words and apply them backwards. They teach that if you have position in the kingdom of God, you must lead as a servant. But Jesus meant us to see that those who first serve are indeed the leaders that others will follow. Position and title are useless in such a scenario. Jesus, of course, is our prime example. He did not have any title or position in this world yet he spoke with authority unlike any man who ever walked the earth.

For delegation to work, the authority remains with the one who grants it to another temporarily only for accomplishing an assigned task. The authority is secure because it belongs to someone above in the chain of command and "covers" the ones beneath who need it for a specific purpose. If the connection breaks, the authority is no longer channeled down.

Jesus's authority did not come from any source other than his intimacy with the Father and the constant empowerment of the Holy Spirit.

When in the church we delegate authority, we connect our people to others for empowerment and permission rather than connecting them directly to God. When people look to other people for all the power and permission in ministry, a codependency is developed that is unhealthy and will not prosper or reproduce.

Distributed Authority and Freedom to Serve

In a flat structure that does not employ a hierarchical leadership model, authority is distributed to each person to accomplish all God has for him or her to do, without needing layers of middlemen to pass the authority down. One's "covering" is found in his or her position in Christ, not in human positions above in the chain of command.

In this manner, each person is endowed with the authority to accomplish all God intends. Permission from other people above is not necessary if God is the one who issues the command. In such a system, spiritual and relational authority are what is needed in leadership.

Many fear that without positions of authority there will not be any leadership. This is a false assumption based on our limited experience of true authority. The strongest authority one can have is spiritual authority. When the words that come from one's mouth are full of God's wisdom and insight, people will notice and follow regardless of position, title, or diploma. This was what was so noticeable in Jesus, especially in contrast to the status-conscious Scribes and Pharisees (Matt. 7:28–29). The strongest and purest leaders do not need to rely on position or title. Their passion, wisdom, and authentic love carry all the authority that is needed. The moment we rely on our position or title to accomplish our work, we are sick and dying because it means that the source of permission and power are human rather than divine.

One of the worst things about a hierarchical structure and operating from positional authority to get the kingdom work done is that most people assume that the King himself, Jesus, is at the top of the chain of command. Therefore people tend to respect those in position over them because they are receiving orders from "on high."

This is a huge problem in so many ways. For one thing, people in authority are often not hearing from God. Worse yet, some are using God to reinforce their position in the order of command, which is extremely abusive.

One of our organic-church leaders worked as a youth pastor at a larger church. He came from a rough background, and his salvation is something he never takes for granted. His own story of redemption is a constant reminder to him to share the Good News with others. He started to reach out to the gang members in the community. Soon some started coming to the youth groups, complete with tattoos, street slang, cigarettes, and baggy pants. Of course the upright parents of the Christian youth were not all that pleased with the "visitors." Some of the gang members were finding Christ and a better way to live, but because they didn't clean up right away and look like the other Christians, there was a problem.

Eventually the discussion reached the highest level in the church—the senior pastor's office. The young leader was called into the pastor's office where he was scolded and told to ask the former gang members not to come back to church. He was to cease and desist from any more outreach to those types.

My friend could not accept that. At first, he tried to reason with the pastor. He appealed to the love of Christ and the mission of the church, but nothing seemed to work. The pastor was adamant. And when the youth pastor said he was unable to obey, he was chastised severely. The senior pastor made it clear that he would be fired immediately if he did not comply. As the levels of their voices started to rise, the youth pastor, not liking the way the conversation had gone, started to show the senior pastor how far off from the Bible he was. To that, the senior pastor replied, "You better be careful. Now you are very close to attacking God's man. You better back off right now."

There are so many things wrong with the pastor's statement. It betrays that the pastor thinks he is indeed higher in God's kingdom than others, not just higher than gang members and youth pastors, but in the highest position of the church. He sees himself as "God's man," untouchable, unquestionable, unashamed. How foolish!

Some people are deceived into thinking that positional authority is the strongest authority to which we can appeal. How unwise it is to abandon spiritual, moral, and relational authority to grasp positional authority, which is not strong. It is infantile and weak.

There was nothing else the youth pastor could do, no one else to whom he could appeal. He resigned immediately and left the church. He is now part of an organic church we started, part of a hip-hop group that recently put out a CD, and serving as a social worker to troubled kids in LA. His life and fruit continue to develop.

Contrasts in Authority

The very nature of delegated authority is selfish and stingy, whereas distributed authority is generous and empowering. One holds all the authority and the other gives all of it away. One requires positions in the chain of command; the other is not dependent on position. One is more concerned with getting the right person to the top of the pyramid; the other is more concerned with getting out of the way so others can be empowered.

Thomas Paine, the Revolutionary War hero, once remarked, "Lead, follow, or get out of the way." This has become the motto of strong leadership today in business, the military, and educational institutions. I have heard of one strong Christian leader who has this slogan on a plaque on his desk to remind him each day of what it means to be a tough leader who accomplishes much. From a traditional point of view, I fully understand this perspective of leadership. It is the philosophy of get the job done or get out of the way so someone else can do it.

Paine's quote presents three options in opposition to each other, and we must all choose one of the options. We are leaders or followers or we are just in the way. Over the years I have come to realize that a good leader is a good follower who knows how to get out of the way. So I have adopted this as my motto: Lead, follow, *and* get out of the way.

13

DOWNWARDLY MOBILE

Following Christ to Humility and Exaltation

It is well to remember that the entire population of the universe, with one trifling exception, is composed of others.

Andrew J. Holmes

The Son of God became a man to enable men to become sons of God.

C. S. Lewis

I am convinced that Steve Martin is one of the funniest men alive. His comedic timing is genius. His early work needs to be rediscovered because it is so funny. I am especially fond of his first movie, *The Jerk*, which is a comedy that makes fun of the stupidity of its main character in a way similar to the movie *Dumb and Dumber*. Martin's character is sympathetic, foolish, and a jerk all at the same time.

The Jerk is a movie about Navin Johnson, who, although Caucasian, was raised by a rural Black family. He sets off into the world to make his mark, but Navin is not the sharpest tool in the shed; in fact he is about as dull as can be—he is *the Jerk*. This is a rags to riches and back to rags story.

Navin invents an eyeglass holder that becomes a big success and makes him a multimillionaire seemingly overnight. Unfortunately, the invention causes people to become cross-eyed. A class action suit is brought against him, and he loses all his riches.

My favorite scene in the film occurs shortly after Navin loses the lawsuit. It is a tragic and revealing moment that is both funny and at the same time insightful. Obviously he had been drinking too much. He is at a desk in his mansion, writing checks to the thousands of people who will divide his wealth into equal parts of $1.09 each. We see him dressed in what appears to be his pajamas and a gray robe. His slow, exaggerated movements are caused by the alcohol he has consumed. His desk is cluttered with checkbooks and envelopes containing checks. Movers are carrying out furniture that has been repossessed.

Navin's wife, played by Bernadette Peters, walks in crying and in the course of a conversation she declares that they have hit bottom. Navin says, "No! Maybe you've hit bottom, but I haven't hit bottom yet. I've got a ways to go. And I'm gonna bounce back, and when I do I'm gonna buy you a diamond so big it's gonna make you puke!"

She replies, "I don't want to puke. I don't want wealth. I just want you back the way you used to be. What happened to that man?"

"Me! What happened to the girl that I believed in, the girl I fell in love with, the girl who believed in me? Well, there are plenty of places I can go where people will believe in me again."

In distress she tells him to go so she can go back to being the girl she used to be.

A wide-angle shot reveals that Navin is wearing his robe over a wrinkled dress shirt and his boxers. "Well, I'm gonna go then," he says, and I don't need any of this. I don't need *this* stuff." He brushes most of the checks and envelopes off the desk in anger. "And I don't need you. I don't need anything."

He pauses and looks down at the desk and sees an ashtray. "Except this." He picks up the ashtray and says, "This ashtray, and that's the only thing I need is this," shaking the ashtray at his wife. He has now come out from behind the desk revealing that he does indeed have trousers on, but they are down around his ankles, though we can see his dress shoes and black socks. He walks fitfully, staggering because of his pants.

"I don't need this or this," he adds, "just this ashtray." He pauses, looks down, bends over, and picks up something. It's a paddleball toy. "And this paddle game. The ashtray and the paddle game, and that's all

I need." He is making his way out of the room and picks up something else. "And this remote control. The ashtray, the paddle game, and the remote control, and that's all I need."

He is now in the hall outside of his office. His pants are still down around his ankles, so he shuffles as he walks. He stops at a small table and says, "And these matches. The ashtray, these matches, the remote control, and the paddle game . . ." He pauses, continues looking down at the table and says, "And this lamp."

He is staggering, shuffling, and carrying more and more worthless stuff as he moves toward the staircase. Trying to hold everything while shuffling a few more steps with his pants around his ankles, he sums up his needs once again: "The ashtray, the paddle game, the remote control, the matches, and this lamp, and that's all I need. And that's *all* I need too. I don't need one other thing. He looks down, pauses, and says, "I need *this*." Though his arms are full of junk, he bends down and adds one thing to his growing inventory, a chair.

"The paddle game and the chair, the remote control and the matches for sure." He is turning, trying to hold all these worthless items close to his chest. He is stumbling along, making his way to the front door.

He turns to look through the hall and foyer at his wife, who is still in the same place in the office watching him in his fit of lunacy. He says, "Well, what are you looking at? What do you think I am, some kind of a jerk or something?" He turns and continues to the front door. He stops, turns, and looks down at another table just before he is out of sight. "And this," he says, picking up a worthless magazine with the only two fingers that are free to carry it.

He proceeds shuffling toward the front door. "And that's *all* I need. The ashtray, the remote control, the matches, and this magazine . . . and that's all I need." His voice trails off as he walks off mumbling an inventory list of his most valued possessions. He is shuffling into the sunlight streaming in from the open front door and he is carrying more worthless stuff than seems possible, with his trousers down around his ankles. He is *the Jerk*.

While this is humorous in its exaggerated way, we must be careful not to be the same kind of jerk. Sometimes we cling to worthless things, stating that we do not really need anything, and all the while walking away from the most valuable thing—the ever-present help of the Holy Spirit for life, love, and leadership.

The Upside-down Kingdom

The Height and Depth of Humanity

At the heart of Paul's letter to the Philippians is a beautiful poem, a song. It is often called the Christ hymn. Most see the hymn starting in verse 5 of chapter 2 and ending in verse 11. Personally I think it starts in verse 1. It may seem odd to transition from *The Jerk* to the Christ hymn, but as we dig into the passage, you will see a clear connection.

This passage has been a lifelong discovery for me. Like many great works of literature, it has beauty, poetry, joy, love, a hero, mystery, blessings, cruelty, tragedy, irony, and victory. It is incredibly practical, intensely personal, and yet is so deep that it has had theologians debating it for centuries. It is an epic story in only eleven beautifully crafted verses. Wow!

This song has endured many translations into many languages, centuries of theological debate, and way too many long-winded sermons, yet is as relevant today as the day it was originally composed. In my opinion this poem, along with 1 Corinthians 13:1–13 and Matthew 5:2–10, are the height of poetic literature in all of human history.

The Christ hymn takes us from the heights of heaven, to the darkness of crucifixion, and then back to even greater heights. It encapsulates the greatest act of injustice in all of human history and then triumphs with the greatest act of righteousness. In the end the cavalry arrives, the good guys win, and the hero gets his bride. It is a sweeping and heroic love story, in a beautiful poem, and it's still a whole lot shorter than *Beowulf* and much easier to read!

I will simply present the song below, taking the liberty to lay it out in the stanzas I see in it. I know you have probably read it before, perhaps dozens of times. Read it once again.

The Christ Hymn

Therefore if there is any encouragement in Christ,
If there is any consolation of love,
If there is any fellowship of the Spirit,
If any affection and compassion,

Make my joy complete by . . .

Being of the same mind,
Maintaining the same love,
United in spirit,
Intent on one purpose.

Do nothing from selfishness or empty conceit,
But with humility of mind regard one another
as more important than yourselves;
Do not merely look out for your own personal interests,
But also for the interests of others.

Have this attitude in yourselves which was also in Christ Jesus,

Who, although He existed in the form of God,
Did not regard equality with God a thing to be grasped,
But emptied Himself, taking the form of a bond-servant,
And being made in the likeness of men.

Being found in appearance as a man,
He humbled Himself
By becoming obedient to the point of death,
Even death on a cross.

For this reason also, God highly exalted Him,
And bestowed on Him the name which is above every name,
So that at the name of Jesus every knee will bow,
Of those who are in heaven and
on earth and under the earth,

And that every tongue will confess that Jesus Christ is Lord,
To the glory of God the Father.

We have a lot of good things to hold on to in Christ—real things with eternal value. This hymn identifies some of them—encouragement, love, fellowship, affection, and compassion. We have been given so much.

The first sentence has implied privilege in it and could easily be translated, "since there is encouragement in Christ . . . consolation of love . . . fellowship of the Spirit . . . affection . . . compassion." These things just are. They are real for those in Christ, and since they are real, we have a responsibility based on these privileges. We are to be of the same mind, continue in love, united in God's Spirit, and intent on one purpose.

Often we go through life unaware of the great riches that are available to us. The Spirit of God brings to us love, encouragement, fellowship with one another, and unity.

Many of us have more wealth available to us in Christ than we realize. We live like paupers when we are indeed royalty. Navin Johnson tried to

The Upside-down Kingdom

hold on to the wealth he had but couldn't. We have more wealth than we realize, and yet we do not grasp it. Through God's Spirit we could be enjoying the riches of love, unity, and lives of purpose. The Spirit of God in us is incredible power. Where there is great power, there is great responsibility, so Paul goes on to tell us what is expected of us as a people and he reveals the secret of unlocking that power and finding unity.

The Secret

The next stanza of the song is the secret to the unity that is expected of those blessed with the privilege of the Spirit's riches. There are two verses in the stanza, both made up of parallel lines:

A Do nothing from selfishness or empty conceit,
    B   But with humility of mind regard one another as more important than yourselves;

A Do not merely look out for your own personal interests,
    B   But also for the interests of others.

In these verses we are presented with a choice: selfishness and empty conceit or humility. Those are the options we have—one or the other; there is no middle ground in this. You are either humble or you are selfishly pursuing empty conceit.

Humility is the cure for so much. If the destination you desire is unity, you cannot get there by taking the "unity off-ramp." To get to "Unity-ville," you must take the humility ramp. Humility is the only way to find unity.

Humility is really a core quality of God's kingdom and of organic leadership. The Bible is clear that God loves humility. It says more than once that "God opposes the proud but gives grace to the humble" (see James 4:6; Prov. 3:24). When we function in pride, we are heading down a self-destructive path, and we do not need to worry about Satan; it is God who opposes us!

The solution presented over and over again in the Bible is to humble yourself so God can exalt you. That is the overriding message of this entire song, demonstrated through Jesus's example. You have basically two choices: humble yourself and God will exalt you, or exalt yourself and God will humble you. Spelled out like that, clearly I would much rather humble myself than have God do it for me. Likewise, I would much rather allow God to exalt me.

So the choice seems obvious: humble yourself. Ah, but that is not as easy as it sounds. Humility is a hard thing to grasp. It is like a bar of soap in a bathtub. As soon as you think you have it in your fingertips, it slips out and is lost in the murky water again.

The moment you think you are humble—you've lost it. It always strikes me as absurdly humorous that Moses describes himself as the most humble man "on the face of the earth" (Num. 12:3). Sounds proud, doesn't it?

Part of the problem is we have a distorted view of humility. The Philippians passage clears it up nicely for us. We tend to think that humility is thinking poorly of ourselves. So often we put ourselves down in an effort to be more humble, usually a joke at our own expense. You cannot think anything good about yourself and still be humble, right? Well, actually, humility is not about self-assessment. Humility is not inwardly focused. Putting yourself down is false humility. If you are truly humble, you are not obsessed with self.

Rick Warren has said, "Humility is not thinking less of yourself; it is thinking of yourself less." The secret to humility, which is the secret to unity, is to consider others more important than yourself. To be concerned with other people's interests is to be humble. If we would all do this, all our interests would be well cared for.

We strive to be unified, but this is the wrong pursuit. We look for things we share in common. We try to tolerate differences under the banner of unity. When we try to be united, we are just made more aware of our differences. But when we pursue humility—true humility—unity is the natural by-product. We cannot get to unity by chasing after it. The door that leads to unity is humility.

The Greatest Mystery

The Bible is full of unanswered questions and mystery. There are concepts that we can know but never truly understand. How can God be three persons and be one God? How can God be sovereign and men still have free will? I love that there is mystery in the Bible. I am grateful that we can still be learning for the rest of eternity, and I do not feel pressured to try to have a satisfactory explanation for everything.

The one verse in the Bible that leaves me most puzzled, however, is verse 5 in Philippians 2. It says, "Have this attitude in yourselves which was also in Christ Jesus." Why is this such a grand mystery to me? Well, you see, it is connected to the previous verses. The attitude of Christ Jesus is the humility mentioned above. Now, that is where I lose my capacity to understand the immensity of this verse. It is telling me that Jesus has this attitude of thinking of me, and you, as more important than himself. The implications of this are too big to comprehend.

The Creator of the universe, who spoke it into existence and holds it all together with his spoken word, thought of me (the guy who can't even balance his checkbook correctly) as more important than himself! The holy One, who never allowed himself to entertain an impure thought for even a second, thought of me (who has a hard time not thinking impure thoughts for even a single day) as more important than himself! Whoa. See, I cannot fathom this mystery. I know it's true; the evidence is throughout Scripture. I know what he did; I just can't comprehend the "why" behind it. That is what gets me. I know he loves me. I have experienced his love throughout my life, and it has never failed me. I do not question his love for me; I question how he could love me like that.

The reformer Martin Luther agrees with me. He once remarked, "The mystery of Christ, that he sunk himself into our flesh, is beyond all human understanding."

The Humiliation of Christ

In verses 6–8 the song shows us that this unfathomable idea—that Christ thought of each of us as more important than himself—is true.

In every way Jesus is the opposite of Navin Johnson—*the Jerk*. Navin was upwardly mobile until he hit a snag that snapped him back to his poor status. Jesus, on the other hand, was downwardly mobile. This is not a rags to riches and back to rags story like *The Jerk*. No, quite the contrary, this is a riches to rags and back to riches story.

It starts with Jesus taking two big steps down.

Step One: His Incarnation

In the beginning Jesus is equal with God! You can't start from a higher place. "Although He existed in the form of God," the verse says. He begins in heaven on his throne. He is the Creator, God Almighty, the Lord of Hosts. But in heaven, surrounded with the glory of all that it means to be God, he valued you and me more.

It says he "did not regard equality with God a thing to be grasped." Navin Johnson felt his place of wealth and privilege slipping away. His response was to grasp everything within reach—ashtrays, paddleball games, matches, lamps, magazines, and chairs. He held on to everything he could fit in his arms. Not Jesus. Jesus had everything in the palm of his hand and let go just so he could reach out to us.

Insecurity causes us to grasp for things. When we fear we are losing, we grab whatever we can. Usually, the things we grasp are meaningless in the scheme of things. For the person who serves Christ, there is nothing he or she can lose that is of value. The child of God has already received heaven and all it contains, so what else is there to grab?

Security allows us to let go. Jesus was secure in who he is. He was more motivated by his love for others than any selfish ambition to hold on to position and privilege.

He let go and "emptied himself." For centuries theologians have debated over what Jesus emptied himself of. This has so monopolized our discussion of this passage that it is often referred to as "the *kenosis* passage" because *kenosis* is the Greek word for "emptied." How sad it is that we let a theological debate become the focal point of such a beautiful and profound chapter of the Bible. That said, Jesus's emptying himself is a wonderful truth that is hard to forget.

Of course, being God, Jesus cannot possibly empty himself of deity. Most theologians think the best explanation is that he emptied himself of the prerogative to use his divine nature independently. In other words, he was no longer an independent operator but was completely submissive to the Father from that point on, becoming a bond slave.

Now, I do believe that Jesus never did anything unless the Father was telling him to do it. He was constantly hearing from the Holy Spirit and obeyed every leading. I believe he lived as a servant and obeyed the Father completely, and there are some very clear statements in the Gospels to support this, so we do not really need this passage to state this theological truth. The problem with using this passage to teach this truth is that it leaves open the idea that prior to the incarnation, Jesus worked independently of the Father and the Holy Spirit, which is just not sound.

So how do we interpret this passage? Of what did Jesus empty himself? Remember that this is a song. The language is poetic. When it says he "emptied Himself," it is referring to his giving himself completely for others. It is very similar to the language Paul uses later in the same chapter when he says of himself, "even if I am *being poured out* as a

The Upside-down Kingdom

drink offering" (v. 17, emphasis added). Now theologians do not debate what Paul meant by that phrase because it is clearly a poetic way to describe his personal sacrifice. I believe the same is true when it says Jesus "emptied himself."

Jesus, who once was in the form of God, was willing to take the form of a bond servant. He was as much God as he was a bond servant. He was both at the same time. He took on humanity and appeared as a man, not an exceptional man, a man like any other.

I am always awestruck by the incarnation of Jesus. At one moment, he was in the form of God. Then suddenly, by his own choice, he was a fertilized egg in an unwed teenager's womb. He chose to be a developing fetus—for you and me. He didn't enter into the world on clouds with a trail of angels all around. No, he entered through a birth canal like everyone else. It was messy, painful, and not in the most sterile of environments.

The Word of God became flesh—and was unable to communicate except to cry. The Lord of the universe dwelt among us—as an infant totally dependent on his mother for everything. The Omnipotent could now bleed. Others would change his diapers. This was his choice. This is what it means for him to be made "in the likeness of men." This is extreme humility.

Step Two: His Execution

Not only did Jesus appear as a man, he allowed himself to be treated like any other man. As if the humiliation thus far wasn't enough, he would step even lower. The song says, "He humbled Himself." This has got to be the understatement of the universe! As if he hadn't quite fully humbled himself yet, he goes farther down.

He was a bond servant. His will was no longer his own, and his submission took him all the way to death. It says he became "obedient to the point of death." That's pretty extreme obedience! You really can't go any farther than that, can you? Well, actually he did. He didn't just die; he died by the cruelest form of execution ever devised by man. It says he was obedient to death, "even death on a cross."

The passage doesn't even say "the" cross. It wasn't even a special cross, just a typical cross that he died on, because it wasn't the cross that was special; it was the man on it. This particular cross wasn't even meant for him. It wasn't Jesus's cross; it was Barabbas's cross; it was my cross. But for Jesus's work, any cross would do, as long as it was a cross, the less spectacular the better for this humiliation.

Jesus didn't just become a man but a servant of all men. He didn't just die but died in a manner as only the very vilest of criminals would—naked to the world and condemned of what would appear to be the very worst sort of crime. It was very public, painful, and shameful, and he went through it for us.

The Exaltation of Christ

The Bible consistently teaches that when we humble ourselves, God will exalt us. Jesus has led the way for us in this. He humbled himself beyond all reason, and for this he was exalted. It says he was "highly exalted." The literal meaning is "superexalted." Though the extent of his humiliation was extreme, in comparison the extent of his exaltation far exceeded it. He took two big steps down and was raised two bigger steps up.

Step One: Lord over Men

The first step in Jesus's exaltation is to be given "the name which is above every name." He humbled himself to be a servant to all, and as a result he is exalted to be over all. The name of Jesus is exalted.

One of the ways he is exalted higher is that now, post-humiliation, "every knee will bow." Prior to his incarnation and execution, while you could say he was higher than all, the truth is that not all would bow to him. Not so now. There will be a day when every single knee will bow to him "of those who are in heaven and on earth and under the earth." All of his creation will bow to worship him, as it should be. Every angel, every human, every demon, Satan himself will have to bow and acknowledge Jesus.

Step Two: Exalted with God

It is not enough that people's knees bow to worship Jesus, their tongues will worship as well. "Every tongue will confess that Jesus Christ is Lord." They may not like it, but they will confess it. The entire created universe will exalt Jesus as Lord, and God the Father will be glorified.

Below is a diagram of the Philippians passage, showing Christ's humiliation and exaltation. This is a song, and the latter part is an inverted parallel to the first part (a chiasmus).

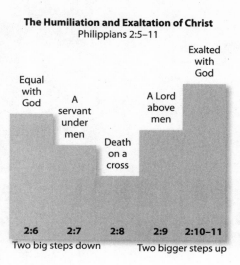

The Humiliation and Exaltation of Christ
Philippians 2:5–11

Equal with God — A servant under men — Death on a cross — A Lord above men — Exalted with God

2:6   2:7   2:8   2:9   2:10–11

Two big steps down   Two bigger steps up

Christ's Example for Leaders

Christ leads the way. It all starts with him. He doesn't ever ask us to do something that he didn't first do himself. He is the ultimate leader who shows us the way by going before us. We learn from Jesus that the way up is first down; ambition should be replaced with humility; a leader seeks to serve first, not to be served.

As we think about organic leadership, the Philippians passage is the foundation of what it means to lead in an upside-down kingdom. It is a pivotal passage on leadership. Of course it is key to everything in Christianity, not just leadership. Why is it so critical? Jesus is showing us how to lead in an upside-down kingdom. He is teaching us how to lead the church to be united and on mission together. It all starts with considering others' needs more important than our own. If Jesus, from his throne in heaven, can think of us as more important than himself, you and I have absolutely no excuse to think less of others. Christian leadership is not about having a more compelling vision and larger-than-life goals, according to this passage. It is a race to empower and exalt as many people above yourself that you can in your short lifetime. That is upside-down leadership, and that is the example Jesus showed us.

14

INCARNATIONAL LEADERSHIP

Christ's Life in You

Christianity is: "the life of God in the soul of man."

Henry Scougal

God became man to turn creatures into sons: not simply to produce better men of the old kind but to produce a new kind of man.

C. S. Lewis

Whom do you take after?"

That was the profound question my mother asked me one night. It led to a conversation that lasted all night and into the morning. From most people, it is not such a profound question, but when it comes from your parent, it becomes interesting.

I grew up in a home that did not have any faith in God. When I was a small boy, a neighborhood friend became a Christian. I distinctly remember my mother pulling me aside and telling me, "Neil, don't you ever become a Jesus freak like Chucky."

So when I became a follower of Christ my freshman year of college, I found it difficult to tell my family, especially my mother. It took me a year to come out and tell the truth. I drove home from college with a stack of books I had never read, each one proposing to defend the rationality of the Christian faith. I placed the stack of books down on the coffee table in the living room in front of both my parents and my uncle and announced, "I have something important to tell you. I have become a Christian, and these books will explain why you should too."

I was surprised to hear my mother say, "Oh, we knew you became a Christian."

I wondered how they knew. Who told them? Could it be that they saw it in me?

My mother wasn't ready to put her faith in Christ at that time, and no amount of books would change that. But she was prepared to continue watching me. And for a few years she watched. She saw me get married. She watched our marriage. She saw me graduate from college and start seminary. It wasn't such a long time that my mother watched me, only a few years really. She would have seen a lot more change in my life if she had lived long enough. But the time she did have, however short it was, was enough for her to see a dramatic difference in me.

I prayed every day for my parents, and it seemed like none of the prayers were getting past the ceiling. My mother was very proud, and I thought that she would be the last person to ever accept Jesus. I remember praying for the Lord to do whatever it took to save her soul. A short time later I learned that she had an advanced form of cancer and had started an aggressive treatment.

One evening after a long day of work, while still in my lifeguard uniform, I stopped by to see my mother before going home. We were talking about my day and her medical treatment when she surprised me with that very straightforward and direct question: "Whom do you take after?"

I said, "Well, you and Dad are the only parents I have ever had, so I guess you both."

She said, "No, you are not like me, and you are nothing like your father. What makes you so different from the way you were brought up?"

"That's Jesus," I replied. "You are seeing Jesus in my life. That's the only explanation."

Then she said, "Tell me about him."

We had a long talk about who Jesus truly is and what the gospel is all about. Before I knew it, the sun was rising. We had talked all through the night. Within a few weeks she had become a follower of Christ.

At one point, close to her death, she sat up in bed and with perfect clarity said good-bye to the whole family. She asked me to read the last chapter of the Bible. She said, "I don't have time to read the whole thing so I just want to hear if it has a good ending." She also wanted the rest of the family to hear the ending as well and to know that her newfound faith was real. I read the last chapter, and she lay back down, behind the dark curtains of the painkillers.

A short time later my mother died. My father has yet to accept Christ. I think he has been watching less than she did.

Struggling with Identity Issues

What do you want people to notice about you? When you enter a place full of people you do not know, what are the traits you want them to notice first so they will like you?

I have been in circumstances when I wanted to impress people. I am sure you have as well. At those times I am amazed at what I put forward as my identity: I am a former athlete. I used to be a lifeguard. I drive a nice car. I have artistic skills. I associate with some cool people. I can be funny in front of a crowd. I am a church planter. I started a business. I am a homeowner. I am an author. I am Dana's husband. I have three beautiful kids that have grown up to love and serve Jesus. My dad is a successful artist. My uncle is a legendary big wave pioneer. I am a Lakers fan.

All of these things are true, and none of them are the best thing about me. These are not my identity; they are facts about who I am but they are not who I am.

Have you ever tried to tell people who you are without telling them what you do, whom you are related to, or what things you like or dislike? It is not so easy. We are, unfortunately, too far removed from our true identity. Like superheroes we keep our true identity secret and go through life with masks on the outside hiding our real self. We cover our souls with bumper stickers that cannot possibly convey who we really are.

Strip away the veneer and reveal the real deal. The real you is who you are when no one's looking. Who you are is truly more important than what you do. Life is designed to strip away all the masks and bring out the true you hidden inside, the you that Jesus has redeemed —*the new you*! I like what Ralph Waldo Emerson once said, "What lies behind us and what lies before us are tiny matters compared to what lies within us."

Marriage is a part of that revealing process. Courting is not—it is about the bumper stickers and the veneer. When we date, we put on our best face. We are cleaner, smell prettier, and act more chivalrous. This is not real.

Most people go into marriage fully deceived, but of course that is part of life. It doesn't really matter, because one of the purposes of marriage is to strip away the veneer. We cannot avoid the surprise no matter how transparent we may have been in the courting relationship. Marriage is such that through the years you will both be peeling away the shallow image to discover the real person underneath it all. Hopefully, you will like what you find.

Spiritual maturity comes when you are willing to strip away the outer shell and allow the redeemed identity of Christ in you to be seen. When we see the value of the stripping process and begin to cooperate with it, we are realizing the necessity of revealing the real person inside. Then we are prepared to help others through their stripping process as well.

Some people have a Christian identity on the outside but not on the inside, which leads to a tragic end. The truth is you have to choose between your true identity and the shallow one you show others. You cannot be two people at once. Either you hold on to the lesser self or you abandon it and allow your real self—the new you—to be revealed.

The Spirit of Christ

In the last chapter we looked at the humility and exaltation of Christ. As I mentioned, most biblical scholars believe that the passage we examined is a poem or hymn about Christ. After the hymn it may appear that Paul begins some random discussion about people and circumstances relevant to Paul's current circumstances and the Philippian church. But the message about humility continues; it doesn't end in verse 11.

The Spirit of Christ discussed in verses 1–11 is displayed vibrantly in the examples Paul uses in the rest of the chapter. Often in his descriptions he employs the same or similar language as he did to describe Christ.

The Spirit of Christ is incarnate in other leaders.

In Paul

The Spirit of Christ is seen in Paul (Phil. 2:17–18). In verses 6–8 the Spirit of Christ is described: "[He] did not regard equality with God a thing to be grasped, but emptied Himself, taking the form of a bond-servant, and being made in the likeness of men. Being found in appearance as a man, He humbled Himself by becoming obedient to the point of death." This same Spirit is seen in Paul when it says, "Even if I am being poured out as a drink offering upon the sacrifice and service of your faith, I rejoice" (v. 17).

Jesus emptied himself in the service of others to the point of death. Paul poured himself out in service to others even to the point of death. Jesus's Spirit lives in Paul.

In Timothy

The Spirit of Christ is seen in Timothy (Phil. 2:19–24). When the Spirit of Christ is in us, we are to be "united in spirit, intent on one purpose" (v. 2). You are not to just "look out for your own personal interests, but also for the interests of others" (v. 4). This same Spirit is seen later in Timothy. Paul describes him as one who stands alone as a "kindred spirit who will genuinely be concerned for your welfare" (v. 20). This contrasts with others: "For they all seek after their own interests" (v. 21).

It is the Spirit of Christ that makes us all one body with one spirit, looking out for each other's interests. Christ's Spirit lives in Timothy. He is a leader who incarnates Christ's attitude for others to follow.

In Epaphroditus

The Spirit of Christ is seen in Epaphroditus (Phil. 2:25–30). Christ was obedient in his service to others "to the point of death, even death on a cross" (v. 8). Epaphroditus, sent by the Philippians to serve Paul, was obedient to his charge . . . also to "the point of death" (v. 27). Christ showed us what it means to be a servant who is obedient to the extreme of death. In serving the Philippian church and the apostle Paul, Epaphroditus was willing to serve even when he was so sick he nearly died.

Paul, writing to the Philippians, wants to be sure they understand what Epaphroditus did. He was one of them, and they may not have recognized in him the Spirit that motivated him. Paul uses the same words—"to the point of death"—to describe Epaphroditus's sacrifice as he used above for Jesus. He too is an example of a leader with Christ incarnationally living through him for others to see and follow.

In You

Is the Spirit of Christ evident in you? Are you living in such a way that others see Christ in you and ask, "Where does that come from?" Are you willing to cooperate with the stripping away of the outer veneer of lesser identities so that Christ can shine more obviously through you? Here are some important questions to ponder.

1. When will Christ be enough?
2. What will it take for the Spirit of Christ to be the most noticeable thing about you?
3. How can you cooperate with the Spirit's stripping process?
4. In light of Philippians 2, what will you begin to look for in the people around you, and how will this affect the way you respond to them?

Ray's Story

All young men have an internal need to have a father who will teach them how to be a man. This unconscious and internal drive pushed me around for a few years, as I searched for a mentor who would love me and show me what being a man and a husband and a father is really all about. My own father taught me how to be an artist and gave me a love for the ocean, but he was not equipped to teach me how to be a godly man. My search ended when I married Dana and was "accepted" into her family. Her father, Ray Walker, was a real man. He was a cop for thirty years on the streets of LA. He worked as a detective in all sorts of neighborhoods and divisions. But he wasn't just a tough guy, he was a godly man who had a great sense of humor and loved everyone he was around. His job was not his master and he could leave his work at the office. When he came home, he was a dad and a husband, not a cop.

Of course, at first, it is intimidating to date a girl whose father carries a sidearm and can open your files and investigate all your records at any time. As I got to know Ray, however, I found him anything but intimidating. He was a very vulnerable and accessible person. I learned what the term *gentleman* means by watching Ray. He was all man and yet always gentle.

He became the godly father I needed, and in a sense I became the son he never had (he had three beautiful daughters). We would tell each other everything and had no secrets between us.

We loved being together. We would watch movies or the big game on TV. It didn't much matter. We would have fun no matter what we were doing. We were not just family; we were best friends.

Ray was best known for generosity and a friendly personality and would come up with a corny joke for any occasion. Too many times to count he covered my needs financially in our young marriage. Sometimes, while trying to support a family of five with several part-time jobs, we would be hungry, and we always had a good meal when we were with Ray. For more than a decade I didn't have to buy a car because he would always give me his old car when he bought a new one, and he always took immaculate care of his cars! They would run for years. Even now my oldest daughter drives one of his old cars.

A few years ago Ray started forgetting things. Small things forgotten turned into big things misplaced, and eventually he was diagnosed with dementia, probably from early onset Alzheimer's disease. He became confused and unsure of who family members were.

Caring for someone like this is not easy. Dana and I took him into our home for periods of time to relieve June, his wife. This was both the hardest and easiest decision we ever had to make. Dana had to stop working, which set us back financially, but this was not a concern.

We looked after Ray. I shaved him, bathed him, dressed him, and cleaned up after him. He was a constant companion, but this was not a burden. It is hard to explain, but I loved the man so much that this was not hard at all to do. In fact I would rather have him in this condition than be without him at all.

So many times I prayed for his healing. At one time he even seemed healed for a moment and then faded back into the gray cloud of the disease. I couldn't understand why God would allow such a good man to suffer such a horrible disease. I still do not have an answer, but I can say that God showed us all something beautiful in this ordeal.

It may sound strange, but watching this godly man live through this horrible disease raised my respect for him, not the other way around. Some people say that when a person suffers from Alzheimer's, the personality changes, and the victim can become an angry and hurtful person. That was not the case for Ray. He never stopped exhibiting the things that I loved about him.

Whenever we were out and a waiter would present the check, Ray would instinctively reach for his back pocket and say, "I've got this." Of course he hadn't had a wallet in a long time but he still had his generosity. It was a great honor to buy his meals after all the times he bought mine.

When we were out, he had a smile and a kind nod for everyone. He would search for a joke that was no longer in his files, but I could tell he still had his sense of joy.

The strangest thing for me was when Ray came with me to our organic-church family. He couldn't remember people's names but he knew the words to the songs and sang them as well as ever. When he prayed, his prayers were articulate and clear. Many times I had to raise my head and open my eyes to see if it was really Ray praying. I realized that the disease could take his mind but not his soul or the Spirit of Christ in him.

Dementia strips away your identity. All the stuff you used to know and things you used to take for granted are violently ripped away. Your mind, your memories, and your sense of identity are all taken from you. But your soul, your true self, is not taken from you. Jesus remained with Ray from start to finish.

I stayed beside Ray until the end. On his last night I stayed by my friend's bed, praying and thanking God for his life while he labored to breathe. His own body was forgetting how to work as the disease spread through his mind with a seemingly unending appetite.

Finally, in a holy moment, I put my hand on his arm one last time, turned to heaven and said, "Lord, take my friend home." In that very moment, Ray released his last breath and his soul left his body. I felt privileged to have been in the room when his mind went from a dark cloud of nothing to fully knowing, just as he is "fully known" (see 1 Cor. 13:13). I looked up and said out loud, "Bye, Ray. I love you."

When Ray's mind was as sharp as a tack, I saw so much godliness in him. It was always evident as we laughed together and walked through life together. Alzheimer's is a horrible disease, but I saw Jesus in Ray throughout. I saw a man walk with God through the darkest night of the soul and emerge victorious. I only hope that I can live my life with the same joy, generosity, and dogged faith that Ray had. He was Christ incarnate for me, even in the midst of serious dementia.

The Bottom Line

You may be inclined to say, "This is not about leadership. This is just about godliness, about being a good follower of Jesus. Everyone should be this way." Exactly. That is the point, friend.

What would the world be like if all followers of Christ lived like this? We tend to think we need leaders who serve, but really we need servants who lead. Servanthood is not an adjective to describe a good leader, as if it is one of many qualities of a good leader. Servanthood is what we need, even more than leadership. Leadership is just a function for the servant. A servant leads others in the path of being a servant, and that is what the church truly needs if we are to change the world for the better. And that pretty much describes Jesus and therefore should describe those who live with the Spirit of Jesus incarnate in their lives.

We don't first find leaders and hope they take on the qualities of a servant. We need to find servants and let them be just that. Servanthood is not the path to leadership; it *is* the leadership that the kingdom requires. Jesus was clear that those who want to be first will be a servant to all, *not a leader to all*. If we had a lot more servants and a lot fewer leaders, we would be much better off. And if we had enough servants, we wouldn't really be lacking in leaders at all.

If we all lived like Jesus, leadership would not be an issue, because it would be a *by-product*! Leadership, or should I say godly influence, would also be prevalent, saturate the world, and bring transformation to our neighborhoods and nations from the inside out. No one would need to know who is in charge. We wouldn't need to fight over who is on top. We wouldn't be competing for influence or audience. And it wouldn't matter if we have position, title, or a fancy business card. To influence, all we need is the Spirit of Christ in us. That, my friend, is the point.

We are the body of Christ. Christ lives in us. You are Christ's hands and feet to reach out in love to this world. This is what much of the world wants to see; they are dying to see it.

Whom do you take after?

SECTION FOUR

THE SIDE-BY-SIDE KINGDOM

Recipes for Homegrown Leadership

All of us are growing in the garden of God's kingdom. We are not the farmers; we are the produce just as much as the person next to us is. If you are removed from the garden and not growing, you are in a precarious place.

Mentoring of others is not a top-down proposition but a side-by-side proposition. In this section we will examine some useful ideas for coming alongside others in a mentoring relationship to help the emerging leaders grow and bear fruit.

First, we will look at the fact that knowledge alone is insufficient to develop leaders. We will examine principles of holistic leadership formation as well as an alternative theological learning system.

You will learn two simple skills that will enable you to lead leaders successfully, and there is a chapter that spells out some helpful ways to mentor people as you walk beside them in life.

This is very practical material that can be used in a natural leadership relationship. And they are proven ideas, learned in the hard-fought battle for the development of the next generation of leaders.

15

KNOWLEDGE IS NOT POWER

Holistic Leadership Development and Theological Education

Who dares to teach must never cease to learn.

John Cotton Dana

The realm of God is dangerous. You must enter into it and not just seek information about it.

Archbishop Anthony Bloom

Morpheus should be dead, but instead Neo and Trinity did what no one has ever done before, they intentionally attacked three agents to rescue their leader. Armed to the hilt, they walked straight into a veritable fortress. After gun battles, explosions, and helicopter crashes, they managed to rescue their friend.

The Matrix is a futuristic science fiction movie that carries several gospel narratives within it. For instance, Morpheus plays a John the Baptist type of character who was prophesied to discover the messianic "One" who would come and set the captives free. There is a Judas character who betrays them all and dies. Demonic "agents" possess people to get their evil agenda accomplished. There is a messianic character who has miraculous power, dies, and rises from the dead to overcome the demonic agents.

From the start, Morpheus felt certain that Neo was the One, the prophesied savior who was to come. Even his name, Neo, is a rearrangement of the letters in One. What he didn't know was that the prophet known as the Oracle, who foretold the coming, had already informed Neo that he wasn't the promised One.

After Neo accomplishes an impossible mission, Morpheus has a see-I-told-you-so look on his face as he turns to Trinity and confirms that Neo is the One. Neo decides it's time to let Morpheus down and explain that the Oracle told him that he isn't the One.

Undeterred, Morpheus explains, "She told you exactly what you needed to hear." Then he adds this piece of wisdom: "Neo, sooner or later you are going to realize just as I did—there is a difference between knowing the path and walking the path."

Educated beyond Obedience

Many of us in the Christian church today need to hear that there is a difference between knowing the path and walking in it. We are very adept at knowing the path, just not so strong at walking it. Most Christians in the West are educated beyond their obedience. More education is not what we need. We need more obedience to what we already know.

The problem is that we have convinced ourselves that knowledge is the key to maturity and growth. We seem to live by the credo: the more we know, the more mature we become. This is not true. Even as you may read the sentence, you probably realized it isn't true; nevertheless, our behavior clearly indicates that we have bought into the assumption.

We are far more influenced by our modernistic society than we care to admit. It is commonly espoused that knowledge is power and that education is the key to overcoming all sorts of evils. The church has bought into this ideology, hook, line, and sinker. But knowledge is not the same as power. Education is not the whole solution to life's woes. Knowing something is not nearly as potent as doing something with what you know.

James warns us clearly about being hearers of the word who are not doers. Those who are hearers only, he says, delude themselves (James 1:21–23). I believe this is a more serious problem than any of us have realized. We are deluded into thinking we are better off than we really are.

When it comes to evaluating leaders, what is it that we are to measure? Is sound doctrine sufficient? From the way most leaders are groomed, evaluated, and selected in the church today, correct doctrine and the ability to communicate it appear to be the dominant measures of a leader.

Sound Doctrine

Paul writes in Titus 2 what he sees as sound doctrine. I would imagine any theologian would be interested in what the great apostle Paul views as sound doctrine. The list is as provocative for what it doesn't include as the things it does have in it. There is no mention of eschatology or the trinitarian doctrine. Instead, the passage on sound doctrine is all about relational character lived out in real life.

There is a problem when we define our fellowship by the subtleties of our doctrines. Then we are forced to decide what we believe on a variety of theological issues and develop a creed or statement of faith by which we determine with whom we will or won't work. We place on this theological banqueting table our best theological assumptions, but also our less certain ones. Unfortunately, all the entrées are treated with the same certainty and given the same authority, so minor doctrines carry the same weight as the major ones. Our view of speaking in tongues is as authoritative as the deity of Christ. Our view of the timing of certain end times events carries the same weight as the inspiration of Scriptures.

When this occurs, the worst thing is not the elevated importance of lesser doctrines, but the diluting of the more important ones. In either case, we have problems.

The Bullet Test

Church Multiplication Associates (CMA), the organization I helped to found, is a diverse movement that has a variety of expressions of Christ's body within it. One of the ways we determine those we will work alongside is the "bullet test." It works like this: Imagine someone put a gun to your head and said, "Renounce this doctrine, or I will shoot you!" If you say, "Go ahead; pull the trigger. I will not renounce this doctrine!" it is a "bullet doctrine"—worthy of taking a bullet.

Now this is a very subjective test, but it is surprisingly useful nonetheless. Of course, there may be some fanatics who would die for their view of when the rapture is to come, but most levelheaded people would not. The threat of death is a surprisingly good way to evaluate devotion.

We work alongside those who share the same bullet doctrines that we do and don't worry about the non-bullet doctrines they may hold, even rejoicing in the diversity of viewpoints on the lesser issues. I know there are many in Christendom who could not function with this sort of organization. I am simply describing our mind-set concerning doctrine. We realize that the bullet test is not a definitive, absolute measure, but it helps people prioritize what they value for the purpose of joining together.

When the Moravian Church came together in Hernhutt under the hospitality and growing influence of Nikolaus Ludwig von Zinzendorf, they were fractured and paralyzed by several competing doctrines. It was the special filling of the Holy Spirit, much like the day of Pentecost, that changed everything and unleashed something that would change the world. Love prevailed among them from that moment on. They developed a motto that continues to this day: "In essentials, unity; in nonessentials, liberty; and in all things, love." This began a movement that eventually ushered in modern world missions. The Moravians sent out hundreds of church-planting missionaries all over the world. At one point they had two people in the field for every one at home. And those who remained at home were not idle. From there, prayer continued twenty-four hours a day, seven days a week, for an entire century!

CMA, at its core, hopes to be a movement that follows this example. We unite on the essentials, grant freedom on the nonessentials, and desire to be controlled by our love for Jesus and one another in everything.

Rediscovering the Mystery in Theology

The thing that alarms me most is how confident we are about the things we know, when, in fact, what we think we know is often pure conjecture. There are some things we cannot know for certain, yet we treat them with the same absolute authority as doctrines that are indeed sure. Based on some of these less-than-sure doctrines, we identify those with whom we are able to be joined together.

Perhaps the doctrinal area that causes the most problems is that of eschatology, or the doctrine of last things. Many denominations do not work together simply because they land on different sides of this doctrine. Pastors are evaluated for candidacy based on what scheme for the end times they believe is true.

The denomination I'm associated with (Grace Brethren) has two statements about end times in its statement of faith, thus effectively disqualifying some from leadership if they lean in another direction. This is interesting because the denomination is older than the system of theology it espouses, meaning that we were born and existed as a movement for a century without these statements. Now we need them to discern who is in and who is out.

When I teach on end times I have an exercise I use in the beginning just to help all see the speculative nature of such things. I put up on the screen lists of the ingredients to three very different candies available at every market in America. The first list I show is the major ingredients. And I ask people what the candies are. Usually some of the guesses are close and some are not. I then put the names of the candies up on the screen next to the lists—Peanut M&M's, Snickers Bar, and Reese's Peanut Butter Cup. We all know how different these three candies are. One is hard and melts in your mouth but not in your hands, the other two will melt all over your hands. One is a candy bar, another is a small bite-sized hard candy suitable for a candy dish, while the other is a soft chocolate cup filled with sweet peanut butter. The expression of these similar ingredients is very different in the end product.

I ask the audience to match ingredients with the candy and usually that is difficult. Finally, I list the fuller ingredients and eventually some are able to figure out the candies, usually by the process of elimination.

My point is that all of us have the same list of ingredients, and we are all struggling to figure out what the end will taste like. You can't really know what it will taste like just reading a list of ingredients. There is a difference between knowing the path and walking the path. This exercise helps people to understand that this is conjecture and speculation. Some may be closer to the final makeup of the events that culminate all things, but none will actually know what it will truly taste like.

I am a firm believer that everyone will be surprised in the end, for better or worse. I will say this: if you are not comfortable with mystery, the New Testament is hostile territory for you. The plain truth is that our God has not given us all the facts about everything. He leaves much room for our God-given imaginations and the joy of discovery. God loves mystery, and so should you if you really want to be a sound theologian.

It is not bad or wrong to explore and even speculate about things. It is a good exercise to try to piece it all together. Jesus affirms that we should be able to discern the signs of the times (Matt. 16:2–3; 24:32–44). That is not the issue. The problem is that we isolate parts of Christ's body over the ways we construct the recipe, without ever having baked the cake. I am in favor of theorizing and investigating these ideas, just not of judging others based on whether they share our viewpoint.

I am bored with theologians who think they have an answer for all the questions of divinity. I find theologians who live with unanswered questions far more interesting. I fear that some theological systems are so "sound," with categories and boxes for everything, that they simply cannot be true. Faith is not merely an intellectual exercise; it is a journey through new uncharted waters full of unexpected surprises and unexplained mysteries. In fact, "faith" and "facts" are really at odds with one another. If you know something, it is no longer faith; it is now a fact. Faith requires, at its core, unanswered questions. Some of the theological systems that men have forged are more like a logical workout than a mysterious journey.

When two people in suits come to my door with logical answers about every theological subject, I not only find them boring, but I know they are false prophets. If you can explain all there is to know about God, then your god is too small for me. I want a God who is bigger than my 5.5″ × 6.5″ cranium.

One day Augustine was walking along the shore of the Mediterranean, contemplating the triune nature of God. He happened on a small boy who had dug a hole and was running back and forth from the ocean collecting water and then pouring it into the hole. Augustine asked what he was doing. The boy said, "I'm putting the ocean in this hole." Augustine realized that trying to understand God entirely was as ridiculous a proposition as filling a small hole with an entire ocean.

Philipp Melanchthon, the theologian who worked alongside Luther during the Reformation, once said, "It is better to worship the great Divine than to explain him."

Qualifications of an Elder

Theology is a noble endeavor to pursue, but it is not enough to make you a good leader. When Paul lists the qualities to look for in a leader, sound doctrinal positions are not listed. They are all about character.

Why have we made such an issue of people's doctrinal stance on both the minors and the majors, when the Bible does not? Sure, the Bible clearly rejects false teachers, but these are not people who have subtle differences while believing basically the same thing on major issues. The way we have been trained to think is that heresy will run rampant if we do not make sure our leaders are all in a line on their doctrines.

Often I ask a group if they personally know anyone who has started a cult. On a rare occasion one person may raise his or her hand. Then I ask if they know of any leaders who have fallen into immorality, and almost every hand in the room goes up. I comment, "I don't think heresy is really our biggest problem."

First Timothy 3 and Titus 2 contain descriptions of those we would want to emulate in our pursuit of Christ. Character is the issue we should be most concerned with, not theological positions on minor issues. But in my opinion, to treat these passages like checklists for pastors or elders is a mistake. Most of us have used these lists as if there is a ceiling of maturity that some people will break through to become elders.

If we follow the lists consistently, no one who is married without children can be a pastor. And even those who have children must have grown children who all walk with Jesus. If one of your kids doubts for a season, no matter how short, you are suddenly no longer qualified to be a leader. But if the child reawakens to his or her faith, you are suddenly qualified again. This is not a good understanding of the passage.

Rather than seeing these passages as leadership requirement checklists, I suggest we view them as ideals we all pursue, and those who are farther along can lead us in that direction. To treat the passages otherwise can lead us to being guilty of some rather peculiar abuses.

Because the lists are all about character, when we treat them as checklists of qualifications for leadership, unintentionally we release those who are not leaders from very basic character formation. Paul is not teaching this and it is directly against Jesus's instructions. Just because you are not an elder, you are not allowed to have several wives, get drunk, and beat up your boss at work. It is painfully obvious in the New Testament that Christ is calling all of us who follow him to a life of godly character epitomized by these descriptions in 1 Timothy and Titus.

Perhaps we should look at these passages in a new light. Can I suggest the following paraphrase of 1 Timothy 3:1? "If anyone strives to find a mentor, it is a good thing he seeks. Here are the qualities to look for in someone you should follow." The word *office* is supplied in the text by the translators of certain translations. When someone is longing for a mentor, the qualities they should search for and emulate are in this passage.

Holistic Leadership Development

So when it comes to measuring an emerging leader, what should we look at? I believe that we are to grow organically as whole people. God has made us with a mind, a will, and a body. When God develops a leader organically, he develops the whole person, not merely his or her knowledge. We must grow in cognitive development (our knowing), character formation (our being), and skill levels (our doing).

On Being

When it comes to spiritual leadership, your character is the most essential garden to find growth and fruit. As I have already stated, from this garden all else is determined. A leader can know all the right doctrines and have all the right skills but without character this leader is not fit for duty.

We are too enamored with spiritual gifts and not serious enough about the fruit of the Spirit. In the New Testament wherever there are lists of spiritual gifts, you will find that love is accentuated as the most important thing. It is "a still more excellent way" (1 Cor. 12:31). We should look for fruit more than for ministry gifts in our leaders' lives.

Recently a leader of a fast-growing church in my area decided to leave his wife for another woman, believing that with this new woman's support he could do even greater things for the Lord. This is deluded thinking. He has skills and knows his doctrines well but he is not fit to lead a church.

Developing character in another person, however, is a tricky and perilous journey. We can have a set list of basic Bible knowledge and systematic doctrines to teach. We can measure the knowledge with an exam. In a similar way we can have a list of skills and check them off as the emerging leader demonstrates competency in each area, ultimately developing an arsenal of skills. But how do we teach and measure character?

We cannot develop a list of character qualities and check them off as the leader demonstrates them. We may be tempted to do this, but try it. Humility should be on the list. When you see the leader exhibit humility should you check it off as mission accomplished? Of course not. The moment you check it off, you will have to put it back on the list because the candidate will suddenly be infused with pride over having accomplished such a monumental feat.

Many seminaries have realized that knowledge is not enough, so they have taken a more holistic approach to training leaders that involves character and skills as well. Often this will require a practical internship in a church ministry added to their curriculum. The problem is that you cannot teach character by reading a book or taking a class. Character is learned in the crucible of life experience. Students can be taught about character but not given character. Actually, the challenge of paying for the education and persevering in the challenges of the program do more to produce character than the classes or textbooks do.

Character is not something we can teach. Only God builds character in our lives. We can't even produce character in our own lives without God doing the work. As mentors we can teach about character, but we cannot produce it. This is a very frustrating truth for a whole lot of leaders who wish they could produce godliness in people.

As we have already seen in chapter 9, God produces character in us and uses difficult challenges and trials to do so. So what difference can a mentor make when it comes to helping someone in character formation? A mentor can be a mirror and a model to the emerging leader. As a mirror, the mentor can show the apprentice what the mentor is seeing—the good and the bad. Through his or her own character, the mentor can be a model for the emerging leader to follow.

A mentor can teach what the Bible says about choices and present examples of those who have gone before but cannot make the choices for the student. A mentor can teach a person how to hear God's voice and why it is important to follow that voice but cannot choose to follow for them. A mentor can teach the consequences of living a life in disobedience but cannot make the student choose obedience. Character can be learned only as we walk through real-life experiences with our heavenly Father. This is an intimate spiritual experience with which no one can interfere.

On Doing

Skill development is a crucial part of mentoring leaders. In the past this was greatly underestimated. Often leaders would be full of unapplied knowledge and sent out to lead churches without any skill training whatsoever. It was like sending soldiers off to fight with high-powered rifles but no bullets.

Skills must be paired with experience; in fact, they cannot be truly learned any other way. We can teach people practices and methods in a classroom (or even in a book such as this), but in essence we are only teaching people *about* skills. People can truly learn a skill only when it is in a context where they can put it into practice.

We are all bound by our own cultural setting and time in which we live. Skills that work in one setting will not necessarily work in another. Skills that were employed effectively a century ago will not work today. Because our culture is always changing, and changing faster than ever before, it is essential that we are all learning new skills all the time.

We will explore skill training in greater detail in chapters 16 and 17.

On Knowing

The goal of mentoring is not teaching people what to think but how to think. Like the old proverb says, if you give a man a fish, you'll feed him for a day, but if you teach a man to fish, you will feed him for a lifetime. So the goal of mentoring when it concerns cognitive learning is instilling in people a hunger for learning and then teaching them how to discover good information.

There are some other principles needed in this arena, though. We must get better at not educating people beyond their obedience. The way we pour on the teaching without any regard for practice is atrocious. We simply do not understand the damage this causes in our disciples and emerging leaders. We actually teach people in a subtle yet very tangible way that obedience is not necessary; simply knowing the truth is enough. We are, in effect, training people not to take God's truth seriously or personally.

I know that many teachers are concerned with practical application. In lots of cases very solid ideas are taught to help people think through the application of truth. But mentoring must go farther. We must withhold the next lesson until the first one is fully practiced, so that we are building the learning on obedience rather than simply on knowledge. This may be scary, but it will produce far better leaders in the end.

There was a young pastor in Argentina who preached a message in his church. The next week he came to church and preached the very same message again. People thought it strange but they were patient with their new pastor. The following week came and they were ready to hear something new, but he taught them the very same lesson again. Now the people were starting to get concerned, but they gave him another week. Sure enough, the following week he preached the very same sermon yet again. So the deacons came up to him afterward and asked him why he was preaching the same lesson over and over again. He answered, "I will not teach a second lesson until the first one is done."[1]

This is a good practice. It's hard to do, but if we were to do it, our people would be stronger. Never teach a second lesson until the first one is done. I would like to add to this that a lesson is never truly learned until it is passed on to another. Many of us have discovered that we learn more when we teach than when someone teaches us. We should employ this learning method much more intentionally.

TruthQuest: An Alternative Theological Learning System

If after reading this chapter you are tempted to think that I do not view theological education as valuable, you have judged prematurely and inaccurately.

Learning should be a lifelong adventure, a quest. Only fools say they have learned all that is important and have nothing more to learn. You do not graduate from this quest until there is a flat line on the monitor next to your hospital bed. Until then we should all be endeavoring to learn more. God and his Word are infinite and our journey for understanding will never be satisfied this side of heaven.

A New Method

We need new methods of training men and women to serve as leaders in the church in this new millennium. In both the past and present, unpaid missionaries, who do not have a seminary education, have fueled the great movements of God. With this in mind, CMAResources has devised a new system that we call TruthQuest, which can equip a man or woman in basic theological understanding in a year's time and in such a way that he or she can reproduce this method by training others in the same way. It is cost effective and practical to real life. Best of all, it can actually increase the learning of the participants because it is *learning based* rather than *knowledge based, curriculum driven,* or *teacher centered*. This is a whole new way of training people in theology and it could revolutionize church leadership for the coming century.

How It Works

In this new training system the learners are brought together into a once-a-month gathering of no more than eight people and no fewer than five to study theology. On a Saturday or Sunday of each month the people gather and study for approximately eight hours with a couple of breaks. These meetings will last for less than a year.

Theological education in TruthQuest is approached with what is termed as an "incarnational" model of learning. Truth must be "fleshed out" in real-life experience or the educational process has failed. In TruthQuest all theology is examined through a grid of questions for life application, all related to the DNA of God's kingdom life.

Prior to the gathering, each learner will have studied four points of a particular doctrine selected that month. The learners will utilize the Scriptures as well as two textbooks from two different theological points of view (all from an evangelical tradition—i.e., Reformed, dispensational, Wesleyan, and charismatic) to study the doctrine.

Each learner is to complete all the explanations derived from his or her own study for each of the doctrines and come to the gathering prepared to share his or her answers, as well as giving examples that illustrate the truth in real life. In essence each student comes prepared to teach the whole class each doctrine. In the gatherings the learners are called on at random to teach a particular doctrine as it relates to one of eight segments of practical life application. After the learner has finished his or her lesson, the facilitator opens up discussion with the rest of the gathering by first asking if the presenter missed any important facet of the doctrine or if the others would like to challenge the presenter's lesson in any way. Finally, if something goes unsaid or if an unsound theology emerges in the discussion, the facilitator may at that point interject his or her own point of view. Prior to this, the facilitator will lead only by asking questions of the participants.

Some "Brain Bruiser Discussion Questions" are included in each section of the facilitator guide to help stimulate discussion if the learners themselves seem to have stalled. Answers, however, are not supplied. This is to generate discussion. There may or may not be good answers to the questions.

TruthQuest is a *community-based* theological discovery system. The journey is not made alone. In a roundtable format, the truth of God's Word is tested and internalized through the process of discussion, probing, and even debate with a team of peers. This Socratic approach instills a deeper level of learning because it is not merely memorizing facts for a test; it is holding the learned principles up in the crucible of debate and mutual experience and as they relate to the learners' personal lives.

Both the TruthQuest participants' workbook and the facilitator's guide are available at our website: www.cmaresources.org.

On Graduation

I had a seminary professor who once told us the story of a student who made this bold proclamation: "I'm going to finish my education and then I will get married." My seasoned professor wisely commented: "There are two things wrong with this statement: One, marriage is an education; and two, we are never finished with our education."

Leadership development is a lifelong process.

16
THE SECRET TO LEADING LEADERS

Following a Middle School Master

The wise old owl lived in an oak;
The more he saw the less he spoke;
The less he spoke the more he heard:
Why can't we all be like that bird?

Edward H. Richards

Probably my best quality as a coach is that I ask a lot of challenging questions and let the person come up with the answer.

Phil Dixon

Sitting across from me was a man who seemed larger than life. He was a big guy, but there was more than his physical stature. He was somehow tougher than most guys. And he'd lived life to the max. He had the scars to prove it.

His name was Bob. Just Bob. I remember thinking it was sort of an ordinary name for a guy who had done so much.

I was just into my second year as a pastor, fresh out of seminary when we met. He was older than I was, but a brand-new Christian.

He was eager to change the world and just glad that someone would take the time to meet with him. We had lunch at a local hole-in-the-wall diner.

Bob told me his story, and it was a story! He was never the sort of guy who did anything halfway. He was one of those all-in or all-out sort of guys. While a radical youth running with the wrong crowd, he decided to enroll in the army to get straightened out. He went to Vietnam as a Special Forces soldier. Trained to kill, he used his training, saw lots of combat, and saw his comrades die.

It was late afternoon and Bob was still telling me story after story of harrowing experiences. From murder to drug smuggling; from a motorcycle gang to a concert promoter; from the death of his firstborn son to his own salvation—each story was more compelling than the last.

With tears streaming down this tough guy's square jaw, he told each story in graphic detail. That jaw had received quite a few blows in its life, but somehow the tears seemed to hit him harder.

I remember thinking that I didn't want the stories to end. For one thing, they were amazing stories, but more than that, I was afraid of the moment he would stop talking and expect me to say something. That was terrifying me, because I had nothing to say! I rehearsed words in my mind like, *God loves you* and *God forgives you*, but even to me they sounded about as shallow as a bumper sticker slogan. I was painfully aware that I had nothing to give this man to help him with his pain. While I appeared calm on the outside, my heart was racing because I had no counsel for this guy who had lived ten times the life that I had. I felt woefully ill prepared to help someone who had done so many things that he regretted. Not knowing what else to do, I asked him more questions about his experiences, hoping it would delay my moment of reckoning.

Then the moment came. He was finished talking. From across the table, I looked at this guy with both compassion and fear. I had listened to his every word and now I was silent. I said nothing. I just looked at him and smiled. Then he said one more thing that I will never forget. He said, "Man, you are so wise!"

I probably said something that sounded a lot like "Aw, shucks." To be honest, I didn't say anything at all worth remembering—*that entire day*!

On the inside I was thinking of only one thing: a single line from the Scriptures that I had recently read. Suddenly it became real to me in a whole new way. The verse, written by Solomon, the second wisest man who ever walked on this earth, says: "Even a fool, when he keeps silent, is considered wise" (Prov. 18:28).

Once again, the Scriptures proved true. Another proverb in a similar vein is, "Better to be silent and supposed a fool than to open your mouth and remove all doubt." I was indeed a fool masquerading as a wise man simply because I had sense enough not to open my mouth.

Those of us who are leaders have a tendency to overestimate our words and underestimate the value of simply listening to others' words. It is not uncommon to have someone in the church who listens very little and talks way too much. On more than one occasion, I have had to tell someone, "If you would talk less, people would listen more. But because you talk so much, no one really listens to what you have to say."

Learning to listen is a great skill. It will make you a better leader, a better spouse, a better person. When it comes to leading leaders, this skill is even more valuable. It is absolutely necessary. Leaders are not easily influenced. They tend to be the kind of people who must be heard. To lead leaders, you must win their respect, and there is no better way to do that than to listen to them.

The Child Leader

A great example of the profound way that listening can be used to lead leaders is found in Luke 2:41–52. This happens to be the only glimpse we have of Christ in his youth. He is twelve years old, which would be comparable to a middle school kid in the sixth or seventh grade. His family had come to Jerusalem for the holy days. They came and left in a caravan full of family, friends, and neighbors. On the return trip Joseph and Mary suddenly realized that their firstborn son was not in the crowd of travelers.

Can you imagine the panic of realizing that you had left your child in a big city by himself? Mary and Joseph quickly turned around and started the ascent back up the hill toward Jerusalem, probably praying constantly.

Luke records that they found Jesus in the temple in the midst of the teachers. Now to get the full picture, imagine a middle school kid with freckles and a voice that hasn't even begun to crack yet, on a skateboard, his baseball cap on backwards. This kid is among the elite teachers of the teachers, or the rabbis of the rabbis. Picture him at the Evangelical

Theological Society's annual meeting, surrounded by older scholars, seminary professors from around the country. These "suits" gather together to impress one another with deep theological questions. They are discussing the latest paper read, each trying to say something that the others haven't thought of yet.

In such a context, this sixth-grade boy skates in and begins to speak. He wants to add some insight on the hypostatic union or some other deep and difficult doctrine. What do you think would happen in such a case? I am sure the scholars would each be amused at the boy's bold assertions. I am also sure they would not give him much regard beyond an amusing pat on the head and an encouraging word to keep it up so that one day he would grow up and maybe become a teacher too. These men would be too busy and too important to give more than a moment to this boy's words.

That, however, is not the response that Jesus received. Luke recounts that Jesus was "in the midst of the teachers, both listening to them and asking them questions. And all who heard Him were amazed at His understanding and His answers" (vv. 46–47).

Two Skills Necessary for Leading Leaders

When it comes to having influence among those considered by all to be leaders, you simply must approach with a listening ear if you ever hope to get *their* ear. Jesus, even at such a young age, understood what it took to gain an audience from those who normally would not have the time for such a youth. He listened to them and asked insightful questions.

Active Listening

The first skill needed to be a good leader of leaders is the ability to actually listen to people. This is not as easy for leaders, because they tend to be people with answers.

All of us have been with someone who is a good listener. There is actually an entire industry based on people being good listeners— psychological analysts. Because listening is so needed and rare, people will pay up to four hundred dollars an hour for a good listener.

What do you think of a person who is a good listener? Are you drawn to such a person? A good listener is rare and valued. Being a good listener will make you a better teacher, evangelist, leader, father, wife, husband, or mother. You will be a better person for it, and you can help others do the same.

Asking Questions

Asking good questions is a fine art. It takes years of practice to perfect the skill. Asking questions is not an admission that you are ignorant or lacking in knowledge. On the contrary, it can often mean that you are more advanced in learning.

Have you ever noticed in the Bible that it is God, the One who knows everything, who asks the most questions? You do not wade very far into the Scriptures before you find him asking questions. By chapter 3 of Genesis, he is asking question after question. "Adam, where are you?" Now God does not misplace things. He doesn't lose his car keys. He knows full well where Adam is; he is drawing him out with questions, and it works. "Who told you that you were naked?" "Did you eat of the fruit that I told you not to eat from?" Adam eventually comes out of hiding, removes the fig leaf mask, and divulges a full confession, albeit with a little blame shifting.

God knows all the answers. He doesn't ask questions because he is ignorant. He doesn't come into a situation and start asking questions like a parent because he needs an explanation so he can apply punishment appropriately. God is the leader of the universe. Out of love and wisdom, he is asking questions to draw out Adam's confession for healing and restoration. A good leader is skilled at asking questions that will draw out what is best in those he or she is influencing.

With an upset prophet, God asks, "Do you have good reason to be angry about the plant?" (Jon. 4:9). At times we all need to be asked questions from an outside objective source to help us look more clearly at our situation. That is especially true of leaders.

Jesus's Example as an Adult

Jesus asked a lot of questions. You could see how frustrating it may have been to be one of his disciples, because he so often answered questions with other questions. He knew how to pull out people's true values with a simple question.

When Jesus told the disciples to feed the multitude, they asked him how. Jesus answered their question with another: "How many loaves do you have?" (Matt. 15:34). This prompted them to take stock of the reality so that when the miracle came, they would see how incredible it was.

On another occasion a rich young ruler approached Jesus and asked how to have eternal life. Jesus responded by asking him, "Why do you call Me good?" (Luke 18:19).

The religious leaders approached him with a question and Jesus said that he would answer their question if they would first answer his (Matt. 21:23–25).

He approached a man who had been lame for decades sitting by a pool, which was thought to be a miraculous source of healing. Initiating the conversation, Jesus asks an important question that I think all of us in Christian leadership need to learn to ask: "Do you wish to get well?" (John 5:6).

When he was in the presence of religious leaders who were judging others, he asked them, "Why are you thinking evil in your hearts? Which is easier, to say, 'Your sins are forgiven,' or to say, 'Get up, and walk'?" (Matt. 9:4–5).

When he confronted the multitudes, asking them to consider the importance and identity of John the Baptist, Jesus asked, "What did you go out into the wilderness to see? A reed shaken by the wind? But what did you go out to see? A man dressed in soft clothing? . . . But what did you go out to see? A prophet?" (Matt. 11:7–9).

Jesus pulled his disciples aside for a teachable moment and asked two questions: "Who do people say that the Son of Man is?" and "Who do you say that I am?" (Matt. 16:13, 15).

Jesus approached a poor, blind beggar, who was shouting to him from the side of the road, with a question: "What do you want Me to do for you?" (Luke 18:41). Jesus didn't presume to know what he wanted; he asked. No one had ever served this man—except Jesus.

Jesus was a master at the art of asking good questions. We should strive to follow his lead.

In the resource *Empowering Leaders through Coaching*, Steve Ogne and Tom Nebel present ninety-nine good questions for a mentor.[1] Questions can prompt people to think and investigate their own actions and values. We should avoid, however, any sort of manipulative questioning. I hate it when people pretend to be taking a survey when they are really just trying to share the gospel. It is not only manipulative but also deceptive. This is no better than the obvious salesperson who cold-calls you around dinnertime to ask you questions about your current mortgage—it is fishing for an angle, and that is not how we should approach people. Today people are experts at seeing through such a gimmick, so we need to stop it immediately.

Important Skills for Leaders

Listening and asking good questions are two important skills for leaders because they can draw out the emerging leader's learning in life. When we hear someone tell us something, it goes only so far in our understanding and can easily be forgotten. Discovering something ourselves is a much deeper level of learning and is not easily forgotten. Lessons discovered in the course of life are life changing, while lessons learned from another person's experience are shallow.

A mentor should see his or her role as cooperating with the work the Holy Spirit is already doing in the life of the emerging leader. Often it is a challenge for us to observe objectively what our experience is teaching us, because we are too immersed in the lesson itself. Someone who can listen carefully, and occasionally ask a question that helps us connect the dots, is helpful.

I remember listening to one of our organic-church planters who was feeling rejected by a mentor because he so obviously loved another growing leader like a son. In essence, some jealousy had found a wedge into this young man's soul. He may have seen the jealousy, but he didn't have a way to work through the reason it was there or how to settle it in his mind. This situation was damaging his relationship with a very significant spiritual father.

I could have easily scolded him for being childish, told him to suck it up, and sent him on his way. But that would not have dealt with the real issue and nothing would have been resolved. If I had done that, he would now simply add guilt to his already crippling problem. Instead, I took a different tack.

After listening carefully to his feelings, I asked him, "How many children do you have?"

With a smile he said, "I have two beautiful daughters."

Then I asked an unusual question, "Which one do you love the most?"

At first he looked back at me with a puzzled expression that seemed to ask, *How can you ask such a stupid question?* I just looked back at him with a subtle smile, waiting for the light to turn on. My smile informed him that there was more to the question than was at first apparent and it encouraged him to look deeper. In silence I watched him across the table. I could see his mind working. A knowing smile came on his face as he realized that his own spiritual father could love two disciples equally and yet differently. Jealousy evaporated immediately as he thought of how much he loved both his girls equally and yet uniquely.

Instead of merely hearing my opinion of the relationship, he was able to learn from his own life experience and resolve his own issues. This is a deeper level of life change, because it is self-discovery. He couldn't think of his mentor again without thinking of his own love for his daughters.

I have been starting and leading churches for a couple decades now. I have heard a lot of compliments in my life, but most of them seem rather superficial. Occasionally, though, someone says something that demonstrates that I have indeed been doing some good. Those compliments feel the best inside, and I recently received one.

Annie, a woman who has been in one of our organic churches for almost eight years, was reading one of my books, *Search & Rescue*. One thing you have to know about Annie is that she is a person who values authenticity so much that she will always be honest in her comments. She may not be perfect, but she is a woman with no guile. As she was telling our church about how she felt about my newest book, she said, "Well, I don't care much for the lifeguard stories (there is that honesty I was telling you about); they don't excite me. But I really like the rest of the book." Looking at me she said, "I forget that you're a real good Bible teacher." Then she said these words that I really value: "You should have us shut up more often and just teach us instead of letting us talk all the time when we are together for church."

Now that may not sound like a compliment to you, but to me it is one of the nicest things anyone can say. It isn't her words about being a good Bible teacher that made me feel good, but the recognition that I listen more than I speak. I heard this from someone who is under my influence as a leader and always tells the truth. It shows me that the people whom I have been leading recognize that I am more interested in drawing out what the Lord is teaching them than simply telling them what he has been teaching me. That was a far nicer compliment than all the times I have heard people say, "Good sermon, pastor."

I imagine that Jesus's disciples would have much preferred Jesus speak all the time and not ask so many questions. But that isn't what makes a good teacher or mentor.

A Lesson Tested on the Field

An organic-church planter in the Denver area decided to test these principles of listening and asking questions. Tim Pynes went to a popular coffeehouse in the Boulder area with a sign that read: "I will buy you a free cup of coffee if you will listen to my story about God."

Tim sat at a table for hours with his sign, and never did anyone stop to listen to his story and receive a free cup of joe. Occasionally someone, who was sure he was just another obnoxious evangelist wanting an audience, jeered at him.

The next day Tim went to another coffee shop, very much like the previous one, but this time he brought a different sign. It read: "I will buy you a free cup of coffee if you will tell me your story about God."

That day Tim's time was consumed with people who were glad to sit and share their story of God. Tim listened to people. He listened carefully. He never intentionally interrupted or shared his own point of view. He was there only to listen and would only share if asked. And he was asked, repeatedly. As people told him their stories, they were struck by his rapt attention and became curious about this man. Each asked him to tell his story, which he promptly did. Some left and told their friends they needed to go to the coffeehouse and hear that guy's story.

Tim remarks that he rarely had to buy anyone coffee; many times others would insist on buying him coffee.

This experiment reveals something that Jesus already knew at a young age, but most of us go through life never learning: people respond better to those who will listen to them first.

In his highly successful book, *Seven Habits of Highly Successful People*, Steven Covey prescribes this very powerful principle for those who hope to be successful leaders: "Seek first to understand, then to be understood."[2]

A Simple Tool

CMAResources offers a very simple tool for use during mentoring appointments. This tool, the M2M Mentoring Guide, is a single 8.5" × 11" page for taking notes when meeting with those being mentored. Two of these pages are printed together on NCR paper, so that as the mentor takes notes, those words are also printed on the second sheet.

This way both keep copies of the important things covered at the end of the meeting. M2M stands for "mentoring to multiply."

On the sheet there are six sections for note taking and a portion for recording any goals accomplished, assignments given, or next steps (with due dates), and when and where the next meeting will take place. By far, the heart of the tool are the parts that reveal the intersection of active listening and asking good questions as they relate to the DNA of your life. Remember DNA stands for divine truth, nurturing relationships, and apostolic mission.

There is no place for the mentor to tell the apprentice what to do; the form reinforces the concepts of listening and drawing out solutions by asking questions. It focuses the attention of both the mentor and emerging leader on the DNA of the apprentice's life.

One certainly does not need to use this tool to mentor effectively. It is merely a suggested aid. A seasoned mentor will take note of all this naturally. At first, using such a tool is awkward; it doesn't feel natural. There are some occasions when I do not use the tool, because of the context, even though I created it.

The Mentoring Guide can be a useful and practical help, however, in the following ways:

1. *It keeps a record of the development of the emerging leader's life.* As meetings accumulate and the notes are kept in either a file or a binder, both the mentor and the apprentice can begin to see personal patterns and trace God's hand in the learning process. While at first it may seem strange to the apprentice to have someone taking notes, after a while he or she will learn the value of the notes. More than one of my apprentices have actually been disappointed if I failed to bring the Mentoring Guide to a meeting.

2. *It keeps track of assignments and appointments so that a mentor who is investing in numerous lives at once can keep each meeting in mind.* Juggling the mentoring of a handful of leaders all at different stages of development and each with different gifts, calling, and roles is not easy. This tool can help the mentor keep up on everything that is going on. No longer will the mentor need to ask the apprentice for a recap. The notes can also remind the mentor of how to pray for each apprentice.

3. *It sets a simple pattern for the emerging leader to replicate when it comes time for him or her to start mentoring others.* As emerging

Name: _____

Mentoring Guide

M2M
mentoring2multiply

Reflect
(Active Listening)

Refocus
(Asking Questions)

Resource
(Action Plans)

Goals Accomplished:

Next Steps:

Next Meeting:
(Date/Time/Location)

Divine Truth

Nurturing Relationships

Apostolic Mission

© 2006 Neil Cole

leaders go through the mentoring process, they are being trained in how to replicate it as mentors. They can start immediately to mentor others, using the Mentoring Guide. Mentoring leaders can have confidence that the emerging leaders are sound in practice if they are utilizing the tool because it encourages active listening and asking good questions, and it has no place for giving answers.

The M2M Mentoring Guides are available at our website: www .cmaresources.org.

You too can be considered wise even if you have nothing good to say, just by listening and asking good questions.

17

WAX ON AND WAX OFF

Life-on-Life Mentoring Skills

To lead people, walk beside them. . . .
As for the best leaders, the people do not notice their existence.
The next best, the people honor and praise.
The next, the people fear;
and the next, the people hate. . . .
When the best leader's work is done the people say,
"We did it ourselves!"

Lao-tzu

The only real training for leadership is leadership.

Antony Jay

Mr. Miyagi was a wise master teacher to his apprentice Daniel-san. The 1970s movie *The Karate Kid* actually left us with a vocabulary for hands-on training in a mentoring relationship.

Young Daniel LaRusso (played by Ralph Macchio) sought out karate training from the old man (played well by the late Pat Morita). The lessons start with Daniel washing and waxing all of the vintage cars Mr. Miyagi has. But Daniel must do the job right—especially the buffing of the wax. With a specific circular motion, Miyagi explains,

"Wax on." Then with the other hand in the opposite direction but the same circular motion, he says, "Wax off."

At first, it seems that the washing and waxing of old cars is just payment for the training to come. But after painting the man's fences, painting his house's siding, and sealing his deck, Daniel loses patience, sure that the old man is taking advantage of him. He assumed that all the strict techniques for how to apply the paint, wax, or sealant were only to make sure he took good care of the teacher's possessions. As we find, appearances are not always what we think they are.

Miyagi explains that this is learning karate. LaRusso says he hasn't learned any karate; he's just done all his work for him around the house.

In a telling scene Miyagi has his student do the very same movements that he had reinforced with much practice while washing cars, painting fences, and sealing the deck. "Show me wax on. Show me wax off." As Daniel makes those movements, with his arms now sore from all the work, Miyagi throws fists and kicks at him and Daniel finds he knows how to deflect attacks using those same movements reinforced over and over again with hard work around the yard of his master's house.

Over the years, since this movie was released, I have heard more than one pastor refer to experiential mentoring with a simple expression: "Wax on; wax off." I believe we need to apply some of that wax in our church leadership experience and clean up our act. Life-on-life mentoring is the only way for young leaders to shine. In this chapter I will share some of the principles I have learned over the years about mentoring.

One-on-One Training

Mentoring is the only way to build leaders. You cannot effectively mentor classes of people, you can only truly mentor people, one at a time—*life-on-life*. We are tempted to think that we will go much faster, cover much more ground, and fulfill the Great Commission faster by training several people at a time. The truth is that this method trains a lot of people in very little that is helpful, and it actually takes more time with less results, whereas investing in people one at a time can yield far greater results for generations of influence. What you can teach in a classroom setting or a conference may be helpful, but in the grand scope of things, it is a shallow learning experience and no substitute for one-on-one, life-on-life training.

One key difference is the multiplication factor. The Bible calls us to multiply leaders, not just add them to the mix. Organic leadership reproduces itself, and as in nature, reproduction always occurs life-on-life. The best way to multiply leaders—in fact I believe the only way to multiply leaders—is to do so one at a time. So while you may cover a lot more ground with large groups of people, your training will not be reproductive. If, however, you train a few, one-on-one, you can make sure they are growing holistically until they too are training others one-on-one. This is how we reproduce as leaders, and the result can be exponential, rather than merely incremental, growth.

Multiplication will reach the world in a relatively short time if we are all committed to it. Continuing the same thing we have been trying to do for centuries will not.

I also believe firmly that people need to learn in groups as well as one-on-one. In fact, my book *Organic Church* explores smaller communities as ones where viable learning and growing can take place. Peer learning is very valuable, but when it comes to mentoring leaders who multiply, you simply cannot replace one-on-one, life-on-life mentoring to get the job done.

Principles for Mentoring One-on-One

I keep three sayings in mind when I meet with someone I am mentoring to remind me of what is important for each of our appointments together. They are:

1. *First things first.* As I meet to mentor an emerging leader, I take an inventory of the basics that need to be learned and dealt with. If there is some obviously glaring weak area, I address it first. If there is an obvious area of challenge in the person's life at that time, which is clearly on the Lord's agenda, I focus on the area. In this way I let the Holy Spirit lead the mentoring process in the life of the emerging leader, rather than simply following whatever comes next in the curriculum workbook.
2. *One thing at a time.* So often we teach more than people can learn. The results are ineffective learning. In my experience, if I try to teach just one thing to an apprentice and do well with it, the emerging leader is always learning something. If I try to teach three or four things, there is a good chance I will teach the person nothing. Our memories are just not that good. If I

can get across one lesson that will be remembered forever, it is far better than covering three that are remembered for only a couple of days. When I focus on the apprentice learning just one thing, I can devote more attention, prayer, and creativity to that training.

3. *Always one more thing.* Over the course of mentoring, I am always looking a little ahead and asking the Lord what is next for this leader to learn. In this way we do not have any dead time in the process. I do not presume to know what is next; I ask the Lord to reveal it. As a mentor, the sense of anticipation for what the Lord wants next is always on my mind. This means I am, in essence, studying what God is doing in this person's life.

Two additional principles I keep in mind when mentoring people one life at a time are:

1. Each person learns at a different pace.
2. Each person has a different style of learning.

PACE OF LEARNING

When we attempt to train a large group of people rather than one-on-one, problems occur because people all learn at a different pace. Some are quick learners, and some need to marinate and stew with the lesson a while before they internalize it. Usually, when we lump everyone together in one group, we go too slow for the fast learners and too fast for the slow ones. We go at an average pace and thus raise average leaders.

Most Western teaching methods are linear in direction and lead a classroom full of people in the same direction at the same pace. So everybody must finish the curriculum at the same time.

The problem is that your pace of learning does not always equate to the depth of your learning or understanding. We have adopted language that favors the fast-paced learner. When we speak of someone who is not as intelligent, we tend to call the person a "slow learner," which can be a serious misnomer. Just because someone is a slow-paced learner, it doesn't necessarily mean he or she is not as smart as the fast-paced learner.

I know some people who have minds that work at lightning speed, but they miss a lot of information in the process and actually do not learn as much or remember as much. Being in a hurry is not always the best condition for learning.

I know others who learn at a snail's pace, but what they learn, they really know well. There are many stories of some of the most intelligent people who have ever lived, like Albert Einstein, who were slow in their cognitive development. People thought they were not as smart as their peers because they were so slow to learn to speak, for example. When they did speak, however, they spoke very well all at once, and Albert Einstein had lots to say!

Of course, it can also be true that some learn very fast and retain what they have learned. We all probably wish we could be like that, but my point is that everyone learns at a different pace and should be mentored uniquely.

STYLE OF LEARNING

There are a variety of learning styles. People take in information and assimilate it differently. Our bodies are designed with multiple sensory intake mechanisms, and people tend to favor some over others. These sensory modes are gates to the mind. As a mentor it is important that you recognize the unique learning style of each emerging leader with whom you are walking. The sooner you discover your apprentices' learning styles, the sooner you can effectively fuel their growth. Trying to force people to learn in a style that is not suited to their needs is not a good use of time.

Along the way I have encountered four dominant learning styles. There are visual learners, audio learners, kinetic learners, and verbal learners.

Visual Learners

Some people are visual learners, meaning the information they retain the best is what they receive through their "eye gate." I am this type of learner. People like us find visual aids, such as diagrams and charts, helpful when we learn or teach. This is the reason movies play such an important role in my teaching. I use charts, diagrams, images, Power-Point animation, and film clips in my teaching because that is how I receive information. Trained as an artist, I think visually more than in sentences, and even when I write, I want to paint a picture. I use lots of stories to convey ideas. For visual learners a napkin and a pen are important tools in a mentoring appointment. Give them a whiteboard when they share and several different colored pens and they will be like a giddy child on Christmas morning. These learners enjoy the Internet, but websites with lots of words are not as interesting as those with visual images and flash animation.

The Side-by-Side Kingdom

Audio Learners

Audio learners need to hear information for their best learning. The "ear gate" is the predominant channel of information to their deepest memory storage, and they learn well through devices such as audiotapes, CDs, and MP3 recordings. This person is able to receive and apply verbal assignments and will tend to feel that charts and diagrams only clutter the content and are distractions. When this person is on the Internet, the flash animation and images are secondary and usually ignored; he or she is looking for the written content. Wanting to hear what they are reading, these people often prefer to read out loud, and though they have been trained not to do so publicly, you may notice their lips moving as they read and hear the words in their mind.

Kinetic Learners

Kinetic means movement. There are people who learn best by doing something physical to reinforce the lesson. The kinetic learner's mind is wired in such a way that when his or her body has to take certain actions, it helps the person to process and remember data. Learning is processed through the "touch gate."

These are people who like to work with their hands. If you tell them what to do, it may or may not sink in, but if you show them what to do, they will learn it fast and never forget it. Some great athletes are this way. The Xs and Os on a coach's whiteboard are not really their language, but when you walk through the offense or defense in practice, they will be the first to understand. When an instructor has an audience break into groups and do exercises, it works well for the kinetic learners. The audio and visual learners may roll their eyes when asked to role-play, but the kinetic learner starts the learning process at this point.

My son, Zach, is this type of learner. Giving him a list of tasks to complete is not always a good idea because none of it gets very deep in his memory files. Walking him through the house and pointing out the work is far more effective. When I want to teach him something on a deeper level, I have to be creative and come up with something physical we can do together that will get the point across.

When Zach was turning fourteen, I wanted to teach him what it means to be a godly man. So we did something very masculine—we went camping on an island off the West Coast. Around a campfire, we talked about five important qualities of being a man: initiative, influence, intent to finish well, integrity, and identity. I used a different finger for each of the qualities and together they form a fist. The next day he became a warrior.

In the morning we went for a scuba dive to have a little adventure. It turned out to be more of an adventure than expected. My rented air tank came loose under about fifty feet of water in a kelp forest. My son helped restore my tank and rescue his dad.

When we returned home, I presented Zach with a sword, which hangs in his room to commemorate his passage into adulthood. In ancient days a soldier who was really trusted and honored by his peers would be given a sword. You do not give a lethal weapon to someone who hasn't earned your trust. To this day Zach has a daily visual reminder of my trust in him as a man who is becoming a spiritual warrior.

Because he is a kinetic learner, all of this communicated to him on a deep level; he was receiving information through his kinetic channel. It was a memorable experience for him that he'll be able to tell his own son someday.

Verbal Learners

There are a few people who learn by saying something out loud. Many include this under the audio learning category, and it may well be that these learners are in that category. Personally, I find verbal learners unique and fascinating. They must conceptualize the idea in their mind first by articulating it in their own words, but then also by trying to counter the idea. We may be tempted to say this person learns through the "tongue gate" but it is actually the "mental processing gate."

Toying with a concept deepens the verbal learner's understanding. When these learners retell the concept in their own language, they are learning at a deeper level. It is not always enjoyable to mentor these people because they come across as argumentative on just about everything that is important. The reality is that they are simply processing the lesson as best they can by internalizing it verbally. Just because they take the opposite point of view doesn't mean that they are against what is being said; it means they are trying to understand it the best they can.

In the early days of CMA we had a team member who was this kind of learner. He is one of my oldest friends and we shared an office space early on in our ministry. Because I knew that he was a verbal learner, it was fun to see him process information. For those who didn't know what was going on, it could be a nightmare. I was drawing pictures and Chris was arguing *every* point. Our voices would rise to higher decibels with each level of understanding. Anyone in the room who did not know us thought we were fighting. We were not fighting; we were learning. In fact, our love for each other and bond are stronger for having walked together through this process. The reason this has worked is because we know each other and I know what it takes for my friend to internalize concepts at a deep level.

Enhancing the Learning Process

Find out how your apprentice learns and fuel that with experiences about which he or she can be excited. If you pay close attention to an apprentice's strengths, passions, and learning styles, you can greatly enhance the learning process. You can even help the person expand his or her learning style to a degree and increase the person's exposure to good material.

For instance, I was mentoring one young man who wanted to become a church planter. He hated to read, except for novels. In fact, he loved novels and would read them with a voracious appetite. When I gave him a nonfiction book, he had little time or taste for it. I took stock of his learning style and passions. I decided that reading fiction was a start, but I wanted to expose him to other writing that could greatly increase his learning.

Having realized that a nonfiction book had little impact on him, I assigned him some fiction works with strong lessons in the areas that were especially pertinent to him. He was coming from a more legalistic background, so I chose *Wisdom Hunter* by Randal Arthur and *The Screwtape Letters* and *The Great Divorce* by C. S. Lewis, which are fictional but very helpful at exposing the way people think. Then I assigned Lewis's *Mere Christianity*, thinking that he was ready for it, but I had gone too fast.

He enjoyed the fiction works and learned from them, but he still didn't like the nonfiction book. So my next assignment was a small step, not a huge leap, into nonfiction. I gave him an exciting biography, which he enjoyed because it was a story, though a true story. After he read the biography, I gave him a smaller book written by the one whose life story he had read. He enjoyed it because he knew the life behind the words. Once he enjoyed a nonfiction book that wasn't a story, I felt a degree of success. I did this a couple times—biographies followed by works written by the person. Eventually this apprentice developed an appetite for nonfiction works. He may never be a voracious reader of nonfiction, but he has expanded his learning.

Just-in-Time Training

The timing of training is important. Unfortunately, timing is often not even considered as most curricula simply follow the linear order of the workbooks or lessons. But an individual's learning is tied directly to his or her experience, and experience never follows a linear path.

We learn best when it's something we feel a strong need to learn. If we don't feel a strong need for the lesson, we will learn in a superficial way. We never fully own the lesson when it is abstract and unrelated to our own personal life experience. But if we feel a deep need for what we are learning, the lesson will never be forgotten; we will own it, and pass it on to others.

Training that is personalized and following the Holy Spirit's unearthing of needs in the apprentice's life is what I call Just-in-Time Training. Rather than the mentor determining the order of lessons or the priority of learning, regardless of the apprentice's real-life needs, Just-in-Time Training cooperates with the work we assume God is already doing in the learner.

The following three principles help guide the Just-in-Time Training process.

Need-Oriented Training

Never teach a skill until there is a need for it. Need-oriented training sticks longer and deeper than that which is unconnected to real-life experience and often simply slips off the surface of a learner's consciousness.

I do not mean that the mentoring relationship is strictly focused on the person and his or her interests. Not at all. What I mean by "need" is that the learner senses the need to learn the subject on a personal level. It is not just about meeting selfish desires, because that would not be consistent with the life of following Christ.

The Holy Spirit will bring to light issues in a person's life that create such a need. The mentor can sometimes see the need coming, even before the apprentice does. At times, an alert mentor can even help awaken the apprentice to the need.

As you listen to the Lord in prayer for the emerging leader, be asking the Lord what is next. Sometimes this can be clouded with your own biases, but sometimes your instincts may be right, so be sure you have heard from the Lord when deciding how the training should proceed.

As the Holy Spirit directs an emerging leader to recognize the real needs in his or her life, the trainer follows the Holy Spirit's lead and does not set the agenda for the person's development. Soon the learner will recognize that God, rather than the trainer, is teaching him or her, and so the lessons will be learned better and be more memorable. The mentor may not even know why a specific skill is being taught at the time, but the Holy Spirit does.

One time I felt that the Lord was telling me that one of my apprentices needed to learn public speaking. At the same time a pastor in our area asked me if I had anyone who could fill his pulpit for him while he was on vacation. Seeing the two very different circumstances as more than coincidence, I presumptuously said yes and gave him Joe's name.

At the next mentoring appointment, I asked Joe if he wanted to learn how to preach a sermon. He got excited at the opportunity to learn this, but as of yet didn't really feel a strong need for it.

I told Joe, "Good, we will learn how to develop and deliver a message in the next couple weeks. You need to learn fast because on Sunday two weeks from now, you will be giving your first sermon in front of one hundred people at First Brethren Church of San Bernardino!"

Well, needless to say, Joe was a very attentive learner, and he did a great job with his first sermon. I didn't know it at the time, but this was actually vocational training for this emerging man of God, who has had a great career in training and sales for the Red Cross and has used his public speaking skills throughout.

The point is that we look for what the Holy Spirit is doing in the person's life and try to cooperate with teaching what is pertinent. If you can help create a need so that the person's learning will be deeper, all the better. Often, however, the Holy Spirit will have already created the need. Then you can design assignments that require the emerging leader to learn a skill that will help magnify the need. Pay attention to what God is doing and look to connect the lessons with legitimate needs in the learner's life so that the learning is deep.

One Lesson at a Time

Never teach a second skill until the first one is learned. As was mentioned in chapter 15, most Christians in the West are already educated beyond their obedience. It is far better that we train people one lesson at a time and do not teach a second lesson until the first one is learned.

Learning by Teaching

A skill is never truly learned until it is taught to another. Perhaps the best example of creating a need in an apprentice I am mentoring is having him or her teach the lesson to others in a formal setting. When someone is accountable to learn something because he or she will have to apply it in a real-life situation, the person will pay closer attention and learn much more deeply.

Anyone who has taught others knows that we learn more by *teaching* others than by being taught *by* others. In fact, I don't think anyone has ever truly learned a lesson well until he or she can and does pass the lesson on to others. This is a learning principle that we can use intentionally. It is all part of the intentional learning process.

An example is when I was teaching Joe about some basic evangelism skills. First, the Lord had awakened him to the needs of his family and friends who do not know Christ, so his desire to learn how to evangelize was prompted by the Holy Spirit, not me. As I said above, this is important. Then, at his request, I gave him some tools to help him learn some skills in evangelism. On a day and time that he set, he reported on how his evangelism experience went.

We had a great time as he reported the positive response he received. But the training was not done then. I had him identify others to whom he would like to teach the same skills. After he had taught what he had learned, I considered the lesson complete—for now. The truth is we do not ever finish the learning process.

This principle, often overlooked by leadership training, is very significant. It encapsulates the others because it reinforces teaching based on a recognized need and proceeds one step at a time. But it is more than that. It also takes the training—the needed extra step of reproducing the learning in the lives of others. If we are training leaders, we must see them lead.

We use these principles in the way we train organic church planters in CMA. Our training in organic church is called the Greenhouse. It is a good training system that has equipped thousands of church planters across the world to make disciples and start organic churches. There are at least two presenters for every Greenhouse we conduct in the States, so there are two sets of eyes and ears and two stories to tell. There is also some training of trainers going on behind the scenes. The Greenhouse casts the seed of organic-church planting very broadly and effectively, but it is what I consider the "back end" of the system that gets me most excited.

The Greenhouse is our farm system for emerging organic leaders. We use it to identify these proven leaders and then take them to the next step of influence. Those who have been through the training and are effectively doing the work in their own context are called to join us in the training process. We have found that when they start teaching the principles to others, they grasp the concepts on a much deeper level. They become organic-church evangelists of a sort who pass on the DNA of our movement. The more they teach the principles, the more the principles become their own. They learn the concepts on a deeper and more personal level than if they had just heard others teaching the materials.

On-the-Job Training

All of the above principles are reasons for learning on the job, as opposed to simply learning in a classroom or with a book. The truth is leadership cannot be learned any other way. A leader is an influencer. You cannot learn to lead unless there are people you can influence. You can learn theories about leadership, but you cannot learn how to lead without experience on the job with people.

If you have learned to ride a bike, it wasn't by reading a book about the physics of inertia and balance. It was because someone put you on a two-wheeler and ran beside you as you learned on the street. You learned with help, and if you're like the rest of us, you learned by falling down a few times. There is nothing like scraped knees to teach us the principle that we have to continue to move forward or we will fall.

If you know how to swim, it isn't because someone taught you in a classroom with charts and diagrams on a whiteboard, explaining the physics of buoyancy and hydrodynamics. You learned in a pool and you probably choked on the water a few times in the process. Leadership must be learned in the fluidity of real relationships, and the emerging leader must "choke" a few times to get it right.

It is the reality of life that validates the importance of what we learn. When we learn in a sterile classroom, removed from real life, we cannot have the discernment necessary to know if what we are learning is true. Hebrews declares that the mature are those "who because of practice have their senses trained to discern good and evil" (Heb. 5:14).

I remember clearly sitting in on a seminary class in rural America where students had moved to gain an education. They were young and, in this learning institution, isolated from their places of ministry. The classroom and library had become their learning environments, not a church setting or relational groupings.

In this class the professor went off on a tangent speaking about animal rights activists who were causing all kinds of problems with their misplaced priorities. The students gave him their rapt attention, laughing at the professor's extreme examples. The thing is, while there are some stupid things that people do because they love and even revere animals, I do not know of any ministry or church that really has problems with animal rights activists. Maybe it occasionally exists, and I don't really need some of you to write me stories about it. The point isn't that people do not have these problems, but they aren't a high priority when it comes to preparing people for leadership in the church. Experience would have given the students better discernment. Then they would know from their life experience that this subject is not that important. When we are living in the midst of people (problems and all), as opposed to being isolated from people, we begin to understand what is valuable and useful and what is not.

There are lots of things that can be taught in the sterile environment of a classroom, but leadership is not one of them. Neither is riding a bike or swimming. There is no substitute for learning on the job with people's messy lives. You have to get wet, you have to fall down, and you have to make mistakes. That is how we learn the skills we need to apply in the future and pass on to others.

Mentors must also create environments that allow for mistakes. Anyone reading this book knows that failures and mistakes are often the best learning experiences. We should consider this and allow for it. Intentionally build failures into the learning process, and then expect them, allow for them, and even encourage them by encouraging apprentices to try new things. We will produce more learners, and therefore more leaders, if we do.

Obedience-Oriented Training

There is one principle that is extremely valuable in training people on the job. It is a principle that can save literally years of your life and keep you from untold frustrations. When it comes to investing your life into another, invest in what is proven, not in what is potential.

Everyone has potential. Six and a half billion people on the planet *all* have potential. Some just happen to have more than others. Potential is a wonderful thing to have when you are young, but not so wonderful later. No one wants to have it said at his memorial service, "He had so much potential." Potential is nothing—it is a zero. Potential is the hope that one day there will be something. When you invest in nothing, the yield may be nothing.

When you invest in what is proven, you are investing in something far more concrete. The proven is substantive; it is, well, proven. You can count on it.

A Small Challenge

Some feel that I am being mean when I tell others not to invest their life in potential. Actually I am being loving, both to the one I am instructing and the one in whom they would invest. The idea is not that you disassociate from people, but that you first challenge them to obedience to the Lord. If at first they cannot follow the Lord in even the simplest and most basic steps, and you invest your time, energy, and emotions in them, you will be very disappointed.

So to invest in what is proven, begin by presenting an individual with a small challenge. If he or she rises to the challenge and accomplishes the small thing, challenge him or her to greater things. I suggest you withhold your time and energy until you have seen the fruits of some obedience. Mentoring is a whole life investment. I would not waste it on someone who will not value it.

When I start mentoring, I begin very casually and informally. As we simply go through life, I may listen and ask a question or two. I do not immediately set up appointments and start investing my life in the person. At first, I will suggest a simple and biblical practice related to the person's spiritual life experience to date. If he or she takes the suggestion and practices it, I will have confidence to suggest something a little more challenging. After doing this a few times and seeing him prove himself in a few things, I will begin to formalize the mentoring relationship with appointments for our getting together.

Again Joe provides us with a great example, because he surprised me so much. He came to me fresh out of high school and asked me to mentor him. He was young, thin, and still had braces on his teeth. He looked even younger than he actually was and was called Joey at the time. I didn't honestly think he was ready, but to be true to my own convictions, I challenged him to start an LTG and let me know when he had done that. (An LTG is simply a once-a-week meeting with one or two others who desire to follow Christ and remain accountable to the things that make that possible.) It can't ever hurt to do this and could always pay off with great dividends.

The next week at our church meeting, Joe told me he had started an LTG. Then I encouraged his faithfulness with a challenge to multiply the group and come back to tell me when that was done. To my surprise, a month later he had multiplied the group. Then I challenged him to do so again and see if he could gather the people into a small group for a weekly meeting. After he did that in a relatively short time, I started to mentor him more intentionally and did not regret it.

A Biblical Principle

This approach to mentoring is a good and needed filter. Not only does it filter out those who are not faithful with the small things so that you do not entrust things of greater importance to them, but it can also help you realize that someone you didn't expect is actually the right one to invest in—like Joe.

This type of filtering is not just for my protection. This is the best thing for the emerging leader. It is all part of the one-on-one, obedience-oriented, just-in-time, on-the-job training process.

This is a biblical principle. Jesus commended those who are faithful with a few things to be given greater things (Luke 16:10). Deacons must first be tested, then appointed to serve (1 Tim. 3:10). Solomon was a wise man. He instructed us not to hire those who simply pass by and are available. It will result in damage and painful loss. Instead, he instructs, put your confidence in one who has proven to be trustworthy (Prov. 26:10; 25:19). Albert Einstein once said, "Whoever is careless with the truth in small matters cannot be trusted with the important matters."

A man I consider a mentor, George Patterson, first taught me obedience-oriented training.[1] Years of experience on the mission fields of Honduras taught him much about starting churches that reproduce by training leaders that reproduce. He suggests seven biblical commands that are useful in training leaders to obey Christ.[2] They are:

1. Repent, believe, and receive the Holy Spirit.
2. Be baptized.
3. Love God and neighbor.

The Side-by-Side Kingdom

4. Celebrate the Lord's Supper.
5. Pray.
6. Give.
7. Disciple others.

Imagine what the world would be like if every Christian followed through on just these seven basic commands in the New Testament. When you see someone who has a heart to obey Christ and is willing to follow through on the challenges of simple obedience, that is someone worthy of the investment of more of your life. Try to balance your life investment with the person's proven obedience in each of the lessons God has granted as you walk together in a relationship.

As the relationship matures into more formal mentoring, it still follows the same obedience-oriented path. The amount of investment is always contingent on the emerging leader's obedience to the previous lessons Jesus has taught him or her.

This will guarantee greater fruitfulness for your life. It will not, however, guarantee that you are never disappointed again. It will reduce the amount of grief in the mentoring relationship but it will not eliminate it. Jesus had Judas, Paul had Demas, and you will be disappointed in life, even by some who have been proven. Then the disappointment will hurt on a much deeper level because of the more trusted relational investment. It is still worth the investment, however, in spite of the pain. It is the only way to change the world—one life at a time.

Some Exceptions

Now friendship is something else entirely. You will find that you have deep friendships with those you have mentored and who have mentored you. But friendship goes beyond the ideas expressed in this chapter. I do not suggest you respond to your spouse with the same principles I am espousing in this chapter (the previous chapter, however, would greatly benefit your marital relationship—read it again!). Your wife or husband is not your project and will resent being treated like one. You can, however, certainly apply some of these principles in raising children.

Of course you will have friendships that are not mentoring relationships. The principles I give in this chapter are best kept in a mentoring relationship. I am not teaching you to avoid friends or people in your church family because they do not measure up to the obedience suggested. I am saying that when it comes to investing in leadership development, what is proven is a far better foundation than simple potential. Unfortunately, many churches are so desperate for leaders, they don't even require potential—just a pulse is enough!

The Show-How Skill-Training Method

When it comes to training people in skills, the best way is the show-how method. This is not a new idea, but sometimes ideas last a long time because they work.

The show-how method of skill training follows a very simple formula with any sort of task. Sometimes this method is called the MAWL method of training:

Model: I do; you watch.
Assist: We do.
Watch: You do; I watch.
Leave: You do; someone new watches (the process begins again).

This is so sound and so simple that it really doesn't need any more elaboration.

When we train the Greenhouse trainers in CMA, we employ this simple and straightforward method. As I already mentioned, after leaders have had the training themselves and put the concepts to work in their own context, we recruit them to become trainers. We give them a workbook, a PowerPoint presentation, film clips, and an actual audio recording of the whole weekend's training to study in preparation.

The first step is for those leaders to come to a training event, where they will hear it all again but with a different set of ears—because now they are learning so that they can eventually present the material. A need has been created that fosters a deeper level of attention.

Their first assignment at a training event is what we refer to as providing "color commentary." With any televised sporting event, there is usually a play-by-play announcer who carries the weight of the presentation, and beside him or her is a color commentator who will share inside information about players, coaches, and strategies. Similarly, the first experience for new trainers is to tell their own stories and to help answer questions, but they are not responsible to carry much of the training itself.

The next time they are called on to help with a Greenhouse, they will be beginning trainers. They are to select and teach the portions of the material that they are most comfortable with, and the lead trainer is beside them to help in any way necessary.

The third time they are involved with a Greenhouse, they will be responsible to teach the portions they didn't teach before, but at this point they will have heard them a minimum of three times. After this experience, they are prepared to lead a training session all by themselves, and we then consider them a lead trainer in Greenhouse. Their next step is to train others in the process.

We are constantly developing proven trainers so that our pool is increasing. We have just passed a milestone where we are averaging a Greenhouse training every week, and we estimate, on average, a new church every day. For the first time, we have names of people on our training list with whom I am personally unfamiliar. Our trainers are reproducing themselves.

Balancing This Over-the-Top Training

Some leaders have been doing the math since this chapter began. They can't help themselves; they are responsible for so many people that they have not been able to concentrate wholly on the chapter. They know from experience they can mentor only so many people personally and are responsible for a whole lot more than that. How can they apply these mentoring principles and still be faithful to their call? Often we do things the way we do simply out of the necessity created by the demands of our responsibilities. It may not be the best method but it is all we can do.

There are limits to the number of people you can personally mentor one-on-one. I have found that twelve to fifteen is about the max anyone can handle at one time. Jesus focused on twelve, so perhaps we should do the same.

But what if the demands of your ministry call for far more than twelve new leaders, and your life does not allow for the time to train more than that? What can you do then? The solution is in the quality of the leaders that can be produced with this mentoring style, as opposed to the shallow leaders produced with a more programmatic and curriculum-based method. With this leadership formation method, leaders are produced who are capable of reproducing. Thus the number of leaders increases exponentially as each new leader reproduces other leaders.

Another thing to consider is that each of the twelve on whom you focus your mentoring will be at a different place in the scope of development. Some will make less intensive demands on your time than others. So at any one time, not all twelve will require weekly attention; some will need only monthly contact, and you will meet with others only as needs arise. The leaders who do well with this method do not need a long-term commitment of the same intensity. If the leaders you are mentoring need this kind of commitment, you are not choosing your apprentices wisely and are wasting their time and yours.

Jesus spent three years with the Twelve. Even if we stretch it to five years, the demand will not be constant over those five years. There will be a season of more intense and formal meetings, but later there will be a season of only occasional meetings. If you are mentoring well, your leaders will be spending more and more time with their own emerging leaders, leaving less time for them to meet with you.

There are some natural stages in the process of forming leaders that we should take into account. Development should occur naturally and develop via reproduction from the micro to the macro. The chart below illustrates this. A developing leader should grow from one level to the next based on proven reproduction at each previous level. At any one time, a good mentor will be developing leaders in various phases simultaneously. Each phase demands a different level of intensity and formality of mentorship.

Natural Phases of Organic Leadership Reproduction
Reproduction should occur naturally at every succeeding level of complexity, beginning at the smallest and simplest level.

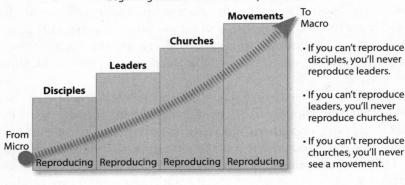

The following bell curve diagram shows the increasing and decreasing amount of intensity needed to mentor people in the organic-growth process. In my own experience, some leaders need only a biweekly appointment for an hour. For others, it may be monthly. Those who are

The Side-by-Side Kingdom

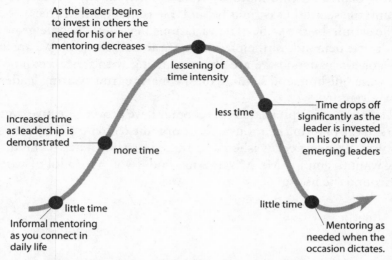

Over-the-Top Training
Balancing Time with Multiple Apprentices

As the leader begins to invest in others the need for his or her mentoring decreases

lessening of time intensity

Increased time as leadership is demonstrated

more time

less time

Time drops off significantly as the leader is invested in his or her own emerging leaders

little time

Informal mentoring as you connect in daily life

little time

Mentoring as needed when the occasion dictates.

A single mentor can balance up to twelve leaders at a time. Each of the apprentices will be at a different place on the curve and will need less or more time depending on his or her development. In this way you should always be able to bring new apprentices in as you send mature leaders out. Jesus invested in twelve leaders over the course of three years, which is a good ratio to follow and could produce two hundred-plus reproducible leaders over a lifetime.

at an earlier disciple-making level will demand a weekly meeting, and we recommend an LTG for such meetings, as much for your benefit as theirs.

In Southern California we have a lot of property development with new houses and shopping centers, especially out in the extremities, as the urban sprawl spreads. We also have a reputation for our palm trees, so tree farmers grow the trees that others buy and plant on their new properties.

One day I realized that I could learn more about how to develop leaders organically from these farmers than from a lot of the seminars and conferences I had attended. If a farmer were to plant a single row of seeds and tend the plants over the years, from seedlings to twenty-five-foot palm trees, he might not be inclined to sell them. Since he had poured a lot of attention into his single row of trees, he would be attached to them. And once he sold them all, he would have had nothing left. He'd be out of business. But of course, tree farmers do not run their business this way.

A tree farmer plants new seedlings every year, so he has trees at a variety of heights and maturity levels. When he sells off one row of mature trees, another is right behind. He is never out of trees.

We should be the same. The variations in the way people grow and the diverse demands of their learning are actually helpful. We are never in want for leaders if we are always starting with fresh seedlings, all the while finishing and sending off the mature fruit-bearing leaders to new adventures.

The methods expressed in this chapter have proven effective over the years in the planting of thousands of organic churches. They may not, however, get your car washed and waxed or your fence painted. You may want to employ Mr. Miyagi's method if you have a lot of work to do around the house.

18

CATALYSTS
FOR REAL CHANGE

Leadership Tools That Multiply Impact

Sometimes the questions are complicated and the answers are simple.

Dr. Seuss

The value of an idea lies in the using of it.

Thomas Edison

have traveled all over the world, training people to do organic-church planting. This is a great privilege but also a responsibility that I do not take lightly. At the risk of sounding arrogant, I must mention that this is what we were aiming for when we first started our ministry called Church Multiplication Associates. We set a goal from the very beginning that our strategies would be used all over the world. And, although there are many goals we have not seen come to fruition, this is one we've achieved.

Granted, I love to travel, but that is not the motivation behind the aim. Complete global domination is also not in our hearts. Ours is not some ugly American, arrogant desire to be the best and the biggest. No, the goal was very strategic from the moment we set it. We understood that the Great Commission is fulfilled only if it touches the ends of the earth. Frankly, while every ministry should have such a motivation, I am relieved that many do not. The American church has already exported enough ridiculous ideas that do not work in other cultures. We have exported a Western model of church into hundreds of cultures where it doesn't work—and shouldn't work.

So why did we set such an outlandish goal? Here is some of our thinking: Goals can be more than just a wish list; they can also be guides to our values. Goals should be a reality check for what is important, and, of course, a test of how well we are doing.

We aimed for global influence because we value the multiplication of ministry principle and believe it will fulfill the Great Commission to the ends of the earth. As such, we understand that if we want something to truly multiply beyond culture, tradition, language barriers, or national borders, we have to come up with transferable strategies that transcend all those obstacles. We set this as our goal from the start so we would be successful only if what we did in California also worked in Calcutta. This is more than a standard of success, but also a criterion by which our progress can be measured. If we found something that worked in Phoenix but not in Phuket, we were failing. Most leaders ask the question: what works? We ask the question: what multiplies?

In CMA's office we have what we call our Shelf of Shame. It is a shelf full of resources, most of which we created and tested over the years and found they do not reproduce and are culture bound. Some of these tools have been quite successful for church growth and would be valued by churches around the country. Some of these resources are quite impressive and cost us lots of time and money to create. We could make back that money and more if we offered these resources to churches hungry for tools that work. Instead, they collect dust on our Shelf of Shame as a monument to our learning process. If it doesn't multiply, we shelve it. If it doesn't work across cultural barriers, we shelve it. It's that simple and that important to us.

Now, our training can be found all over the world in a wide variety of languages and cultures. Often cross-cultural missionaries are attracted to our materials, even before American pastors are, because they can recognize the transferability of what we produce.

I was asked to present some of our teaching in Turkey to many cross-cultural missionaries from Central Asia. After the training, my daughters and I went on a tour of the seven churches of Asia Minor

The Side-by-Side Kingdom

(addressed in Revelation). On the bus with us were some of the missionaries from the conference.

On the last night of the tour, a few of the missionaries decided to take advantage of the moment. They all came at once, surrounded me at the dinner table, and asked me the tough questions. One man from Kazakhstan said, "I've been here on the mission field for fifteen years. Often we have American leaders come over and teach us stuff that works in their world. It always sounds exciting at first, but when we try it here, it doesn't work. What makes your material different from that?"

This was a good question. I explained our original goal and some of our effectiveness, but there was more to his question. He wanted to know our thinking about contextualizing our strategies for different cultures.

I wish American church leaders were asked this question. Too many of us find something that works for us in our home context and assume it will work anywhere else, so we have become notorious for exporting strategies that do not work overseas, or even in other contexts in our country, for that matter. We leave behind burned-out pastors all over the world who bought our sales pitch but did not find our product helpful.

The Frustration of Following Models

There are diverse factors involved in finding something that works in a variety of environments. Just because it works for a high-caliber leader like Bill Hybels, in a growing and affluent neighborhood such as South Barrington, Illinois, during the eighties and nineties, doesn't mean that it will have the same effectiveness somewhere else. I am not singling out Willow Creek as a negative example but making the point that if we simply try to duplicate what worked for one person (an exceptional person at that) and expect the same result in a different context, we will be disappointed. I know many leaders who followed Rick Warren's experience with expectations of starting the next Saddleback, only to fall short of the mark they had set, though their ministry could be seen as a success by any other standard.

I know of one leader who left a megachurch in Southern California, which had thirty-five hundred in attendance each week, to plant a church in another community. The church plant went from zero to almost three hundred people in just a couple of years, which should be considered phenomenally successful. Unfortunately, the church planter's model of success was a church of more than three thousand people. His church plant also happened to be in the shadow of Saddleback at the same time as its dramatic growth. The church planter felt like a failure and resigned.

When Rick Warren started Saddleback in 1980, he asked a series of questions about what people expect in a church. Many times since then I have seen promotional pieces containing the same questions. Each piece is printed with a different church name and logo on it. It's clear that people think, *If it worked for Rick Warren, it should work for me as well.*

When we operate in this way, we are being lazy leaders who think of the church as nothing more than a fill-in-the-blank, plug-and-play exercise. Many of these leaders, even if they have good hearts and sound strategies, may not find success if for no other reason than that God does not want to reinforce a weak understanding of what the church truly is. God is concerned about this after all.

Our problem is that people are lazy thinkers. They would much prefer that someone else figure out the solution so they can just plug it in. We want to have someone else tell us what model we need to follow to build a successful church. A step-by-step manual is very attractive to someone who wants success but is unwilling to put in the time needed to think, pray, and fail for that success.

Descriptive and Prescriptive Teaching

Joseph Myers, in his book *Organic Community*, does a good job of articulating the difference between *descriptive* teaching of ministry patterns and *prescriptive* teaching of what has worked for someone else. Describing successful ministry patterns allows us to learn the principles of why a method worked, whereas prescriptive teaching tells us to do the very same thing to get the same results. In other words, follow the recipe.[1]

When we only follow the patterns that others created somewhere else, it is a paint-by-number approach to ministry and it produces very disappointing results. Formulaic answers to our ministry demands are dangerous and leave behind scorched earth. So many pastoral leaders feel like failures because they bought the "tool" at a conference, plugged it into their own environment, and expected the same results that the "successful" megachurch pastor experienced. Often they assume the

The Side-by-Side Kingdom

problem is with them or their people, not the process. This leaves behind many leaders who suffer from a failure complex.

Many assume that I also teach a prescriptive and formulaic pattern. I fully understand this critique and take it to heart, because all of us have been burned by such ministry models. In essence, this is why the missionary from Kazakhstan was asking me why I thought what I was teaching would work in his environment. He had been burned before, and he deserved a thoughtful answer.

No How-to Manual

Most ministry models contain much promise but little is ever delivered. The problem, however, is not just a lack of fulfillment. Simply following ministry models also feeds and fuels a lack of faith in Christ. This approach shifts our hope for a genuine life in Christ to a poor substitute. Faith and expectations are placed on the model rather than on the Master.

I guess this is the reason I get a little frustrated when my ministry is summed up as just another prescriptive model of church. We work hard not to present a model, and we have many diverse churches in our movement. All of the ministry resources we create are working in a wide variety of church models around the world—from microchurches to megachurches.

It's not unusual for people to get frustrated with us because we will not give them a how-to manual of organic church. We have one answer for a myriad of questions: you have to listen to God in your own environment and figure out the answers for yourselves, and let others do the same.

Many people assume that, since we teach some practical methods, we are simply proffering another model of ministry. That is a natural assumption that I understand. The reality is that a great deal of thinking in this area has gone into our resources, which separates them from the usual church model approach.

It's ironic that some people accuse us of not giving enough of a model and others say we present too much of a model. I guess this is because we are trying to balance practicality with not being too prescriptive.

We can give people practical help without presenting a fill-in-the blank manual of the latest church model. It means we have put a lot of time into thinking about, practicing, and editing our material. Knowing what to eliminate is as important or more important than knowing what to include. Being discerning about the material we include, packing it in a simple process, while maintaining the profound nature of the method, is a fine art. As Antoine de Saint Exupéry once said, "Perfection is achieved not when there is nothing more to add, but when there is nothing left to take away."

The Breakdown of Complex Curriculums

Unfortunately, most of us have been trained with a curriculum approach to learning, and so we practice the very thing we have learned. A curriculum approach, however, does not reproduce well for the following reasons:

1. *Curriculum is linear, and life is not.* Perhaps life would be more convenient, certainly more predictable, if it followed a linear pattern, but it doesn't. Life comes at you in unexpected ways.
2. *Curriculum is usually culture bound.* We develop our curriculum from our experience in our own culture and rarely do we rise above and analyze it free of cultural bias.
3. *Curriculum is typically time bound.* What worked in the eighties will probably not work in the nineties. Life in our globally shrinking world goes at such a rapid pace today that what worked two years ago may not work anymore.
4. *Curriculum is typically humanly dependent.* Curriculum is usually created to help a teacher teach. It is therefore dependent on a leader who is able to pass the information on to others. Granted, the gospel is usually dependent on a human vessel (Rom. 10:14). But simply being a presenter is different from being the interpreter and translator and accepting accountability for its application. Most often our training is far too dependent on the expert leader, which keeps it from multiplying rapidly.
5. *Curriculum is often not divine truth but uses the Bible for its authority.* In training, people usually pass on to others a practice or belief they have internalized. They adopt Bible verses to lend authority and substantiate the materials, but rarely in such curriculum does the Bible speak for itself.
6. *Curriculum usually does not fuel all parties simultaneously.* Most training resources require that a leader teach a student. With this pattern, not only is a dependency created from the start, but the

leader is usually not receiving anything from the content and is merely used for the benefit of the follower.

7. *Curriculum does not reproduce easily.* By far, the majority of ministry resources and curriculum created today are too complex to multiply rapidly. Simple things are easy to pass on, while complex things are not.

A problem arises when we decide that church models and the curriculum that created them do not work when exported to other places. We may decide that nothing practical can be passed on, and this reaction is as flawed as thinking everything can be passed on. I believe that some ministry tools are culturally transferable, but only after they have been refined and tested.

Anthropologists have determined that there are some culturally universal practices, needs, and values. And though this may be true, I do not believe that we all need to be anthropologists to figure out what will and will not work cross-culturally. We already have a universal benchmark that we can trust will apply in every culture and to every man.

The Scriptures are universal. They are true in every people group and in every generation, so they are a powerful tool to bring the kingdom around the world. It takes some effort, but when we allow the Bible to speak for itself, we empower people to hear from God in any language.

Simple and scriptural solutions are patterns that others can follow without the complexity of curriculum. The authority is the Bible, and we must encourage thinking and interacting with it, not with our materials. Empower the person with the Scripture instead of borrowing scriptural authority for human teachings.

Viral Methods That Cross Cultural Barriers

In the bestselling book *The Tipping Point*, Malcolm Gladwell says any epidemic type of expansion requires a "stickiness factor."[2] In other words, the pattern must stick with people in such a way that it is unforgettable and easily passed on to others. It is not enough for it to be easy; it also must capture the imagination and affection of those who will pass it on. They must want to tell others about it because it's good news worth telling.

Paul passed on to Timothy truths that were so profound that he would not forget them. They gripped his life and never left him. At the same time, however, the things Paul passed on were simple enough that Timothy could in turn pass them on to others who could then pass them on to others (2 Tim. 2:2). Everywhere Paul went, he used a universal pattern to produce quality disciples who could transfer the pattern to others. The gospel is the most profound truth humankind has ever received, yet it is simple enough for a child to understand and pass on to others! It is not enough that people *can* pass it on, they must *want* to pass it on. The gospel is good news, and like a profound secret, it should be something we all want to tell others.

My friend and mentor Thom Wolf is a biblical genius. He was the first to unlock from the New Testament the missional concepts of *oikos*[3] and *person of peace*.[4] *Oikos* is the Greek word for household and is often used in the New Testament to describe the social web of relationships with which all of us are connected. It was via the natural bridges of *oikoi*, one to another, that the gospel spread across the known world of the first century (Luke 10:1–4). In each *oikos* that is prepared by the Lord of the harvest for the gospel, a person of peace is already prepared there (Luke 10:6). He or she is like the first domino in a relational chain reaction to the Good News within his or her *oikos*. The flame then spreads to other *oikoi* closely connected, and a movement begins.

It was Thom who first revealed that the apostle Paul had a universal pattern for spreading the Good News and making disciples that was easily reproduced. The characteristics of this universal discipleship pattern (described in detail in *Organic Church*) are mentioned below.[5] For multiplication to occur from one life to another, certain characteristics must be evident in the people so a simple pattern emerges that is reproductive. Paul had such a pattern and constantly referred his spiritual disciples to it.[6]

The pattern needs to have the following four characteristics if it is to initiate a multiplication movement:

1. It must be *incarnational*. The pattern must be internal and work its way out into behavior. Paul challenged the Philippians to follow his example and that of others who lived by the same pattern (Phil. 3:17).
2. It must be *viral*. The pattern must be contagious and simple enough to pass on to other generations of learners. In 2 Timothy, Paul refers to this pattern when he reminds Timothy of the things he heard from him among many witnesses and that are now passed on to three generations (2 Tim. 2:2).

The Side-by-Side Kingdom

3. It must be *transformational*. Because the pattern is so life changing, people will pass it on because they have been so affected by
   its positive transformative nature. Paul mentions to the Roman
   believers, whom he had not yet visited, "though you were slaves of
   sin, you became obedient from the heart to that form of teaching
   to which you were committed" (Rom. 6:17).
4. It must be *universal*. The pattern must work across all racial,
   economic, political, social, language, and cultural barriers if it
   is to change the world. Paul wrote to the Corinthians about the
   pattern and said, "be imitators of me. For this reason I have sent
   you Timothy, who is my beloved and faithful child in the Lord,
   and he will remind you of my ways which are in Christ, just as I
   teach everywhere in every church" (1 Cor. 4:16–17).

We need systems that are practical and profound. They must be
both simple and significant—significant enough to tap into the Christian's internal motivation, yet simple enough to be easily passed on
from disciple to disciple and across cultural barriers. Such a system
can strengthen the church and allow growth that is both qualitative
and quantitative.

In *Organic Church* I mention simple criteria we at CMAResources
use to determine if our tools or strategies are worth producing. These
criteria are adapted from Thom Wolf. When we go about thinking up
a new strategy, we ask ourselves certain questions. Strategies we adopt
can be:

1. *Received personally.* The strategy has a profound implication, able
   to be internalized and to transform the soul of the follower. This
   is where it is most essential that the Scriptures speak powerfully
   for themselves.
2. *Repeated easily.* The strategy has a simple application. It can be
   passed on after only a brief encounter.
3. *Reproduced strategically.* The strategy communicates universally
   and can move across the globe by being translated into a variety
   of cultural contexts and languages.[7]

Roland Allen, the Anglican missionary whose works, written almost
one hundred years ago, are now being rediscovered, once said, "The
spontaneous expansion of the church reduced to its elements is a very
simple thing." Truly, it can *only* be a simple thing. Complex things

break apart in the transmission. Simple things hold their integrity as they are passed on to multiple generations of people. We must strive to find the beauty and the power of simple things. Einstein once commented, "When the solution is simple, God is answering."

Keeping the Focus on What Is Important

Another reason simple methods are better than complex ones is that they do not take the glory away from Christ. Unfortunately, many methods are so impressive that people cease to notice Christ. Yet Christ chooses to work through weak vessels so he retains all the glory. If people are so impressed with our wineskins (our systems and strategies) that they stop noticing the wine (the message and person of Christ), there is a big problem. Simple strategies keep the focus on Christ, not on the plans or on the people dreaming up the plans.

As we have developed culturally transferable systems, and shelved a whole lot more, we have learned some key things that guide us in the process. I call these the ABCs of useful tools. Below are three thoughts to keep in mind as you work to develop something that can be effective in other contexts and cultures:

Access to God. We want to turn to God for answers and enlightenment rather than depend on human leaders. A good resource doesn't think for the disciple but challenges him or her to seek God and discover truth.

Bible is the authority and is not simply used to grant authority to the tool. The Bible speaks for itself without human filters. When curriculum is saturated with Scripture references to support its biblical posture, it is, in essence, using the Bible to grant authority to the curriculum. It is far better to let the Bible keep its authority and stand alone without our help. People who obey the Scriptures are far more potent than those who obey men's ideas, with Bible verses tacked on for support.

Compassion for others is the natural outcome when the Spirit, using real catalytic tools, causes life change. It is not necessary to force compassion through guilt, shame, and fear when it is a natural fruit of being Spirit-filled. Obedience is the result of a changed life, not the other way around. We do not change our life to be obedient; we are obedient because our life has been changed from

The Side-by-Side Kingdom

the inside out. We love, because Jesus first loved us and gave his life as a ransom for us. If we are not moved to obedience because of love, the work is futile and will end in rubble (1 Cor. 13:1–3).

Reproducible Tools

Simple and significant tools that allow Scripture to speak to the person are catalysts for change. A catalyst is a chemistry term for something that accelerates the change process by increasing the rate of a chemical reaction without itself undergoing any change. A catalyst maintains its own integrity so it can continue to contribute to the change process as the chemical reaction spreads. Because it does not change itself, but heightens the change process of the other elements, very little of the catalyst is needed.

In a ministry environment we want a system that is solid and simple while bringing together the spiritual elements that induce change. Because the system is simple, it can maintain its own integrity without breaking down and can release a chain reaction with the power of spiritual life.

The Life Transformation Group

A ministry system is not what changes a life, and this is important to remember. In a Life Transformation Group, for example, two or three people come together in safe and honest relationships and read Scripture, confess sin, and pray for others. It is a simple and reproducible system. And it works in any culture.

An LTG is a catalyst; it doesn't change people but brings together the elements that do change people in a way that accelerates the process and maintains its own integrity over the course of many generations.

When developing such a resource, we ask ourselves which Bible teachings are absolutely necessary for life transformation. Then we ask, How can we bring those ingredients together in a simple way that does not get in the way and does not take any authority away from the Bible? We intentionally design highly reproducible methods that bring together life-changing elements. A Life Transformation Group is one example. Another is a tool called The 7 Signs of John.

The 7 Signs of John

A tool that exemplifies the content of this chapter is what we call The 7 Signs of John. It is a simple evangelistic tool that had not even been written down until Jaeson Ma included it in his book *Blueprint*.[8] Because it is so simple, oral transmission of the concept has proven quite sufficient.

The 7 Signs of John is based on the words that the apostle John writes near the end of his Gospel. He said, "Therefore many other signs Jesus also performed in the presence of the disciples, which are not written in this book; but these have been written so that you may believe that Jesus is the Christ, the Son of God; and that believing you may have life in His name" (John 20:30–31).

Apparently, though John was with Jesus from the start and saw all the miracles performed, he selected particular miracles and included them in his book in a specific order[9] for a purpose—to open the eyes of the unbeliever to have faith in the real Christ and gain eternal life. This is not my opinion; this is what the Scriptures say. Consider it this way: the Holy Spirit is telling you that the miracle stories in the Gospel of John are the stories that best present the true Christ to an unbelieving heart. It is quite common for American Christian leaders to exaggerate the effectiveness of a method, but in this case it is the Holy Spirit making the claim, not me.

The 7 Signs can be applied in any size group. You can easily use this tool one-on-one, in a small group, or even in a stadium full of people.

The seven signs from John are:

1. The turning of water into wine (2:1–12)
2. The healing of the royal official's son (4:46–54)
3. The healing of the paralytic at the pool of Bethesda (5:1–17)
4. The feeding of the five thousand (6:1–14)
5. The walking on water (6:15–25)
6. The healing of the man born blind (9:1–41)
7. The raising of Lazarus (11:1–46)

The way it works is that each week the person or persons you are sharing with are encouraged to read one of the stories once every day. So in the first week, they read the story of Jesus turning water into wine every day. At the end of the week when you get together and read the passage, you ask four simple questions and have a discussion about the passage. The questions are:

1. What does this story say to you about human nature?
2. What does this story say to you about the person of Jesus?

3. In what ways does this story affect your way of thinking about your own life?
4. With whom should you share this story?

Discussing the answers to these questions with anyone who is a spiritual seeker can easily be done once a week over a cup of coffee. Every organic church I have ever started began going weekly through these stories and simply answering the questions. I have yet to go through this process and not have someone commit to following Christ. I am not guaranteeing you the same results, but we can take the Holy Spirit's word for it that these stories will help people believe in Jesus.

This simple and profound ministry tool crosses all cultural barriers because it is simply the Bible speaking for itself. It easily reproduces, because anyone can ask a few questions. This is not a model of church or a human curriculum. It is simply unleashing the power of God's Word to do what it does in a life. The only way you could say that this doesn't work cross-culturally is to say that the Bible doesn't work cross-culturally. Even in an oral culture that is not literate, this tool will still work because it is basic storytelling.

This is an example of the sort of resource that is practical, transferable, and truly biblical. There is no workbook or specialized training needed, and it is not dependent on a highly trained person. A Bible is all that is needed. Because it is so simple, it doesn't easily break down when reproduced. It maintains its own integrity throughout many generations and is a catalyst for transformative movements.

A Jaded Missionary Sees the Power

I explained all of the general content of this chapter to the missionary to Kazakhstan that evening at dinner. It was probably a lot more than he was expecting, because most American Christian leaders do not really take the time to ask these questions and find reproducible solutions. At the end of the discussion, to make the idea tangible, I felt it would be helpful to offer an example of a tool that meets all the above criteria. I presented on a napkin at the table The 7 Signs of John. I thought this was the end of the impromptu training, but I was wrong; it was just the beginning.

Our tour guide for this trip was a moderate Muslim. He was also clearly seeking the Lord. At our first stop I sat with him for a cup of

Turkish coffee while all the other participants explored some ruins and the hot baths of Hieropolis, which is near Laodicea. I was recovering from surgery on a torn Achilles tendon and was not able to explore like everyone else, so I took advantage of a moment to share with our guide.

I discovered that he had been given a Bible and had been reading it. He told me that he was starting to love Jesus. I smiled, looked him in the eyes, and said clearly, "Jesus loves you more than you could ever realize." I think the combination of the words he heard come out of his own mouth and my own confident assertion took him by surprise. He was thinking about this for several days.

After our unscheduled training around dinner on the final night of our tour, the speculative missionary decided to put my theories to the test. A couple of the guys found our guide and went through the first miracle story of John's Gospel with him—the turning of water into wine.

I was not there, so I only know what I was told. The next day, after our tour ended, one of the gentlemen told me that our guide had decided to follow Christ. Then he was given the same napkin and told to bring together his family and friends and go through each of the stories and ask the same questions. Who knows how far this simple catalyst will bring change to a Muslim culture in Turkey? None of us are there to oversee and manage the work, but God is there, and he is very capable.

There were two conversions that night at the last stop of our tour: our Muslim guide who had been searching for God, found him, and a jaded and suspicious missionary who had tried so many fruitless, American-made teaching models in the past, found one that would work.

SECTION FIVE
THE PLUGGED-IN KINGDOM

The Life, Power, and Provision in God's Upside-down Kingdom

There is unknowable power and provision in the kingdom of God. And they are not from the place the world would expect. Access to God's provision in his kingdom requires no ATM card, and the password is very different from that of the world. In this section we will address two very important topics: power and provision.

First, we will look at empowerment and exit strategies when mentoring others so that the influence outlives the leader.

Then we will look at the first question leaders often ask me: how can I make a living at this? We will look at who is supported in the New Testament and how that support is released for effective leaders.

In the conclusion there is a true story, a story about rare new leaders whom God has given for this special day. I am blessed to know these men and women who are gifts to the kingdom. Until now only a few knew about them, but I want to change that. I want to let the whole world know what God is up to these days, because I see it as significant.

We live in unprecedented times. This may sound like an exaggeration, but I don't think so. It is not hard to find moments in history when God moved the pieces so that the right people were in the right place to ignite a revival in a certain region of the globe. Today God is doing something unique. He's bringing revival, not on a regional basis, but on a global basis. Not since the first century has the kingdom of God seen such open opportunity worldwide.

19

EMBRACE DEATH AS IF YOUR LIFE DEPENDS ON IT

The Cure for All That Ails Us

Christ bids us: Come and die.

Dietrich Bonhoeffer

All changes, even the most longed for, have their melancholy; for what we leave behind us is a part of ourselves; we must die to one life before we can enter another.

Anatole France

In every city of America there is at least one church with a building worth hundreds of thousands (if not millions) of dollars. This church meets every Sunday morning with only eight to ten silver-haired women and one or two balding gentlemen for a "service." They sing a hymn or two, one of the stately gentlemen shares a few opinions of things in the world today, they say a prayer, repeat amen, and then go home.

269

Empty parking spaces, silent pulpits, and dusty pews cry out for days of glory gone by. The church has been dead for years, perhaps decades, but has been kept alive unnaturally by an artificial life support system. The soul is gone, brain waves have ceased, but mechanization keeps the lungs breathing, the heart beating, and the door opening every Sunday morning at precisely 10:00 a.m.

Why does this happen? We are so desperately afraid to admit failure that we will keep a church alive as long as we can. It is as if the continuity of Christianity depends on this one church staying open. If the church dies, God has failed, and we cannot allow that.

Why are we so desperate to keep churches going? While I know that the church is special to Jesus (we are his bride!), I think we have lost touch with something very spiritual—death. Can it be that death is as spiritually right as life?

The Sin of Self-Preservation

While we clearly avoid a theology of death, the opposite is not a theology of life, for life is not what you will find in churches that strive to avoid death at all costs. I don't know how it happened, but sometime in history we bought into a theology of *safe*. We think we should do what is safe, for ourselves, for our families, and for our churches. We are convinced that anything that is unsafe must be outside of God's will and is thoroughly un-American and un-Christian. A theology of safe is put in place as a defensive measure to avoid death. This leads us right down the path of self-preservation.

Jesus is not about safe. He is the one who said things like: "I send you out as sheep in the midst of wolves" (Matt. 10:16). "I did not come to bring peace, but a sword" (v. 34). "He who loves son or daughter more than Me is not worthy of Me" (v. 37). "Follow me, and let the dead bury their own dead" (8:22 KJV). These are not safe and wholesome, family-friendly words; they are words that shake us up and toss us out in the deep end, way past what is safe.

We often approach church and ministry with a theology of SAFE:

Self-preservation = our mission
Avoidance of the world and risk = wisdom
Financial security = responsible faith
Education = maturity

Does this not describe many of the churches or ministries you have encountered? Some of you have been on elder or deacon boards that are perfectly described by this acronym. I know I have. It almost seems like our default response. Our instinct is to preserve our lives. It seems so natural to surrender to the current that is self-preservation. It is a fight to stay close to a theology of death.

Johannes Hoekendijk, a Dutch theologian who taught at Union Theological Seminary in New York during the 1950s, had a great impact on expanding the mission of the ecumenical church movement beyond merely extending the church-ruled culture of Christendom. He believed that the *missio dei* was more than establishing larger church boundaries. He once defined the church's well-being as, "when she cannot count on anything anymore but God's promises." That is life!

Self-preservation is actively choosing an alternative to the life of our God. It is a direct move away from faith in the life-giving and sustaining Savior. God created us with an instinct for self-preservation. It is not a sin to want to live. It is human instinct to want to survive, but it is a sin to want to live without God's life source. Use your desire to live as motivation to die, for this is the only path leading to true life in God's upside-down kingdom.

Preserving oneself separate from God's life is not just a sin, it is blasphemy. It is taking for yourself the place of life-giver. Self-preservation means that you are the one who gives and sustains life, which is blasphemous.

It is also the path to self-destruction, not life. As Jesus said so strongly and repeated often: "He who has found his life will lose it" (Matt. 10:39). As a consequence of the sin of self-preservation, literally tens of thousands of Christians and churches are deceived into a "churchianity" that is carried out by men, for men, in the name of God. I wonder if God likes getting the credit for all the crap we do.

When the servant of God is presented with the choice between self-preservation or the cross, there should be no choice. We follow Christ to the cross or we do not follow him at all. He said, "If anyone wishes to come after Me, he must deny himself, and take up his cross daily and follow Me" (Luke 9:23).

Just as Jesus picked up our cross and died in our place, we need to pick up his and die for him. Dying to oneself is not easy at all and runs contrary to one's instinctive response, but it is right nonetheless. Choosing not to go on the path of death and, instead, choosing to preserve your life is in reality choosing death. As I have explained in chapter 11, the kingdom of God is counterintuitive.

Carrying Your Cross

Death is more than just an important idea for discipleship—it is absolutely essential. Without a death, there is no disciple. Without dying to self, we do not have a life within us.

Jesus said clearly, "He who does not take his cross and follow after Me is not worthy of Me" (Matt. 10:38). The cross is a sacred symbol to us, coming to us with the baggage of two thousand years of religious worship and celebration. It is far removed from the cross of the New Testament. We wear gold crosses around our necks. The image adorns our buildings and probably hangs somewhere in your home. The symbol has come to represent Christianity, and in some respects, rightfully so. The cross is the hinge of all history. It is the centerpiece of all we believe and hold dear.

We have heard sermons of how the burdens of life are "our cross to bear." We must jettison all that and look at Jesus's statement that we must take up our cross for what it meant, literally, to those who heard the words for the first time. They knew the reason a man carried a cross. They had seen the horrific act many times. It meant only one thing, and suffering the struggles of life was hardly it. Carrying a cross was a death sentence fulfilled. The man who carried the cross had no way out. His life was over, and he was about to suffer the most humiliating and painful execution ever devised by man. He was a dead man walking, dragging the device of his own demise.

When Jesus was speaking these words, the disciples may not have understood that Jesus was about to carry a cross to his own vicious execution, but they knew what it meant to carry a cross. Wearing a cross around your neck is like wearing a guillotine around your neck or an electric chair—only worse.

The cross was an instrument of capital punishment but more severe than any other. It was so severe that Roman citizens were exempted from ever having to suffer such a fate, no matter what crime they committed. Carrying the cross was a death sentence, and the disciples understood that much. Ironically, we are the ones, with a clear view of history and centuries of learning, who do not.

We are unworthy of Jesus when we resist our own death to self. He was willing to give his life for us and, unless we are willing to return the favor, we do not deserve to bear his great name.

Embracing a Theology of Death

Jesus went on to say, "He who has found his life will lose it, and he who has lost his life for My sake will find it" (Matt. 10:39).

Why is death to self so important? Well consider this, without death you cannot have a resurrection. Without death there would be no gospel or salvation or even life itself. Perhaps it is time that we embrace a theology of death.

This is what a theology of death looks like . . .

Dying daily to who we are

Empowering others (not self) as our life

Accepting risk as normative

Theology as not just knowledge but practice

Holding tight to Christ and having an open hand with all else that we "possess"

Unless we are willing to die, we will not live. It is that simple. Death is the path to life. Conversely, holding on to life appears to be the path to death. We are to die to self because it is the only way we can live for Jesus. We can have only one master. Either we will live for ourselves or we will live for Jesus. This is the reason we must put ourselves to death every day.

Organizational Application of Jesus's Words

In the West the cultural mind-set tends to see the individual first and foremost. We read verses in the Bible that use the second person plural and apply it to ourselves as individuals, when in fact it is addressed to a community as a whole.

There are many people groups, however, that do not see the world this way. They see life as a community first and an individual second.

The words of Jesus having to do with death are usually only applied to an individual—a disciple. And the verse should be applied in this way. I have found, though, that the truth contained is a universal principle, which also applies to any organization made up of disciples, such as a church.

More than once I have found myself in a place where I was the voice of leadership to a dying organization. A few times I have "pulled the plug" on a ministry.

It's ironic, though, that all the organizations I have had the courage to lead toward death *have never died*. If anything, they were already dead; I simply said it out loud. When we actually "pulled the plug" publicly, the ministries were reborn with new life and new vision. This is when I discovered that these truths Jesus is giving to us have a corporate application as well.

Jesus said, "He who has found his life will lose it, and he who has lost his life for My sake will find it." And I've seen this every time I have acknowledged a dying ministry. When we have decided to die, we have actually chosen the very thing that brings life!

Some readers of this chapter will think what I am writing about is morbid, mean-spirited, and not necessary. If that is your thought, you are wrong on all counts. According to Christ, dying is the only way to find life, and for me to tell you otherwise would indeed be the most wicked thing I could do. If you hear a voice telling you to do whatever it takes to stay alive, do not listen to it. Choose the cross instead. You will not be disappointed.

When we fear death, we have lost sight of the gospel. Perhaps that is why we are so ineffective in preaching the Gospel—we don't really believe it! If we did believe it, we would accept the words: "Death is swallowed up in victory. O death, where is your victory? O death, where is your sting?" (1 Cor. 15:54–55).

I have come to believe that the health of any organization can be evaluated in direct proportion to its willingness to die. The more vested they are in self-preservation, the less health they will have. The more willing to die so that the kingdom can flourish, the healthier the organization is. Perhaps you should take a minute and do a little self-evaluation in this regard with your own church or ministry.

A Dangerous Leader

The topic of this chapter has important implications for Christian leadership. It is important that we leaders go first. You cannot lead where you do not go. We must all go to the cross; that is where leadership begins.

Once you have been crucified, you are a different person. Old things have "passed away" and new things have come (2 Cor. 5:17). A dead leader is a dangerous leader. Such a person has nothing left to lose. No personal glory is at stake. Ambition is dead. There is no agenda, only what Jesus asks. Reward is not an issue because the leader is already dead. A dead person has no possessions to protect. You can't even really tempt a dead person; corpses feel no pain and have no lust. Once we pass through death, what else is there to fear?

The cross is where everything begins for the leader. All the weeds mentioned in the first section of this book are resolved at the cross. It is the ultimate solution, the cure, for all that ails leadership and the church. Yes, the best cure for illness is death. It kills the cancer every time!

When you have died with Christ, you see people differently. You are no longer looking out for your own personal interests; you can have concern for others. Your interests are all dead and gone; you can live for others. Your decisions are not about what is best for you but what is best for someone else. This is the beginning of empowering others. In a sense, the way to empower others is to stop trying to hold on to power for ourselves. Ironically, that is also the way to attain true spiritual power.

Exit Strategies and Empowerment Strategies

In a day when top leaders are seen as indispensable, I have ambition to be the very opposite. I have come to believe that the real role of a leader who has died to self is to equip others so that he or she is no longer necessary. In a sense, I long to become a disposable pastor—one that is useful for a time but eventually becomes used up and is no longer needed. Like a plastic bottle, once the contents have been poured out, I am done and can be discarded.

Ironically, the more disposable I have become, the more valuable I feel, because it is exactly what God wants of us—and it is rare these days. I have found value in teaching others how to become disposable. If I do my job right, even my role will no longer be needed. This is the true calling of a leader in God's kingdom. The one who wants to be great is a servant of all. This is the difference between being a doer and being an equipper. When you are doing a job for people, others notice you. When you are equipping others to do the work, you do not get the attention.

With this point of view, I have started to value having an exit strategy. More leaders need to have a plan to no longer be necessary. Jesus had the grandest exit strategy of them all. He modeled the way of submission to the Father in everything. He demonstrated the power of being constantly filled with the Holy Spirit. He set a pattern for how to bring change in a grassroots manner. Then he left the disciples with his Word, connected them to the Holy Spirit, and led them in submission to the Father. And he let them go with just that, nothing more. Jesus's exit strategy involved being crucified, and that is where our exit strategy begins as well.

I have found that the best exit strategy is a sound empowerment strategy. If you are unable to empower others to do your job, you will never be able to leave it with the knowledge that others will be able to carry on.

When you exist to help others do the job, you have finally matured to the level of an equipper. The more valuable you are, the less successful you are as an equipper of others. Ironically, the more dispensable you become, the more valuable you are, because there are not that many leaders today who are willing to be dispensable. We have entered into the day of recyclable disciples—transformed from garbage to glory—and disposable pastors. If you are not willing to give your role to another, you do not deserve the role. As a leader in God's kingdom, your success is no longer to be evaluated by what you do but by what others around you are able to do. The only way to begin seeing your life and ministry in this way is by taking the lonely road through the cross. A crucified leader is an equipper of others.

Multiplication and Death

Reproduction always occurs at the microscopic level, even in your own body right now. The hand that is holding this book is made up of millions of cells, and each is multiplying. Your entire body is replaced by new cells all the time—that is health. Every few months there is a new you! For your body to continue to regenerate in this manner, old cells must die for new ones to be born in their place.

Imagine what would happen if the cells in your hand decided to stop multiplying. The moment your cells stop multiplying, you have a serious problem on your hands (pardon the pun). Your hand will shrivel up and die.

Multiplication of cells will continue until you die, but when cells stop multiplying, your body dies. Multiplication stops when death occurs.

And death occurs when multiplication stops. Death and multiplication are intricately woven together in a symbiotic relationship.

On the other hand (no pun intended here), in the spiritual realm, multiplication starts with death. There is a cost involved with multiplication. Jesus used grain as an example of this. It dies to reproduce. Jesus said, "Truly, truly, I say to you, unless a grain of wheat falls into the earth and dies, it remains alone; but if it dies, it bears much fruit. He who loves his life loses it, and he who hates his life in this world will keep it to life eternal" (John 12:24–25).

Surrendering All

As disciples, we must deny ourselves, pick up our cross, and follow Christ. This is all about surrender. This is about confession and repentance. This is about obedience. Where these things exist, there is a dying of self. Only then do we begin to grow and become generative.

We've got to be willing to give up more than our time, talents, and treasure—we've got to start by giving up our *lives* for the sake of his kingdom. If we are willing to pay the price, if we are willing to die to follow Christ, we will see an abundant harvest of souls for the kingdom of God. The Christians of the first century were willing to give their lives for the expansion of the kingdom, and they were able to reach the entire known world with the gospel. Every church throughout history whose members were willing to surrender their lives for the sake of Christ witnessed dramatic and spontaneous growth. This is one reason churches thrive under persecution—the people of God are forced to decide what matters most. They count the cost and pay the price. They die to themselves, their spiritual lives reproduce, and church growth occurs through multiplication.

Exponential Growth

I have heard that scientific and statistical probabilities demonstrate that if a single shaft of wheat is left undamaged and allowed to grow freely and reproduce, it will multiply into a crop large enough to feed the entire world population—for an entire year—within only eight years! It takes only one apple seed to grow a tree. Yet a single apple tree produces enough seeds to plant an entire orchard. Multiplication must start small and seemingly insignificantly, but with time and generational reproduction, it will reach global levels of influence.

How long will it take to reach the world through multiplication? If any one Christian alive today were to lead just one person to Christ every year and disciple that person so that he or she would, in turn, do the same the next year, it would take only about thirty-five years to reach the entire world for Christ! Suddenly world transformation seems within our grasp. But it could be even closer than that. If every Christian alive today were to reproduce in the same way, the world would be won to Christ in the next two to four years. What if all of us decided to put everything else aside and for just the next few years focus on truly discipling another in a manner that multiplies? We could finish the Great Commission in just a few years!

Christianity is always just one generation away from extinction. If we fail to reproduce ourselves and pass the torch of life to the next generation, Christianity will be over in just one generation. Yet, because of the *power* of multiplication, we are also just one generation away from worldwide fulfillment of the Great Commission—the choice is ours.

The Cure for Institutionalization

Early on in the formation of CMA we decided that anything less than a multiplication movement would be a failure for us. With this goal in mind, we realized that one of the greatest threats to being a multiplication movement is institutionalization. When you really think about it, every denomination began as a church-planting movement. Somewhere along the line these movements became sedentary, institutionalized, and the momentum died.

From the beginning we wanted to prevent this from happening to us. At the very least, we wanted to delay its happening for as long as possible. So we tackled the question: how do we keep our movement from being institutionalized? We were not yet a movement, and such questions were difficult to answer, because they cannot be well answered in a vacuum. During our discussions, we found ourselves asking, "What policy can we put in place now that will keep us from becoming institutionalized?" Even as the question came off our lips, we realized the irony of the question. We were close to taking steps toward being institutionalized in our striving not to be. So we simply prayed and asked God to give us the answer.

Once we were in the thick of being a movement, faced with the inevitable decisions, we learned what it takes to avoid falling victim to institutionalization. In answer to our prayers, Jesus's Word came back: "He who has found his life will lose it, and he who has lost his life for My sake will find it" (Matt. 10:39). This is brilliant. It is the kingdom way. The way to stay alive in Jesus's upside-down kingdom is to die regularly. It also verifies what our experience revealed.

When we made decisions that obviously benefited our own existence, the Lord consistently disciplined us. The results of self-preservation are always death and dying. When we have made decisions that, for all intents and purposes, appeared to be suicidal, God has always blessed us with life, resources, and fruitfulness.

As we tell our history, we connect suicidal organizational decisions together into a stream of strategically stupid choices that have brought incredible life and multiplication. Many of those choices had nothing to do with our own spiritual insight—we were just that stupid. Over time and the rich experience of God's favor, though, we have begun to consciously choose death for CMA, because it is the only way to stay alive and multiplying.

Through experience, the Father's loving discipline, and Scripture, we have learned the value of living precariously rather than safely with the wisdom of the world. We have become more content, existing in a place where God must intervene to save us or all is over. In fact, we are growing to like it. Like a long-distance runner who enjoys the endorphin rush, we live for the moments when God shows up at the right moment with another miraculous provision in the heat of the battle.

It is fun to sit together and recount some of the ridiculous decisions we have made all along the way and how God has used them to show his provision of life, power, and resources. The foolish does confound the wise. The weak is strong. The last are first. The dead live. The kingdom is upside down.

Should we intentionally try to be foolish? No, of course not. But if you are like us, you are naturally gifted at it. The point is that if you are not afraid of dying, you will be willing to do things that others will think are foolish. You will then live a life of radical faith. God will become more real to you—and through you to others—because you do not live according to your wise plans but by complete faith in God as your only life.

The path to life begins at the gate called death. It is a narrow and dark gate that is foreboding and intimidating, but for those who know Christ, there is no fear and no pain in it—not even a sting. Abundant life and power await all who would dare enter in.

20

JESUS AND THE MAN-PURSE

Payment for Service in the Church

If ministry is our career, then man can hire us. If ministry is our call, no man can fire us.

Anonymous

He that serves God for money will serve the Devil for better wages.

Sir Roger L'Estrange

Big Dan Teague, a large, fast-talking man with an eye patch, introduces himself to two men in a fine establishment of the South. He sees that they have money, and though he only has one, it is an eye for money.

Ulysses Everett McGill and his associate, Delmar O'Donnel, are unsuspecting of Big Dan's intentions. As he joins them at their table, Everett observes, "I can't help but notice that, like me, you are endowed with the gift of gab."

Big Dan (played by John Goodman) responds, "I flatter myself that such is the case. In my line of work it is plum necessary. The one thing you don't want is air in the conversation."

"Once again," says Everett (played by George Clooney), "we find ourselves in agreement. What kind of work do you do, Big Dan?"

"Sales, Mr. McGill, sales. And what do I sell? The truth. Every blessed word of it, from Genesee on down to Revelations. That's right, the Word of God, which let me tell you there is damn good money in during these times of woe and want. People are looking for answers, and Big Dan sells the only book that's got 'em."

He goes on to say, "I like your style, young man, so I'm gonna propose you a proposition. You cover my bill so that I won't have to run back upstairs. Get your waitress to wrap your dinner picnic-style, and we shall retire to more private environs where I will tell you that there are vast amounts of money to be made in the service of God Almighty."

With that the three move outdoors under a large oak tree to carry on their conversation and enjoy their meal.

This is a scene from the Coen brothers' movie O Brother, Where Art Thou? which is a comical contextualization of Homer's Odyssey, set in Mississippi during the Depression era.

They enjoy the meal in quiet, after which Big Dan thanks them for the extra food and the silence during gestation. Then he asks, "Where were we?"

"Making money in the Lord's service," replies Delmar (played by Tim Blake Nelson).

Big Dan takes the conversation from there: "You don't say much, friend, but when you do, it is to the point and I salute you for it. Yes, Bible sales. Now the trade is not a complicated one. There are but two things to learn. One being where to find a wholesaler—the Word of God in bulk as it were. Two, how to recognize your customer, who are you dealing with as it were. It's an exercise in psychology so to speak. And it is that which I propose to give a lesson in right now." Big Dan rises from the ground and breaks off a large branch from the tree with his bare hands.

Everett remarks, "Why, I'd like to think of myself as a keen observer of the human scene too, Big Dan."

With a knowing grin that betrays more than Everett's keen observation is able to pick up, Big Dan says, "No doubt, brother. I figured as much back at the restaurant. That's why I invited you all out here—for this advanced tutorial." And with that, Big Dan swings the tree branch down onto Delmar's skull.

"What's going on, Big Dan?" Everett asks.

"It's all about the money, boys! That's it!" he says, beating off Delmar, who has grabbed him and is fighting for his life. Delmar is no match for Big Dan Teague and is quickly knocked down and out.

Hardly fazed, the dull Everett remarks, "I don't get it, Big Dan."

With that, Big Dan knocks what little sense was in it out of Everett's head.

He takes the money from their pockets and leaves with the words, "End of the lesson. So long, boys." He laughs as he walks off. "See ya in the funny papers. Y'all've seen the end of Big Dan Teague."

Unfortunately, there are a lot of bullies out there in Christendom who want money and will do what it takes to get it. This is nothing new, the New Testament had similar issues, though I am sure the bullies of today are far more sophisticated in their appeals (see 1 Tim. 6:4–5; Titus 1:10–11; 2 Peter 2:2–3).

The situation is so bad these days that many godly leaders feel it best not to talk about money at all for fear of being misunderstood. Because money is so important to so many people, there is a lot of high anxiety over it. Money is a volatile subject, especially in church circles. We are prone to extremes on both sides of the issue of money—asking for it too boldly or not bringing it up at all.

Many leaders and authors in the growing simple church movement would like to say that supporting Christian leaders is wrong in all cases. Personally I do not believe this. The Bible tells a different story. But at the same time, I also believe the way we go about paying Christian leaders is killing us.

Who Should Be Paid?

Whom should the church pay for service? This is a very critical question for the church to ask today. To approach this subject with cool heads and calm hearts, may I suggest we commit ourselves to addressing this from the New Testament rather than from our traditions, practical challenges, and emotional biases? Can we read the New Testament as if we have never read it before? Can we consider this question as if we did not have two thousand years of history weighing in on our perspective? Can we ask it, divorced from the concern of where our

The Plugged-in Kingdom

next paycheck will come from or worrying about career choices and educational investments? Is this an impossible request? Yes, probably, but we should at least try.

It is my personal belief that two things dictate much of our theology of church finance. We are heavily influenced by the Old Testament principles of supporting a centralized religious government, and by our need to support a new, centralized religious institution. Frankly, I believe we use the Old Testament to support our idea of a centralized religious institution because the New Testament is found lacking in this regard—not that the New Testament is lacking in content about finances; principles of financial stewardship are prominent in the New Testament. Jesus spoke more about money than about heaven and hell, but the New Testament does away with the centralized religious institution. All of us are priests. All are servants empowered by the anointing of the Holy Spirit for the work of the ministry.

Have we hurt the church by making her responsible to employ her leaders like a business? I believe the answer to this question is yes, in *many* ways. Besides draining her of resources, perhaps the worst detriment is how we have segregated the body into a professional class that does the ministry and a nonprofessional class that works hard to pay them.

As I have studied the New Testament with the question in mind of whom the church should pay for service, I have discovered that only the people filling two roles in the church are expected to make their living from the church. If we could pay the people who filled only two roles in the church today, which two would we choose? Senior pastors and missionaries? Pastors and worship leaders? Denominational executives and pastors? I'd probably want to include a gifted secretary in the mix, but that's more reflective of my own weakness than of any understanding of the Bible. I am confident that whatever two roles we chose, they would not be the two mentioned in the New Testament. They are the role of apostle and the role of the widow.

Apostles

In 1 Corinthians 9 Paul makes a case for his right to make a living from the gospel just as the other apostles do. He even cites the Lord as the source of the directive (v. 14), perhaps a reference to his commissioning of the Twelve and his telling the seventy to take no purse with them, for a laborer is worthy of his wages (Matt. 10:9–10; Luke 10:4).

Paul and Barnabas, however, forgo their right for such payment and choose rather to work to support themselves. Paul worked as a tent-maker while starting the church in Corinth, at least until others arrived to help, so as not to be a burden to the emerging church.

Apostolos, the Greek word translated "apostle," means one sent on a mission as a representative or a special envoy. They are the ones to lay a foundation for the expanding church in every region and among every tribe and nation. An apostle is not limited to a single church in a given region, but is commissioned to serve the church of an entire region. Apostles are not likely to manage an existing church, but lay the foundation on which others build. Then they will probably go somewhere else and do it again.

Paul says that apostles have a "right" to make a living from preaching the Good News (1 Cor. 9:3–9). It is important to note, however, that this right can be laid aside and surrendered for the sake of the church, as Paul and Barnabas chose to do. This right should never be demanded to the detriment of the church.

Personally, I have not received money from the churches I started. This conviction is based upon the example set by Barnabas and Paul. I do not ever want to offer the gospel at a charge to those who are hearing.

That said, I do make my own living from CMAResources as I function in an apostolic role. My support comes from grants and gifts from those who are friends and supportive of what we are about. This is not wrong. Paul did not collect money from the Corinthians when he was there planting the seeds of the kingdom. But he would receive support from the churches he had planted after he had left and moved on to plant that same seed somewhere else. Neither I nor the leaders of CMAResources see this as a compensation for work as much as for a release to do more work for the cause. I am not really treated as an employee at all.

Widows

The second role defined in the New Testament as needing full-time support is what Paul calls "widows indeed" in 1 Timothy 5:3–16. Paul delineates clearly what the qualifications are for this role and what the job description is. A widow is to be at least sixty years old, have no family to support her, and have been faithful in serving the Lord and his people. It appears as though she is to make a pledge to serve the Lord

The Plugged-in Kingdom

and not to remarry. For this reason younger women are exempt from the role. Her sole job description is to pray continually, night and day.

With God's plan, not only is a woman without means granted stable provision, but perhaps even better, the church is blessed with constant prayer bombarding the throne of God! This has got to be a powerful partnership. Not only is this woman given financial support, but she is also granted a meaningful purpose for her remaining days. She is given a privilege of great significance.

Wow! I wonder what our churches would be like if we had apostles starting churches all the time in new areas and among new peoples, and the churches were supported by full-time prayer warriors—*night and day*! I can't think of a better investment of kingdom resources. The church would be investing in spiritual endeavors of kingdom expansion, and we would be investing in spiritual battle with full-time prayers and intercession.

In this cast-aside society where people are routinely brushed off as not valuable because of a lack of vocation or a handicap of some sort, this principle could make a huge difference. In God's economy there are no useless Christians who are welfare cases. An elderly, arthritic woman, who can barely rise to answer the door, is an extremely valued servant who is needed to break down walls of separation, destroy spiritual strongholds, and set captives free! She has a calling on her life and is supported full-time to serve in this way.

I can see why Satan would not want us to use such spiritual widows. He'd much rather we pay a full-time staff person to keep our youth entertained and focused while the adults have fellowship and teaching. Could it be that the Enemy is more threatened by this old woman than the highly educated professional pastor? Ouch.

Paul makes one thing clear in this passage that he also made a point of in 1 Corinthians 9—the role is not to be a burden to the church if it can be helped (v. 16). We've grown accustomed to seeing the church as a burden to the pastor, but Paul saw things the other way around. I think our concerns are often misplaced because our values are far removed from those of the New Testament.

Double Honor to Preachers and Teachers

Paul mentions giving "double honor" to elders, and especially those who work hard at preaching and teaching (1 Tim. 5:17). I am in favor of giving honor and double honor to godly elders who shepherd, mentor, and teach the churches. But I have a hard time interpreting "double honor" as a full-time salary and benefits. We have come up with the word *honorarium*, based on this expression in the New Testament. When we present a speaker with a financial token of appreciation, I think we are closer to Paul's intent in this passage.

To be fair, Paul does say, "The laborer is worthy of his wages," which is a quote from the Old Testament, mentioned by Jesus as well. Probably it is a reference to paying for a day's hire rather than a yearly salary. We should definitely be generous in sharing "all good things" with those who teach us (Gal. 6:6), but the goal is always the strengthening of the church, not the sapping of her strength. I also think we are rather limited and uncreative if we think that money is the only thing we should give to those who teach us well.

I believe the principle of the New Testament is to release the servant to be able to fulfill a specific need in the church. Also I think the precedent is that the servant will have already been performing the service before the honor is given, rather than it becoming in advance a condition of service.

Pastors

Should we pay pastors to shepherd the church? We have so many godly people who would be without income if we put a stop to this. So many have spent lots of money and gone deep into debt to be prepared professionally to be pastors. What would become of this investment if we no longer paid pastors?

The scope of this chapter will not allow us to satisfactorily cover this question. I will however say this: it is in the context of shepherding sheep that our Lord himself makes a contrast between those who are true shepherds and those who are merely hirelings. If you're not willing to shepherd the flock without pay, then you're not qualified to do so *for* pay. If you can't lay your paycheck down for the sheep, you certainly won't lay your life down for them.

In the context of organic churching, where churches are intentionally smaller, more intimate, and rapidly reproducing, there is no need to pay someone to pastor. The bar for ministry is down low enough that it is easy to shepherd ten to twenty people without needing to be paid to do so. In such a context, the whole body is more easily mobilized to serve, and ministry is not as dependent on a single professional leader.

The Plugged-in Kingdom

While it is not a *sin* for a church to employ someone, I do think it may not be the best investment of kingdom resources. It is investing in our weaknesses and throwing more fuel on the separation of the clergy and laity. A huge pool of anointed, underappreciated, and certainly underused servants are sitting in pews every week.

More Important Questions

The question of whether or not people should be supported is not as important as asking, *When* do we support them and *why*? When we approach church like a business and look for employees to hire, we have already started down the wrong path in my opinion. Job descriptions, office hours, performance reviews, raises, bonuses, vacation days, sick days are all things that belong in a business, but we should think hard about operating the church this way.

Once I heard a church consultant instruct a roomful of high-powered pastors and Christian leaders not to use the vocabulary of "family" when talking about church but instead use the language of "team." He said the reason we should make the shift is because you can fire someone who is on your team for not performing well, but you cannot fire someone who is in your family. This sounds much more like a business than a church. The New Testament uses a great many analogies for the church, and arguably, family is used more than any other. Business is not used much at all, and only in terms of the value of buying into and investing in the cause. Never is it used to describe how we relate to one another.

Then how should we relate to one another with our financial commitments? Jesus did speak a lot about money. He also gave directions on how leaders are to find their financial sustenance. As I already pointed out, he once said, "A laborer is worthy of his wages." But what is the context surrounding this statement? What did Jesus actually instruct his disciples to do for their needs?

Weakness Evangelism

When Jesus sent out the disciples to do kingdom work, he said, "Go! I am sending you out like lambs among wolves. Do not take a purse or bag or sandals; and do not greet anyone on the road" (Luke 10:3–4 NIV). Whenever my wife asks me to hold her purse at the mall while she tries on something, I quote this verse and say, "No, Jesus said, 'Do not take a purse.'"

In the New American Standard Bible, *purse* is translated as "money belt." It is your wallet. When Jesus sent out the disciples, he instructed them not to raise money or take any money with them at all! They were to go out completely dependent on God and the kindness of strangers.

There are books out today on a variety of ways to do evangelism—servant evangelism, prayer evangelism, prophetic evangelism, and even power evangelism. Jesus's method is what I like to call "weakness evangelism." It is actually quite the opposite of most of our strategies. The disciples were not to go in strength and rescue the people of the world; rather, they were to be completely in need.

Not that they were to be helpless bums—they did have strength. They were to preach the gospel of the kingdom, heal the sick, cast out demons, and raise the dead (see Matt. 10:7–8). Yes, there is a place for power in your evangelism, but do not miss the point that they were totally dependent on the hospitality of those to whom they were ministering.

Usually when we do evangelism, we sweep in with some sort of hero complex. We host a huge crusade in a football stadium with professional musicians and speakers. In our best efforts we build hospitals, schools, homeless shelters, and halfway houses and we exercise our strength in an attempt to impress the community with the compassion of the church. In the end, in the best-case scenario, we may have impressed a few people who will say, "Those Christians are really nice."

The Strength of Weakness

Do not hear me wrong. All those things are good, and we should do them. We should be salt to the world, doing good works that glorify our Father in heaven. We should do all of this and much more. The question isn't *if* we should do them but *when*? My point is that today we *never* come in weakness as evangelists, missionaries, or church planters, and there are good arguments for this being the *first* way we should come.

There are actually a lot of strategic reasons to come first in weakness.

1. *The indigenous people are empowered from the start*. When we come in weakness, the new churches we plant do not start by being dependent on the missionary. It can be the opposite. The new churches begin with empowerment.

2. *Multiplication of missionaries is much faster.* When the new church is empowered, the next generation of churches does not have to wait to get the strength needed to perform at a higher standard. If building hospitals and schools is our first wave of missions, there will never be a second wave, because any second wave of a true movement should come from the indigenous church itself, which could never afford such methods.

3. *The missionary starts with complete faith in God.* Being a missionary is an exercise in humility and faith in God's power, not an exercise in using your own abilities. When humility and faith are modeled, they will be passed on much quicker to the next generation.

4. *God gets all the glory.* When the evangelist is seen as a normal human who needs assistance but who also has a powerful God who grants him or her what is needed, God's provision is not just part of the story, it is the story!

5. *The missionary is not better than the indigenous people.* When we have nicer homes, cars, schooling for our kids, and more discretionary money than those whom we are trying to reach, there are a lot of negative side effects. In any society if missionaries live at a level above those they are trying to reach, it disempowers the indigenous church. Jesus told those he sent out to stay in the homes of the ones they were trying to reach and to eat and drink what they ate and drank. This puts the missionary at the same standard of living as the people.

6. *It keeps the missionary's motivations truer.* When an evangelist or missionary goes out in weakness, his or her motives are not in question. When someone goes out without pay and does the job just to please Jesus, it is definitely not just a career move. We can have confidence in those who have proven their heart on the fields in this way.

7. *It keeps the indigenous Christian's motives truer.* The new Christian's motives are also kept truer, because the evangelist's coming in weakness doesn't offer some false hope that by becoming a Christian, one's standard of living will be raised. Coming in strength may give the new Christians a poor incentive to be saved and serve as missionaries. This happens all over the world. In many places there is a monetary incentive to become a Christian, and especially a Christian leader. Your standard of living rises instantly as Western money supports your life. An American family giving

up a daily latte can feed a family for a month in many parts of the world. This is cheap labor for the church, but it messes with the new Christian's motivations and separates the indigenous Christian worker from the very people he or she is best suited to reach. Suddenly the Christian worker moves into an entirely different social class. In such cases, serving the Christian God and his church pays well but messes up the priorities and motivations of indigenous leadership.

The more I have studied the passages of Luke 10 and Matthew 10, I have an increased appreciation for Jesus's missiological strategies. He does know what he is doing.

Learning Dependence

Many will say that people in the time of Christ were much more hospitable than cultures are today, so this sort of missionary method could be used then. True, but I do not think Jesus's words are to be classified as irrelevant because the culture has changed. I believe his words transcend culture. The focus is not on the hospitality of the people, the focus is on the dependence of the sent one on God's daily provision. This is a lesson needed in every culture and generation! Also I've found, when doing cross-cultural missionary work, there are some societies just as hospitable as the one in Jesus's day.

Jesus shows us the value in training missionaries to go in this manner in a later passage of Luke's Gospel. Near the end Jesus pulled the disciples together and asked them, "When I sent you without purse, bag or sandals, did you lack anything?"

"Nothing," they answered.

Then he said to them, "But now if you have a purse, take it" (22:35–36 NIV). (This is what my wife can say back to me in the mall when finally I agree to hold her purse.)

Why does Jesus first instruct his disciples not to take a purse, and later tell them to take along a purse? Does he want them to go without or to go with financial resources?

As I said earlier, the issue is not whether workers are supported, but *when* they are supported. Going first in weakness and dependency is important. After people have shown they will do the work without support, we can then support them more confidently. It's a testing process but much more than that. It is a growth process. It is as much an opportunity for the missionary to test God as it is for God to test the missionary. The disciples came away from their first venture, believing in God's provision, and with stories they would tell the rest of their lives. This is a foundation on which to build.

Once Dallas Willard was sharing on this very passage at a workshop on ministry in a postmodern world. He asked the question, "Why would Jesus tell them not to take a purse at first and now tell them to take a purse?" His answer: "You don't know how to handle a purse, until you know how to go without one."[1]

We learn something when we trust God's provision and he comes through. What we learn sets a course for the rest of our lives. When we have gone on faith and God shows us his miraculous care and provision, it changes the way we see everything. We view God differently. We view ministry differently. We view money differently. When the tough times hit, and they will, the old lesson will refuel our faith. It's a reminder that we are not in it for the money.

This is a far better foundation for a life of service than simply deciding on a career move. Even when leaders are supported "full-time," it's still not a job but a life calling.

CMA's Lesson

When we first started planting churches, we hired church planters at a full-time salary that decreased in amount over the course of three years. We planted a few churches this way, but obviously it was costly. Because we were hiring people from the outside and needing to be responsible stewards, we also had to have them professionally assessed as church planters before we would hire them. This was also costly. Because we were investing so much in this, we also made sure we did everything we could to ensure the church planter's success. We sent them through church planter's boot camp, made sure they had experienced coaches, bought each one a church planter's toolkit, and gave each one a start-up package of resources so they could buy a sound system, office equipment, and advertising. All of this was very expensive. We set up systems upon systems to ensure success but saw very little. We spent a lot of money to learn that organic-church planting is far more economical and reproductive.

Eventually, however, we did learn and then decided to stop paying church planters any salary. We feared that could be the end but we were wrong. When we decided to stop paying church planters, a phenomenal thing occurred that we had not anticipated. We received many more church planters, and they were of a higher caliber!

Why? Well, we were attracting the kinds of people who are sold out to the cause and would do it whether they were paid or not. That decision was really the final breaking point for our movement. After that, all things changed. Momentum took over.

We found that we no longer needed to buy all the paraphernalia. The churches were simpler and more reproductive. We didn't need assessments. Coaches came naturally from within the movement.

In our old paradigm of church planting, we hired an unknown person and paid him or her full-time. When the person succeeded at starting a church, we would gradually reduce the pay until we no longer paid the church planter. Then we could begin paying someone else.

The new paradigm is the opposite. We do not hire anyone. We cast out the call for people to start reaching their lost friends, family members, and co-workers. Those who succeed will reproduce the church a few times over. Eventually a network of churches develops, which could actually financially support a leader. Indigenous churches reproduce themselves without needing outside resources. That is not the only way it is done, but it is one way that has worked repeatedly in our movement.

Those who know how to get along without a purse prove they are capable of handling the purse. When no dependency is created at the start, kingdom resources are invested in proven leaders.

We do not cower to the bullies anymore. Money is nothing to be afraid of. Our movement is no longer desperate for money or dependent on financing from others. We are experiencing much more freedom this way, and no one is left peddling the Word of God like a Bible salesman looking to get rich.

CONCLUSION

Rare Heroes for a New Day

Example is not the main thing in influencing others; it is the only thing.

Albert Schweitzer

If you would not be forgotten, as soon as you are dead and rotten, either write things worth reading or do things worth the writing.

Benjamin Franklin

The mission I am asking you to volunteer for is exceptionally dangerous," came the command of the colonel to men whose faces looked too young to receive them.

"Take a look at the man beside you. It's a good bet that in the next six weeks you, or he, will be dead. Everyone brave enough to accept this, step forward."

With those words, an entire line of select young men stepped forward to accept a top-secret mission under the command of Colonel Doolittle.

Shortly after the Japanese attacked Pearl Harbor, this mission was put into motion under the direct orders of President Roosevelt. Dramatized in the film *Pearl Harbor*, Doolittle (played by Alec Baldwin) trains and leads this small band of warrior-pilots on a mission to drop bombs directly on Tokyo in response to the December 7 attack.

In a scene just before the mission, while the men prepare on the deck of the aircraft carrier they will leave from but not return to, Colonel Doolittle makes a strangely prophetic comment to his associate.

293

He says, "You know, Jack, we may lose this battle, but we're going to win this war."

He then asks, "Do you know how I know?"

Jack shakes his head and answers, "No."

Pointing to the men preparing for this one-way trip to China over Tokyo, he says, "Them, because they're rare. At times like these you see them stepping forward."

Then the scene ends with his words: "There's nothing stronger than the heart of a volunteer, Jack."

You Get What You Pay For

There are books, seminars, and other resources available today to help pastors motivate volunteers to serve in the church. This is essential because, quite frankly, in churches these days volunteers do not come frequently or with great zeal. In most cases, working with volunteers in church can be frustrating, which is one reason churches that can afford to hire people to serve do so. In some cases, the old axiom proves true: You get what you pay for. Cheap labor is, well, cheap labor.

But why is that? Why is it that church volunteers are so unmotivated?

Often, if the job is big enough, the volunteer is a far superior worker than the one who is paid. The reason the church sees such poor results when she calls for volunteers is because we are asking so little of people. We are asking people to donate a couple of hours each month to babysit in the nursery or greet people and hand out printed brochures at the front door of the church. These tasks may be helpful—I do not mean to demean them—but they are hardly worthy of a life commitment. We get weak volunteers because we ask them to fulfill weak jobs.

Many people actually want to give their lives to something important, but frankly, changing diapers in the nursery and chaperoning a youth group activity is not worth dying for. Most see through the appeals. Simply babysitting the young people while the grown-ups have church isn't a very exciting way to invest their life. Probably they volunteer because they see the need, but it isn't a response of their heart to a mission worth their life commitment.

If people were able to see these tasks as just a small part of an overall mission to change the world, they might be more interested in doing the job. If they knew that the time would come for them to be part of something that actually does effect change, they would have more joy in the tasks. Most people do not see carrying on a weekly church service as changing the world. So they volunteer out of obligation, not out of a sense of call to something bigger than themselves.

In this final chapter of the book, I want to tell you the stories of a new volunteer force that is committed to changing the world. They are not your ordinary church volunteers; they are a new breed of leader that God is bringing to us in a day when we need such men and women.

A New Breed of Leader

Today CMA does not pay any church planters a salary, but nevertheless, some of our church planters have found creative ways to survive and even thrive in the service of Jesus. Below I will share a few examples.

Team-Supported Leaders

While Paul was at Corinth, he was a tentmaker. It was the vocation he fell back on whenever needed. It is wrong to assume, however, that he always made tents while he was on his missionary journeys. Even while in Corinth he made tents only for a time. Eventually the rest of his team came and they started working so Paul wouldn't have to. This approach is a growing trend in our movement. Often it is a spouse who works a full-time job so the partner can devote his or her time to the mission.

Tom and Katie Driver are a couple like that in the Twin Cities. Tom works as a contractor and all-around fix-it man, while Katie starts churches and coaches church planters and often works part-time jobs herself. But if you think that Katie is the one doing the ministry work and Tom is just working his job to support the family, you'd be gravely mistaken. These two are a team in every sense of the word, and a for-midable team at that! The reason they are fruitful is they respect one another and work together holistically.

My wife, Dana, and I have a similar arrangement. She has her own unique call and gifting. She is especially gifted at teaching children. Be-yond spiritual gifts, she is so supernaturally gifted for this that I often refer to her abilities as *mutant superpowers*! She has felt a call to reach out to troubled kids in the urban ghetto, so she works at an elementary school in Watts. This also earns enough income that I am able to continue what I do for CMA, while living in an expensive beach community in Southern California on a very modest level of financial support.

Tent-Making Entrepreneurs

Some of our church planters have taken the tent-making approach. Joseph Cartwright, in the Dallas–Fort Worth area, has started his own window washing company. He wants to help people see better, both literally and spiritually. He has helped start many churches in the past few years while washing windows.

Marcos and Sandy Delaguila used to be on staff at some churches. Marcos was a worship leader at some fast-growing churches but was just not satisfied with the expression of church he was experiencing, so they left to start a church and a business. They started a hair salon in a quaint suburb in New Jersey. They have steady customers who spend an hour with them every month. Many people have found that barbers and bartenders are some of the best therapists because they give you plenty of time and they listen. The Delaguilas have been able to lead many people to Christ. They now have an organic church that meets in their hair salon.

Jason Evans started a network of organic churches in the suburbs of North San Diego County. Feeling a strong pull to urban San Diego, he and his family moved to the city. He got a job doing contracting work while they started churches among the urban poor. One of the organic churches Jason leads is featured in the book *Jim and Casper Go to Church*.[1]

After starting a network of organic churches in Las Vegas, Greg Hubbard felt the same conviction that is common to a lot of people these days: he wanted to be a legitimate presence in the workforce to bring God's kingdom there. So after many years on a church staff, he enrolled in UNLV law school. On graduating with a law degree, he passed the bar and is now serving Christ in the legal profession in Indiana. I have known Greg and worked with him for a few years now and can honestly say Greg would be a profound addition on any church staff. He could easily find a job in ministry if that is what he wanted.

The Vineyard Central Story

Vineyard Central, in the Cincinnati area, was a typical Vineyard church plant. They were meeting in a community center. One Friday, the city officials informed pastor Dave Nixon that the next Sunday would be the last one when they could use the center. That Sunday Dave stood up before the church and had everyone go to a different corner of the room. Those who lived on the north side of town were to go to one corner, south side to another, east and west to opposite corners. Everyone thought this was going to be some sort of experiential learning time. Instead, Dave informed them they no longer had a meeting space. "Choose a leader, a leader-to-be, a home where you can meet, someone who can lead worship, and someone to love the children. Look around. Now this is your church until you hear from us." Stunned, the people did what he asked, and they were suddenly a network of organic churches.

Well, actually it takes a little more to become a network of organic churches, but this was a start. Under the leadership of one young man, Kevin Rains, Dave saw some new life. A single house church started not only to grow but to multiply. Feeling the leading of the Holy Spirit, Dave felt that Kevin had the right gift mix for this new season of the church, so he asked Kevin to become the point leader and Dave would support him. Wow! Now *that* is a rare hero. Not many insecure pastors in today's church world would have the courage to make such a move. Dave is humble enough and in touch with the Spirit, so he not only made the move, but many years later they are still thriving together. Dave is the closest example I have seen today of the spirit that Barnabas had.

A Roman Catholic church building in the center of their community became available, so the Vineyard church moved in on Sundays to worship together again. The Catholic church asked Vineyard Central if they wanted to buy the building—they told them to make an offer.

The first offer they threw out was a ridiculous $10,000 and was immediately turned down. Their second offer was also ridiculous, $150,000, but the diocese accepted it and this church plant bought an entire city block, which included a huge cathedral with tall ceilings and stained-glass windows, a two-story education wing, a 5,000-square-foot convent, and a 5,000-square-foot rectory.

Once again they were back to the normal church thing, albeit in some unusual surroundings for a Vineyard church. But the people were changed. They had tasted a more organic expression of life together and they didn't want to go back to the way things were. They considered what to do with the property. The building, while beautiful, was old and required a lot of repairs and upkeep. They discussed their options and realized that the stained-glass windows alone were worth more than the whole mortgage. They shopped them and found a buyer. The church decided to sell the windows, knock down the building, and create a park for the community. At the last minute, however, the buyer backed out and the Lord seemed to say they should keep the building.

It was almost an Abraham and Isaac test: Were they willing to give up the building? They passed the test.

Today they use the building for community events, such as art shows and quarterly network meetings of all the churches around the city. They use the convent and rectory for living together in community and for holistic mentoring of the leaders they send out.

Kevin was supported full-time by the church but felt the conviction that he needed to be an ordinary guy like everyone else, while a leader in the church. He decided to give up his salary and go back to work for his dad, who owned an auto body repair shop. His father wanted to retire, so Kevin took over the family business. Because of Kevin's entrepreneurial and apostolic gifting, the business expanded, and they started a second shop just a few blocks from the church building. This keeps Kevin deeply rooted in the neighborhood to which God has called him. About eighty other people have intentionally relocated to this same neighborhood to be an incarnational presence there. Many have purchased homes and others have started businesses in the neighborhood.

Not only has Kevin's dad retired, but Kevin has plans to retire soon too with a comfortable level of income as a retired owner of the business, so he can go back to using all his time for kingdom work without taxing his network of churches. Kevin also started reaching out to the guys at work. They began a church after work called Jesus at the Pub, where Kevin would meet with the guys and talk about Jesus and his kingdom, and Kevin would buy the first round!

Woodworking Opens Doors

David and Marcia Lantow moved from Long Beach to San Francisco to start organic churches. There they connected with Ken and Kelley McCord. They fell in love with the city and together have been reaching out for several years. They have had lots of good experience starting churches, but none have lasted for very long, though their team has grown and developed well. Eventually support ran low but their call remained. Efforts to find a job using David's teaching gifts did not yield enough to support the family.

Ken came up with an idea. He wanted to buy a franchise business that refinished wood floors and cabinets. David was at first hesitant, as he had had no experience in wood finishing, nor had Ken, and neither had ever run a business before.

Church planters, though, tend to be risk takers, so they jumped in and started a refinishing business in San Francisco. They hired lots of the people from their team, setting up the business with some basic organic training. Each job site had two workers, one a leader and the other a trainee. They would spend a whole day working together, talking about kingdom stuff, refinishing a floor, and making money. They found some unexpected things occurring.

First, the people who hired them would not just leave their homes open while strangers worked there. They would stay all day while the two worked hard to transform their old wood and talk about spiritual things. Often the owners got caught up in the conversations about kingdom things. Lengthy conversations about the kingdom were taking place naturally in the homes of the people in the city.

Second, they hired some seekers to learn the trade and spend time with a disciple maker out on the field. Some would come to Christ, and the emerging leaders were mentored as well as taught a trade.

Third, for years they tried to reach out in San Francisco, which I believe is the hardest city in America in which to do ministry. The city is inclined to be suspicious of Christian workers. There is also a larger turnover of residents in San Francisco than in most cities. It has become the expectation that those who come to do ministry there will soon leave without having made much of a difference. So people would be very hesitant to put much confidence in friendship with the Lantows and McCords.

When they started the business, however, that changed. Now they are a part of the community, not just sent in from outside. They are now small business owners in a city that values the small business. Since they own a small part of the fabric of the city, they have a vested interest in what happens at a higher level. They are welcomed into people's homes and they do a good job, so people refer them to others.

A simple woodworking business unexpectedly has opened doors that no amount of evangelistic events or community service projects could. In 2007 they were awarded the franchise of the year for their business. The woodworking business is good. The kingdom business is good too.

The Kingdom Comes to a Resort Community in Colorado

Scott and Tina Wilson pulled into the small community in the Rocky Mountains of Colorado with three small children and a fourth on the way, expecting to be used by God. After trying to start a traditional church in the traditional manner, they soon realized that their gifts and desires would not produce what they were assigned to do.

Scott is an evangelist and has led literally hundreds to Christ in Breckenridge, Colorado. They have started several organic churches that have in turn started others. They have assisted the homeless, sent a response team to New Orleans after Katrina, and are often the first called when any emergency occurs in their quaint town. In fact Scott is the chaplain for the emergency services in Summit County.

Scott and Tina have also started several businesses—a firewood business, a hot tubs maintenance business, a business hanging Christmas lights, and a business that rents snowmobiles in the winter and all-terrain vehicles (ATVs) in the summer months. Business has been good, and God has blessed all of their efforts.

The city of Breckenridge loves the Wilson family and is very grateful that they chose to come to live there. Most church planters want to take people from the community to help their cause. Once they start their church, they expect to build a building and not pay any taxes. We wonder why city officials seem biased against churches. Scott and Tina have turned the tables completely around. They do not take from the community, they give to it in so many ways, and the city is grateful for their being part of the town.

Mr. Baker Goes to Globe

Dezi and Susie Baker have been successful youth workers and church planters for decades. Dezi is a man of God who hears from God and obeys. He serves with me on the leadership council of CMA as our prophetic voice. So when God says move, he does, and he heard God say, "Go to Globe." Globe, Arizona, is a small town in the wilderness. It is an old copper mining town and best known as being near the place where the Apaches were slaughtered by being forced off a cliff to their death on a ridge called Apache Leap.

Dezi and Susie were not entirely sure why God wanted them there, but they had no question it was where they were supposed to be. They were also sure that they were to bring the kingdom of God with them, and they were not to be employed by anyone. They were solely to be God's servants there, not slaves to anyone else.

Moving from the Phoenix area to this small town meant they could sell their old house and buy two houses in Globe without any mortgage payments. At first, they felt God leading them to simply trust him. There was not any direction to find employment. There was not any direction to raise support. God just wanted them to live and trust him, so they did. For two years they lived month after month completely on faith without a job. They never solicited funds; they simply obeyed. Now, to be honest there were some circumstances that aided in this venture. They didn't have a mortgage payment or any other debt. They receive a small stipend from the government for having adopted a couple of special-needs kids, one of whom is physically handicapped. Also Susie has a hobby of buying and selling antiques. But none of this could ever explain how a family of five could live for two years without employment. (They also have two grown children who don't live at home.)

All they knew was that God wanted them there in Globe and not to be employed by anyone. God met their needs fully. They did not go into debt nor go hungry. During this time, I have been personally blessed and impressed with Dezi's example because on top of everything else, he would fly into LA on a bimonthly basis for our leadership meetings, *on his own dime*! I must say that the level of commitment from leaders like this is a true example to me, and I am humbled to be associated with them.

Many know Wolfgang and Mercy Simson from his writing and speaking. They also have lived for a few years based completely on faith that God will supply their needs. Their road has been more challenging financially than that of the Bakers, but I admire their willingness to follow God on faith, every single day.

The Bakers are still in Globe. They are still not employed by anyone else, but things have changed—a lot! In the town of Globe there were not any social gathering places except for a few bars and a casino, which all did good business in this depressed town. Dezi heard the Lord direct him, so they rented a space and started a coffeehouse that has become the center of the town's social life. His oldest daughter moved to Globe, and after a brief time as a chef in a restaurant there, she started a catering business and helps run the cafe. Their grown son and his family also moved to Globe and started a Web design business. They started some churches in town and all of this has brought life to a small town.

God had a plan for this place, and Dezi was an instrument to get some of it rolling. There have been some remarkable changes. The old mines were fired back up, as copper once again increased in value. A revitalization of the whole town has come about to such an extent that recently Dezi was asked to run for city council—unopposed.

Dezi is not the only one of our organic church planters to run for office in the city where they have been called to make a difference. Luke and Tiffany Smith live in the city of Logan, just outside of Brisbane; it is the second largest city in Queensland, Australia. Luke has been a pastor on the staff of a church, a denominational leader, and a church planter. In more recent times he felt led to serve the city as an agent of the kingdom and not as a professional Christian, so he resigned his pastorate and started a business as a videographer. He also rose early every day to deliver milk (I guess they still do that in Australia). He served for a time in the Logan City community center. Then an incumbent on the city council asked Luke to run for office and take his place. Luke is now in his second term on the city council of Logan City.

These are men and women who are not just using a city to start a church. These people are moving into their city as God's agents to bring his kingdom and the changes that come as a result. They contribute to the health and well-being of the city, in some cases, so much that the city wants them to lead.

Paying It Forward

Brad and Cari Fieldhouse came back to Long Beach, where they both grew up, to start organic churches. Brad had come to our very first Awakening Chapel (the network of organic churches I was part of starting) and fell in love instantly with this expression of church. He found the group living out what, until then, he had only read about.

On graduating from seminary, Brad's denomination was excited to invest in his church-planting strategy. At that time they were looking to invest half a million dollars into every new church plant. They were surprised when Brad was not interested in their very generous church-planting financial package. He did not request to be funded at all; he was asking for no money! Instead, he pursued employment in the marketplace so that he could start churches as an ordinary workingman, because that was his conviction.

The denomination still wanted to give him some money, so Brad accepted thirty thousand dollars, with one condition: to save it and invest in other church-planting works rather than their own. Brad and Cari wanted to show the denomination that it doesn't cost money to start churches. If this lesson were learned, literally millions of dollars could be saved!

Brad served as the operations manager of a local business and started a network of organic churches called Cross Roads. Along the way, he felt called to bring health and wholeness to the city, and not just plant churches. So he started a second nonprofit ministry called Kingdom Causes. Now Kingdom Causes has offices in several cities and brings together people of the community both to help realize the hopes and dreams of neighborhoods and to tackle the issues that are most damaging to a city's welfare.

Three years into their church plant, Brad fulfilled his original plan. He paid forward every cent to projects that were birthed from their network of churches. Today the nonprofit ministry Kingdom Causes supports Brad and his family as well as many other proven organic-church planters.

Hope for Tomorrow

What separates these leaders from others? Each has had a place in the traditional church structure that met their needs but, based on their conviction, they set out on faith to bring God's kingdom into the workforce and marketplace. They have trusted God for their provision, and with great sacrifice they have engaged the world as fellow workers. Trust me when I tell you that each and every example that I have presented here is a strong and dynamic leader who would do well in Christendom in a more traditional leadership path. Most of them have already done that. They chose the organic church–planting path, not because they couldn't make it in the conventional way, but because, by conviction, they couldn't personally do it any other way.

These are a new breed of leader who are willing to lay aside the security of a salary and venture off with little more than conviction and faith to see what God has planned. And there are more, many more.

These leaders are concerned with improving the city where God calls them, not just improving the church. They have truly brought the Good News to their city—they have brought the kingdom of God and all of its goodness.

Many leaders that have been prepared by the previous paradigm are not capable of taking the risks necessary to launch out and successfully do what these men and women have done. The institution that trained them did not equip them for the world we now face. But of course, the old sort of leadership will not help the church move into either our current or future world. Many leaders will remain the casualties of institutionalization.

I am so privileged to have worked alongside the people mentioned in this chapter and to call each my friend. They all share some things in common. As I have said, they each could easily be on the staff of a more conventional church ministry. They each have as strong a sense of call to what they are doing as any professional pastor or missionary. They are all moving intentionally into communities to bring the presence of the kingdom of God and plant organic faith communities, and they are not doing it for the money. They are living the kingdom incarnationally among the lost and that is making a difference. And for each, the end of their story is yet to be written. They are still learning, growing, and being transformed.

In many cases they are doing better financially than when they were serving in a ministry staff position. Of course this isn't always the case—it's not guaranteed. None of these people launched out into creating businesses thinking they would make more money. They just knew God would provide for them—*and that is a guarantee*!

These are but a few of the growing army of servants who will bring the kingdom of God to neighborhoods and nations. These are the first wave who are hitting the beaches and taking the shores ahead of the rest. But there are many more being called out of the old paradigm to bring hope and good news to the communities of this world. As I survey what God is doing today, I have great hope. We are going to win this war because of people like these.

After visiting her ministry in the slums of Calcutta someone once remarked to Mother Teresa, "I wouldn't do what you do for a million dollars."

Looking back at the observer, the seasoned missionary replied, "Neither would I."

There is nothing stronger than the heart of a volunteer, challenged to do something worth giving one's life to. Come join us.

NOTES

Preface

1. Neil Cole, *Organic Church: Growing Faith Where Life Happens* (San Francisco: Jossey-Bass, 2005); Neil Cole, *Search & Rescue: Becoming a Disciple Who Makes a Difference* (Grand Rapids: Baker, 2008).

Introduction

1. Neil Cole and Bob Logan, *Raising Leaders for the Harvest* (Carol Stream, IL: ChurchSmart Resources, 1995); Neil Cole and Bob Logan, *Beyond Church Planting* (Carol Stream, IL: ChurchSmart Resources, 2005).

Chapter 4 Still in the Dark Ages

1. While some translations have Jesus commanding Peter to "feed" his sheep in John 21:15–18, the word translated as "feed" (*bosko*) is better translated as "tend." Louw and Nida, in their excellent Greek-English lexicon, which is broken down into semantic domains, suggest the word means "to herd animals so as to provide them with adequate pasture and to take care of what other needs may be involved—'to take care of, to herd, to look after'" (p. 518). This is not just feeding them (Johannes Louw and Eugene Nida, *Greek-English Lexicon of the New Testament Based on Semantic Domains*, vol. 1 [New York: United Bible Societies, 1988]).

Chapter 5 Bound by the Chain of Command

1. Neil Cole, *Cultivating a Life for God* (Long Beach, CA: CMAResources, 2008).

Chapter 6 Viewing Life through Faulty Lenses

1. Paul does say that we should never choose to be bound to an unbeliever, or "unequally yoked" (2 Cor. 6:14–18). The reason is that we would not share the most important things in common and our relationship would suffer. But when we come

to Christ already married to an unbeliever, we are to stay in the relationship because our life can have a sanctifying effect on the whole household.

Chapter 7 Parasites on the Body of Christ

1. Church Multiplication Associates is an association of like-minded churches and church leaders who value starting reproductive churches. Our mission is to produce simple systems that are catalysts in reproducing healthy disciples, leaders, churches, and movements. You can learn more about us at www.cmaresources.org.

Chapter 8 The Secret Source of Leaders

1. Steven Covey, *Seven Habits of Highly Successful People* (New York: Simon & Schuster, 1989), 52–54.
2. See Cole, *Organic Church*, 171–92.
3. I recommend that you read *Search & Rescue* to find a disciple-making system that begins with transformation.

Chapter 9 Organically Grown Leaders

1. J. Robert Clinton, *The Making of a Leader* (Colorado Springs: NavPress, 1988), 57–174.
2. Ibid., 43–47.

Chapter 10 Leadership Success

1. Christian Schwartz, *Natural Church Development* (Carol Stream, IL: Church-Smart Resources, 1995), 18, 46–48.
2. Ed Stetzer, Dave Travis, Glenn Smith, and Warren Bird, "Who Starts New Churches?" Leadership Network, 2007, http://www.leadnet.org/Resources_Down loads.asp? IsSubmit=True.
3. Greg Hawkins and Cally Parkinson, *Reveal: Where Are You?* (South Barrington, IL: Willow Creek Association, 2007). You can hear Greg's comments at http://revealnow .com/story.asp?storyid=48.
4. Bill Hybels, Reveal, 2007, http://revealnow.com/story.asp?storyid=49.
5. Ibid.
6. J. Robert Clinton, *Clinton Leadership Commentary*, vol. 1 (Alta Dena, CA: Barnabas Publications, 1999); see also Clinton, *Three Articles about Finishing Well*, available free at www.bobbyclinton.com/articles/downloads/3FinishWellArticles.pdf.
7. See Clinton, *Three Articles about Finishing Well*.

Chapter 11 The New "Up" Is "Down"

1. Jim Collins, *Good to Great* (New York: HarperCollins, 2001), 17–39.
2. Malcolm Gladwell, *The Tipping Point: How Little Things Can Make a Big Difference* (Boston: Little, Brown, 2002).

3. Dee Hock, *Birth of the Chaordic Age* (San Francisco: Berrett-Koehler Publishers, 1999).

4. Ori Brafman and Rod Beckstrom, *The Starfish and the Spider: The Unstoppable Force of Decentralized Organizations* (New York: Portfolio, 2006).

5. For a better understanding of these powerful groups, read my book *Search & Rescue*.

Chapter 15 Knowledge Is Not Power

1. From an audiotape presentation on discipleship by Juan Carlos Ortiz. To learn more about his approach to disciple making, read his book *Disciple: A Handbook for New Believers* (Lake Mary, FL: Charisma House, 1995).

Chapter 16 The Secret to Leading Leaders

1. Steve Ogne and Tom Nebel, *Empowering Leaders through Coaching* (Carol Stream, IL: ChurchSmart Resources, 1995), 2:13–16.

2. Covey, *Seven Habits of Highly Successful People*, 235–60.

Chapter 17 Wax On and Wax Off

1. George Patterson and Dick Scoggins, *Church Multiplication Guide* (Pasadena: William Carey Library, 1993), 198.

2. Ibid., 17.

Chapter 18 Catalysts for Real Change

1. Joseph R. Myers, *Organic Community: Creating a Place Where People Naturally Connect* (Grand Rapids: Baker, 2007), 37–49.

2. Gladwell, *The Tipping Point*, 89–132.

3. See Cole, *Organic Church*, 159–69.

4. See ibid., 181–84.

5. For a more in-depth explanation of the Universal Disciple Pattern from Thom Wolf, go to www.universal-disciple.com.

6. See Cole, *Organic Church*, chapter 8 (109–21), for a more detailed discussion of the New Testament discipleship pattern.

7. Ibid., 110–11.

8. Jaeson Ma, *Blueprint* (Ventura, CA: Regal, 2007), 240–41.

9. It is clear that while the Gospel of John follows Jesus's life, it does not follow a strict chronological order. It is put together more topically than the Synoptic Gospels. The miracles that John writes about are placed in an intentional order. Therefore, following the order as John intended, while not absolutely necessary, has advantages.

Chapter 20 Jesus and the Man-Purse

1. Many believe that Jesus is preparing the disciples for the very vulnerable moment when he is in the grave and the Holy Spirit has not yet come on them. Certainly there is some truth to this idea, and the idea of selling your coat to buy a sword would support that view. But there may very well be more in these words. Perhaps Jesus brought up the first missionary enterprise in the dialogue to remind them of what they had learned about God's provision in missionary endeavors, as preparation for all that was soon to come.

Conclusion

1. Jim Henderson and Matt Casper, *Jim and Casper Go to Church* (Wheaton, IL: Tyndale, 2007).

INDEX

Neil Cole is executive director of Church Multiplication Associates. He is also a church planter in Southern California. He is the author of *Search & Rescue*, *Organic Church: Growing Faith Where Life Happens*, *TruthQuest*, and *Cultivating a Life for God*. Neil also coauthored *Beyond Church Planting* and *Raising Leaders for the Harvest* with Robert E. Logan, as well as *The Organic Church Planters' Greenhouse* with Paul Kaak.

CMAResources seeks to identify missional principles and reproducible methods that can propagate in a variety of cultures and contexts. We aim to empower ordinary Christians to accomplish extraordinary works with the powerful gifts given by Jesus. **CMA**Resources is the resourcing arm of Church Multiplication Associates (CMA), a voluntary association of a multiplicity of expanding networks of disciples, leaders, and churches.

www.CMAResources.org

A few of our many resources about organic leadership formation are:

TruthQuest: A Community-Based Doctrinal Discovery System
A discovery system designed to equip leaders to continue the journey of learning for the rest of their lives. It focuses on training a community of emerging leaders in learning systematic theology. Even more than that, it is also intended to help those emerging leaders to introduce this lifelong journey to others who can in turn do the same.

Mentoring 2 Multiply (M2M) Mentoring Guides
A helpful guide to be used by a leader or mentor to take notes on during their mentoring appointment with an apprentice. A key recording tool for the growth and multiplication of leaders.

Life Transformation Group Cards
A simple brochure to describe two- to three-person Life Transformation Groups (LTGs) with a tear-off bookmark to keep the group on track. This tool is being used all over the globe to grow and reproduce disciples and leaders.

We also offer the *Organic Church Planters' Greenhouse*, which involves practical training and an ongoing support network all over the world. Visit our website to find out more about Greenhouse Training events, other conferences, and workshops, along with locations where they are being offered.

CMAResources.org is the place to order resources, to find training events, or to sign up for our regular e-newsletter. And don't forget to read newly posted articles and browse the archives of our free online library.

CMAResources
1965 E. 21st Street
Signal Hill, CA 90755

phone: (562) 961-1962
fax: (562) 961-1982
website: www.**CMA**Resources.org